PROPOSAL WRITING FOR GOVERNMENT CONTRACTS

PROPOSAL WRITING FOR GOVERNMENT CONTRACTS

HOW TO ORGANIZE AND WRITE WINNING COMPETITIVE PROPOSALS

H. Roger Corbett

SENECA PRESS

Proposal Writing for Government Contracts
HOW TO ORGANIZE AND WRITE WINNING COMPETITIVE PROPOSALS
All Rights Reserved.
Copyright © 2012 H. Roger Corbett
v2.0

SENECA PRESS

ISBN: 978-0-578-08893-8

PRINTED IN THE UNITED STATES OF AMERICA

FOREWORD

I HAVE WORKED in the planning, management, writing, reviewing, and production of competitive proposals for over 35 years, and I have enjoyed the work with a relish that is usually reserved for athletic competitors. I loved winning, and I hated losing. But this field in which one can determine with great regularity how good he or she is, because there is always a winner and there are always losers in the competitive proposal field.

I won many more competitions than I lost, because I learned how to prepare winning proposals. But I learned my craft in one of the most difficult schools that one can ever encounter the school of hard knocks and lost opportunities. I hope that every proposal person can learn from my mistakes and losses and from my victories and wins. I do not wish upon any person the anguish of losing a competition, but I do hope that every reader shares my pleasure in winning.

I could not have won a popularity contest during my work on competitive proposals, but I was one who never accepted defeat and insisted on winning. I was always one who pushed managers and subordinates alike to higher levels in their technical skills, management skills, in their work ethic, and a commitment to winning. I preached the truism that only the best win and that all others are losers. And I am not and have not ever been a loser.

When I present material in this book, please remember that my statements are not arbitrary. Quite the contrary I learned many painful lessons, from which I have developed certain axioms, or rules, that are relevant to all winning or losing proposals. These lessons were learned at great expense to my small business and to my large company employers. I was still learning important lessons on my most recent proposal efforts as a consultant. So, I highly recommend that the reader learn from my painful and expensive lessons and not endure the same pain that I did; I further recommend that the reader avoid the losses that my employers experienced before I was truly a winner.

ACKNOWLEDGEMENTS

I MUST ACKNOWLEDGE the support efforts and encouragement by many people and organizations that contributed to my education in the field of competitive proposals. My friends and acquaintances provided insights, resources, and suggestions on many occasions. And my employers provided me with the resources, the finances, and the commitment needed to succeed in this very demanding business.

The three employers who provided great amounts of precious funds to the preparation of proposals in which I was a lead person include: Science Applications International Corporation The BDM Corporation, and Triangle Research Corporation. Other firms that hired me and assembled proposal teams to work under my direction include: Planning Research Corporation, The Austin Company, and Morrison-Knudsen. I hope that the contracts that they won were an adequate return on the money that they allocated to my proposal efforts.

Key individuals who contributed to my continuing education in the field of competitive proposals include: Stan Harrison of the BDM Corporation; Dr. James Striegel, Fred Giggey, Roger Gruben, and Lew Taynton, of Science Applications International Corporation; Bob Anderson and Hyman Silver, proposal consultants.

Reading as many books on proposals as I could, allowed me to gain new insights into different aspects of proposal work; like providing an understanding of the higher level concerns associated with acquisition management, and presenting strong arguments for high technical merit.

I am very much indebted to the many friends who assisted in the review, editing, and proof-reading of this book. My son, Michael, was of great assistance in the preparation of the graphics and the visual impact items.

TABLE OF CONTENTS

Part II CRITICAL UNDERSTANDINGS NEEDED TO WIN

Part IV: THE MAJOR PROPOSAL MANAGEMENT ACTIVITIES

Part I

THE EARLY ACTIONS
THAT ARE VERY CRITICAL

CHAPTER 1

THE STRATEGIC BID-NO BID DECISION

1.1 THE NEED FOR A HIGH LEVEL CORPORATE BID-NO BID DECISION

THE FIRST STEP in the preparation of a winning proposal is the bid-no bid decision by higher level management. In its bid-no bid decision process, management assesses the importance of the competitive procurement to the corporation, estimates the level of effort needed to prepare a winning proposal, weighs the alternative uses of the Bid and Proposal funds, assesses the likelihood of a win, and determines if the corporation can realistically compete for the contract.

This assessment by high-level managers is characterized by three major features: (1), the people who make the bid-no bid decision are the same ones who control the funds, personnel, and resources needed for the competitive proposal; (2), the bid-no bid decision reflects both the long-term and short-term sales goals of those managers; three, the proposal effort is assured of high level visibility and importance.

A bid-no bid decision is critical to the success of a competitive proposal for many reasons, the most important being:

- Management makes a bid decision at an early date
- Management makes a commitment to allocate resources and funds

- Management provides top-level guidance to the Proposal Manager
- Managers develop a personal commitment to winning

Dale Copeland, of SAIC, once observed that **the chances of winning a procurement are greatly enhanced by the submittal of a proposal**. This humorous observation is important in that a company must make some minimum number of bids in order to stay in business and that the company must invest money and resources in the preparation of winning proposals. So, since there is no way to avoid competitive proposals in the current procurement environment, contractors must make good bid-no bid decisions so that their proposals stand a good chance of winning.

Axiom: **In the competitive proposal world, a bad Bid decision will always inflict more damage on the corporation than any No-Bid decision.**

1.2 THE TYPES OF INFORMATION NEEDED FOR A BID-NO BID DECISION

The SAIC Systems Group had a very simple organization and process for its bid-no bid decision. First the Group Manager established a Bid-No Bid Board comprised of senior managers, technical leaders, marketing specialists, and financial personnel to review all requests for Group and/or Corporate funding for competitive proposals. This Board, which invariably included the Group Manager, met whenever a bid-no bid decision was required.

The work of the Bid-No Bid Board began when any SAIC employee, who was a Bid advocate for a competitive procurement that required Group and/or Corporate funding, submitted a very simple form with answers to only 15 questions. This form, shown in Figure 1.2-1, was reviewed in a formal meeting by the Board, whose membership usually included those managers who would provide the people, facilities, resources, support, and funding necessary to pre-pare the competitive proposal. In other words, those managers who would have to invest the most were the ones who reviewed this form.

If every question in Figure 1.2-1 merited a YES reply, it meant that the marketing and management personnel had really prepared for the procurement and that our corporation could be a successful bidder. If there were four of more NO replies to the questions, it means that the company probably was not ready for the procurement and that the chance of winning was extremely low. However, all YES replies did not mean that a competitive proposal would be submitted as a certainty.

Following a quick assessment of the information provided in Figure 1.2-1, the manager or lead technical person who was advocat-ing a bid decision provided a briefing to the Bid-No Bid Board. The YES answers were explained and documented, the risks associated with the procurement were discussed, the costs for a winning pro-posal were presented, and the impact of a bid decision was addressed at a macro level. It is noted that if there was no SAIC advocate, then a No Bid decision was almost assured. If there was a strong SAIC advo-cate, if all replies were YES, if we could afford the proposal, and if we had a competitive edge, then a BID decision was likely.

There was never any doubt on my part that this simple form, plus the ensuing presentations, had a major impact on the Group's success in competitive proposals. I believe that this form was the single most important consideration in making the bid-no bid decision. We were able to make better Bid decisions and, consequently, we were able to win a higher percentage of the competitions.

1.	Do we know the customer and its key personnel well?
2.	Does the customer know us, our capabilities, and our personnel?
3.	Did we know of the procurement in advance?
4.	Did we influence the RFP in any way?
5.	Have we ever worked for the customer before?
6.	Have we successfully completed similar work with the customer?
7.	Do we know who the competitors are?
8.	Do we know the strengths and weaknesses of the competitors?
9.	Do we have the capability and resources to do the work?
10.	Do we have anything special to offer to the customer?
11	Is this procurement consistent with our Group plans and charters?
12.	Are the key proposal people available at this time?
13.	Do we know how we can win this procurement?
14.	Do we know how much the proposal will cost?
15.	Is it likely that we can win?
16.	If subcontractors are needed, have we identified them?
17.	Have we identified the risks associated with the contract?

Figure 1.2-1 A Bid-No Bid Form Used in the Decision Process

1.3 THE OUTPUTS FROM THE BID-NO BID DECISION

It would seem that the outputs from the high-level Bid-No Bid Board should be a simple BID or NO BID, but life is not always that simple. Some variations of the BID and NO BID decisions can be:

NO BID   Do not bid under any circumstances
           Do not bid as the prime contractor

BID   Bid as the prime contractor
           Bid as a subcontractor to another firm
           Bid if shortcomings are overcome

When the Bid-No Bid Board has made a Bid decision, the managers on the Board have concurrently made a commitment to provide or acquire the resources, personnel, facilities, and financial support needed for the proposal effort. The Board may also provide a wide range of information to the Proposal Manager from its deliberations, including items such as:

- Previously unidentified corporate resources
- Suggested win themes and discriminators
- Views about the customer and the competition
- Suggestions on subcontractors and vendors
- Availability of key proposal personnel
- Money allocated to the proposal effort
- Designated Corporate Officer Responsible

1.4 BID DECISIONS DICTATED BY HIGHEST LEVEL CORPORATE CONSIDERATIONS

At times, the highest level corporate managers make a Bid decision that is based on strategic marketing plans, plans that are unknown to the lower-level managers, the technical staff, and the proposal staff. I have encountered such Bid decisions and I concluded that those Bid decisions were based on strategic matters such as:

Case 1: A Government Contract Officer knows that only one proposal will be submitted for a competitive procurement and that the proposal will be from the incumbent contractor. If only one proposal is received, the Contract Officer may be forced to recomplete the contract with a new, reworked Request for Proposal; such an effort entails many delays and additional costs. So, in order to obtain more bidders when only one proposal is likely, a representative of the Contract Officer may elect to apply pressure on your high-level corporate managers to submit a proposal. This pressure is very successful when your corporation already has a major contract base with that Government office. Since these high-level issues are above the level of the proposal staff, corporate management does not reveal any understanding it has reached.

In such instances, it was very important, and essential, that the proposal team NOT be informed as to the motivation for the high-level Bid decision. I actually had the painful experience of being the Proposal Manager in two such instances, in which I was savvy enough to recognize the situation. I managed the proposals as if I intended to drive a stake through the heart of the incumbent contractor or the pre-destined contractor. We prepared great proposals, but we lost. And the Government was spared much pain and expense.

Case 2: High-level corporate management decided to prepare an outstanding competitive proposal in a situation in which the likelihood of winning ranged from very low to impossible. This BID decision was based on a marketing initiative in which our management wanted to impress a potentially major customer with our corporate capabilities, experience, and resources. Our managers were aware that our lack of a contract base and corporate recognition with the customer meant that we would not win. But we knew that a well-prepared proposal was a great method to establish our credentials and to gain recognition with the customer.

I received the money, people, and resources to prepare a very good technical and management proposal with themes such as: "We want to work for you. We want you to know us. We have the skills and resources that you will need in the future. We do great work, on schedule and on cost." We did not win that procurement, but we did acquire a new major customer and many other contracts later. In the preparation of this proposal, I never let the proposal staff believe anything other than the fact that we were going to win that procurement.

Case 3: In a competition for a technical, scientific, and management services support to a major Government laboratory, we were competing against an incumbent contractor that operated with very low costs. The Request for Proposal included the items normally included in all major procurements, a requirements-driven outline based on the RFP requirements, was prepared in our proposal center. It did not appear that we stood a chance of winning that competition, yet our Marketing person who is an excellent technical person, kept reassuring the proposal team that we could win the competition. I was in charge of the Management Volume, the Staffing Plan, and the Phase-In Plan.

In my analysis of the Request for Proposal, I could not detect the customer's dislike for the managers of the incumbent contractor or the customer's complete satisfaction with the incumbent's technical and scientific staff. Also, I did not appreciate the early efforts by the lead SAIC Group to introduce key SAIC technical managers and scientists who would work with their counterparts at the laboratory. We won the competition, and I was forced to eat my hat, from a company that specialized in such items.

1.5 WHY THIS ACTIVITY IS IMPORTANT

The Bid-No Bid decision is one of the most important activities in the proposal process, because it eliminates futile proposal efforts and focuses proposal resources on competitions that the corporation is most likely to win. So, a good Bid decision means that we save money, win the important contracts, and focus our efforts. It also means that the Group lives within it corporate charter.

CHAPTER 2

THE EARLY DECISIONS AND ACTIVITIES OF GREAT IMPORTANCE

2.1 DESIGNATING THE CORPORATE OFFICER RESPONSIBLE

This activity seems so simple and logical that one would wonder why it merits consideration. Why not just appoint any corporate officer who happens to be walking down the hallway? Well, there are many good reasons for the appointment and there are several important criteria for the selection of this individual. For example, look at the major responsibilities and activities of the Corporate Officer Responsible which are listed below:

- Knows about the procurement.
- Selects the key proposal personnel
- Attends to the financial requirements
- Conducts the daily meetings with the key proposal personnel
- Reports progress to higher-level management
- Selects members of the Gold Team and the Red Team
- Deals directly with subcontractors and vendors
- Approves all major corporate commitments in the proposal
- Deals directly with all other corporate entities involved
- Provides leadership to the proposal effort

- Reviews and approves all planning efforts by the proposal team
- Prepares all teaming agreements for corporate approval
- Acquires needed corporate resources and additional personnel
- Assigns information acquisition efforts to marketing personnel

It is ideal when the Corporate Officer Responsible has a financial stake in the outcome of the proposal effort, since money is probably the greatest motivation factor of them all. It would also help if the job security of the Corporate Officer Responsible was somehow related, however tenuously, to the outcome of the competition. But the principal requirement for the Corporate Officer Responsible is a strong and enduring determination to win the competition. This very important position is not for the faint of heart, the administrator, the disinterested, the lethargic, or the one who merely follows orders.

2.2 ASSIGNING KEY PERSONNEL TO THE PROPOSAL

Some proposal people ask: "Aren't all proposal personnel important to the success of the proposal?" The answer to that question is "YES", but this answer does not mean that some of the proposal personnel are not more important than the others. Those proposal personnel assigned to leadership, management, and special skill positions are designated as "key personnel". The personnel (positions) on the proposal team that are super critical to the success of the proposal effort are shown in Figure 2.2-1.

Within that cadre of key proposal, The Proposal Manager, Volume Leaders, Chief Engineer usually work in a full-time, long-term basis during the entire proposal effort. The Contracts Specialist, Costing Specialist, and Production Coordinator work in a full-time basis on a limited term basis, as a general rule. The Marketing Specialist works in an on-call, part-time basis.

Title	Major Responsibilities
* Proposal Manager	managing the overall proposal effort.
* Volume Leaders	preparing the technical and management volumes
Chief Engineer	directing the engineering design effort
* Contracts Specialist	preparing the cost volume
Marketing Specialist	providing customer/procurement information
Costing Specialist	preparing costing guidelines and computing costs
* Production Coordinator	coordinating art, editorial, and production services
Subcontractor Manager	dealing with the subcontractors and consultants
Plans Leader	preparing the supporting plans

* These key personnel are virtually always required for all proposals, large and small.

Figure 2.2-1 Key Personnel for a Major Proposal
(Like a system development effort)

It is noted that (1) the Chairman of the Gold Team and the Chairman of the Red Team are extremely important people that contribute much to the proposal, but these personnel are not key members of the proposal team; (2) a more detailed description of the authorities, responsibilities, and activities of the key proposal personnel are described later in a section directed to the organization of the proposal team; (3) and smaller proposals will not have the complete array of key personnel listed above in Table 2.2-1, but when all these key personnel are not assigned to the proposal, the functions of the deleted key personnel must be performed by other key members of the proposal team.

2.3 SELECTING THE SUBCONTRACTORS

The selection of the subcontractors to work on the contract after winning the competition is usually an activity reserved for higher-level corporate managers and for the Acquisition Manager, as this activity is not normally performed by the Proposal Manager. These managers should know which firms are favorites of the customer, have successfully completed similar work on other contracts, and have the special skills or resources needed to perform the contract work. Furthermore, these managers are usually aware of the customer's requirements for subcontracting with small businesses.

It is important to select the subcontractors early, preferably in the acquisition planning efforts. The selection must be on the basis of their contract experience, their knowledge of the customer, the resources that they possess, their rate structure, their ability to support your proposal effort, and their willingness to assign personnel to your proposal team. Ideally, the selection should be made as early as possible so that you can use their marketing intelligence and their resources to tailor your proposal to the customers.

Too few managers, high-level or mid-level, have been schooled in the preferred methods for the selection of subcontractors. A few of the basic rules for subcontractor selection that were taught to me by the management of the BDM Corporation are:

1. Never select a firm as a subcontractor who has a history of taking a contract or a customer from the prime contractor.
2. Never select a firm as a subcontractor whose past performance is spotty; check the customer's data base on contractor performance.
3. Never select a firm as a subcontractor who has extremely high labor rates that must be compensated for by your company bidding very low labor rates.
4. Never select a firm as a subcontractor to perform work in an area in which your company is exceptionally qualified and who expects to perform that work also.
5. Never select a firm as a subcontractor with which you have had a bad experience in earlier proposals or in other contract performance efforts.

2.4 DEFINING THE INTERNAL CORPORATE AGREEMENTS

Earl Williams, President of the BDM Corporation, has a sign on the wall of his office that said: *"We Have Met the Enemy, And It Is Us-POGO".* What a true statement. Some of the fiercest pre-proposal arguments I have ever encountered were related to the division of the contract funds after contract award among the various groups and divisions within the corporation. In some proposal efforts, the President had to step in and make an executive decision, to resolve the conflicts.

Within your corporation, there must be a lead organization that is in charge of the proposal effort, and all other corporate organizations become relegated to a subcontractor-type role. The lead organization must prepare a corporate teaming agreement in which the division of contract work is specified in detail and the terms and conditions for performing the contract work are also specified. This agreement should specify that the share of the contract work would be a direct relationship to the investment of the various organizations in the proposal itself.

I once read an article that said, in effect, that: "the pettier the issue, the fiercer the arguments". That certainly applies in the matter of competitive proposal work. Just accept the fact that high level management may prefer to stay out of these dogfights and decide to wait until a victor has been identified before announcing their decision.

2.5 IDENTIFYING THE KEY PROJECT PERSONNEL

When the Government or customer uses the term "Key Personnel", it means that the people designated as key personnel in the proposal are committed to work on the project after contract award. No ifs, ands, or buts. While the terms for the replacement of key personnel may be specified in the Request for Proposal, the customer still expects to see the key personnel bid in the proposal working on the contract, as promised. I strongly suggest that every Proposal Manager read the Federal Acquisition Regulations on this matter and review several court cases related to these FAR requirements.

The key personnel bid in the proposal are critical to the winning of the contract. The key personnel on major procurements must attend Technical Clarification Meetings and Gray Beards meetings prior to contract award. In these meetings, senior technical and management personnel, some of whom are consultants from Federal Contract Research Contractors such as MITRE or ANSER, pose very difficult questions to the key personnel. Such as:

- Describe your technical approach and the specific activities in each step.
- How will you minimize turnover and replacement of key personnel?
- Explain what other alternative technical approaches did you consider.
- Describe your system for acquiring corporate resources quickly?
- How do you intend to minimize risks?
- If one of your key vendors goes out of business, what will you do?

Such questions mean that the key personnel must be familiar with the Request for Proposal, the Specifications, the references, plus intimately familiar with the proposal, the design activities, the corporate resources, and support. The variety and toughness of the questions or requests mean that the key personnel must be able to think on their feet and to respond well to tough questioners. Remember, the answers to these types of questions at pre-award conferences become part of the RFP and the Contract.

> **Advice to the Naïve** - Remember that as the Proposal Manager your personal reputation is on the line. When the proposal states that key personnel will be assigned to the project and will report to the project after contract award. It is wise to disregard the general statements of management on the availability of staff members that they have designated as key personnel. Require the Division Manager to stake his honor on the matter of assigning a key person to the project after contract award, and require each key person to make a personal commitment to you and stake his honor on the matter.

2.6 CONTINUING THE INFORMATION COLLECTION EFFORT

In my experience, marketing people love to make presentations in which they cite about 40 different information items, but these items are invariably about 40 different procurements. What you need as a member of the proposal team is the answers to 40 questions about your procurement. So, as soon as possible after the Bid-No Bid decision and the analysis of the RFP have been completed, provide the marketing types with a detailed list of the questions that you need answered. But remember that the questions must not be illegal and must not compromise your chances of winning the contract. Some of the legal questions that will help the proposal team include:

Who are the members of the Source Selection Evaluation Team?

Who is the Source Selection Authority and the Contracting Officer Representative?

Who will be the Contracting Officer Technical Representative?

Who are the lead technical personnel working for the customer?

Which cost estimating system or software does the customer use?

What is the customer's tolerance for technical risks?

What technical papers has the customer's staff presented in recent years?

Which companies have a major contract history with the customer?

What are the strengths and weaknesses of the competitors?

Who prepared the Statement of Work in the RFP?

Which people will participate in the Gray Beards sessions?

Who will monitor system demonstrations for the customer?

Will the customer have an outside organization participate in the proposal evaluation?

Where does the customer prefer the contract work to be performed?

Which competitor was a major contributor to the Statement of Work or Specifications?

Perhaps the Acquisition Manager or the Marketing specialist concerned directly with the competition can answer these types of questions, but it seems that an additional information collection effort is always needed in most procurements. It is the responsibility of the Proposal Manager and the Proposal staff to prepare their questions as early as possible after reading the procurement documents.

> **As a Point**: Some Government organizations, such as the White Sand Missile Range, publish a list of the Source Selection Evaluation Board members, along with information about their credentials and organization. So this type of information is legal.

Perhaps this is not truly an information collection matter, but the Proposal Manager must assign someone the responsibility for establishing a library and reading room for the proposal team as early as possible. The library and reading room must include all references cited in the RFP, the RFP and its annexes, the corporation's marketing and procurement information, proposal directives, and a listing of available corporate resources.

2.7 DEFINING THE PROPOSAL PROCESS TO BE USED

At SAIC, we had a standard proposal process, or system, that we preferred to use in all competitions. This process breaks the proposal effort into the following major phases, milestones, and activities that are integrated into a smooth flowing series of work efforts by the Proposal Manager and the Volume Leaders. It seemed that most of the proposals that lost had a checkered record in regard to these eight major items.

1. Pre-proposal planning and organization
2. Gold Team Review
3. Proposal team writing

4. Blue Team Review
5. Proposal team writing
6. Red Team Review
7. Proposal team writing/revising
8. Proposal production

The line organization responsible for preparing the proposal has several options available for the preparation of its proposal. For example, the line organization can:

- Contract for the services of a corporate proposal center that provides facilities, production support, and other resources for a fee.
- Manage and write the entire proposal with its own resources and personnel without outside support or services.
- Manage and write the proposal with its own resources and use the corporate production capability to prepare the final version.
- Contract for a full array of facilities and services at a remote proposal site and/or hire an outside proposal consulting organization.

Whatever the choice, the line organization should make its decision in this matter as soon as possible after the Bid Decision.

Proposals for the design of a major system require a design team that functions under a different, but concurrent set of activities, phases, and milestones.

I have been the entire proposal team in efforts during which the proposal process was very abbreviated, but these efforts, invariably, were associated with special circumstances. During the preparation of two severely page-limited proposals in which our Bid decision had been delayed, it was impossible to recruit and organize a proposal team. So, I planned and wrote one 20-page proposal and 16 pages in a 20-page proposal, each in less than one week. The reviews were conducted immediately following my approval of the smooth draft of each page, after which skilled *production personnel took over. Both proposals were winners, with one contract being worth over $20 million. Of course, if the proposals had lost, I would have been the only person facing the corporate equivalent of a firing squad.*

CHAPTER 3

DETERMINING THE RESOURCE REQUIREMENTS

3.1 THE TYPES OF PROPOSAL RESOURCES REQUIRED

3.1.1 THE PROPOSAL FACILITY REQUIREMENTS

Proposal Team facilities will always include offices, conference rooms, and work bays; the facilities can include teleconferencing centers, food service areas, and administrative support areas. Normally, the Proposal Manager has a separate office; on large proposals the Volume Leaders may have an office also. The writers and plan leaders have shared offices or work bays.

Design Team facilities will include offices, conference rooms, work bays, design areas, and special work sites. The Chief Engineer will always have a separate office. The Design Leaders may have an office, although they usually share an office with a senior person. The design personnel, non-supervisory, will normally work in big bays.

Production facilities will include offices for word processing centers, art/graphics, printing and binding, and editorial specialists. The Production Coordinator will virtually always have an office, graphics specialists and editors probably will have an office.

Special Work Sites will include such diversity as the System Demonstration Facility used by the Design Team, the security vaults used by the Design Team and Proposal Team for code-word proposals, the TEMPEST-approved computer centers used for classified software development.

3.1.2 ADDITIONAL PROPOSAL RESOURCES REQUIRED

The Corporate Officer Responsible, the Acquisition Manager, the Chief Engineer, and the Proposal Manager (which in small companies and on small proposals can be the same person) are responsible for assembling the resources needed by the proposal team and the design team. For the proposal and the design team, the physical resources can, or should, include such variety as:

Library-Reading Room	Storage Areas	Food Service Area
Micro-computers	Printers	Scanners
Computer Software	Local Area Networks	Office Supplies
Chalk Boards	Proposal Databases	XEROX Machines
FAX Machines	Voice Mail	E-Mail
Telephones	Safes	Security Vaults

For the system design team, the resources will include the above resources plus many additional critical items such as engineering data bases, design software, drafting boards, computer services, Tempest-tested facilities, inter-facility data networks, large-size printers, and large-size displays.

The non-physical resources required by the proposal and design teams include corporate support in areas such as security, travel, accounting, procurement, subcontractor negotiations, vendor quali-fication, receptionist services, food services, delivery services, office services, computer rental, proposal center services, and administrative services. The number, type, intensity, and duration of these other re-sources will depend, on the exact requirements of the proposal effort.

While most of these resource requirements are very obvious, the timing associated with the prompt arrival of these items can have a major impact on the costs of the proposal and the schedule for the proposal. A two-day delay in the availability of resources for a 20-per-son design team can easily mean a cost overrun of over $3,000. So plan and execute well.

3.2 THE PROPOSAL PERSONNEL REQUIREMENTS

Many companies have prepared planning factors for the person-nel requirements essential to a winning competitive proposal. Some of these planning factors include:

- The Hughes Company, many years ago, stated that their pro-posal personnel requirements were based on one smooth page for every two days of labor
- Hyman Silver, the legendary proposal expert, estimated labor costs to be somewhere between 2 percent and 7 percent of the contract value.
- Several proposal experts have said that the proposal writers should produce one finished page per man-day, not including the other personnel involved.
- In his cost estimating book, Stewart estimated the number of man-hours by labor category required for each page of tech-nical documentation.
- In several high-intensity and very short-term proposal efforts, I wrote a maximum of four pages of smooth text per day. Since graphics, editorial, and production man-hours were extra, the production rate was probably slightly less than three pages per man-day.

Estimating the proposal personnel requirements can be based on several algorithms, but all such algorithms are driven by: the number of pages to be prepared, the complexity of the material on those pages, the availability of existing material, and the work required to make existing material fit the current proposal. Also, the scope of the proposal has other impacts on the man-days required to prepare the proposal. For example:

- On very small proposals, the Proposal Manager and Volume Leaders may be the only proposal writers. They will be supported by production personnel.
- On very large proposals, the Proposal Manager is seldom a proposal writer. The Volume Leaders and the Proposal Planner may not be proposal writers.
- On medium-size proposals, the Proposal Manager may write the Executive Summary and the first page of each section or chapter and Volume Leaders will also be proposal writers.
- On proposals with severe page limitations, the entire proposal may be written by one very skilled person with support personnel, of course.

Some very important people in the proposal process, some of whom may be on the proposal team, are not considered in the preparation of the personnel requirements. These will include the costing specialists and contracts personnel assigned to the cost volume, the managers and consultants assigned to the external review teams, and the subcontractor specialist assigned to the proposal team.

It is suggested that in estimating the number and type of personnel required for a typical competitive proposal that the following guidelines be used:

- On proposals of any size and any format, the production rate for the technical and management writers on the proposal team should be a low of one page per two days and a high of one page per day. This includes time for meetings, reviews, research, writing, and preparing rough drafts of graphics.

- On proposals of any size, the editing and proofreading support should be based on a minimum rate of six pages per person per day and art/graphics support should be based on two items per day. The printing and binding of the proposal will require a minimum of one man-day.
- On system development proposals, the Proposal Planner will require a minimum of four days to prepare the list of proposal requirements and the requirements driven outline. On small study or services proposals, the Proposal Planner will require a maximum of two days for the listing and the outline
- The effort to prepare for a formal Gold Team Review will require about four days of intense effort by the Proposal Manager and two days by the Proposal Planner. The time required for a typical Red Team Review will require two days of effort by the Proposal Manager, plus the time associated with production.
- The preparation of a single subcontractor data package that describes the scope of work to be bid; the deliverables and terms and conditions, and the special instructions, will require at least two days each for negotiations and writing by the Proposal Manager and the subcontractor administrator. Data packages for additional subcontractors will require only one day for the Proposal Manager and Subcontract person.

3.3 THE PROPOSAL FACILITY REQUIREMENTS

The proposal facility requirements will include those associated with the proposal team and those required by the design team. The proposal team should be provided with most, if not all, of following facilities and hardware items listed below. Note: These items are provided by the corporate proposal center or from the line organization's own resources:

- Work space (usually a big bay) for the writers

- Office space for the proposal manager and volume leaders
- Large conference room with chalkboards and posting walls
- Microcomputers, scanners, printers, and local area network for each person
- Word processing and graphics software for each computer
- Office supplies (paper, pens/pencils, folders, staplers, etc.) in a pool
- Office furniture (desks, file cabinets, book shelves, etc.) for each person
- Reference material, data bases, and books in a reading room
- FAX machines, XEROX machines, binding equipment
- Safes, vaults, and secure containers for classified proposals
- Refrigerator, microwave, sink, water dispenser

The Design Team will require all of the above items, plus some very costly additional items, including:
- Computer Assisted Design hardware and software
- Technical references, handbooks, vendor catalogs
- Drafting hardware and software, plus special drafting paper
- System Demonstration Facility
- Special security spaces and work areas

3.4 THE SPECIAL PROPOSAL SUPPORT REQUIREMENTS

Every proposal effort requires support from corporate management, administrative organizations, subcontractors, consultants, and other sources. The general types of support from these sources to the proposal team include:

Contracts Specialists Prepare the cost volume, compute costs, and provide instructions to the proposal staff.

Procurement Specialists Solicit interest from vendors and suppliers, evaluate vendor/supplier capabilities, issue procurement documentation for bid purposes, and receives bids.

Subcontract Specialists — Issue the subcontractor data package for bidding, serve as the corporate point of contact for subcontractors, and deal with the subcontractor managers on proposal matters.

Security Specialists — Approve work spaces for classified proposals, handle security clearances for all personnel, review security procedures, handle visitor clearances.

Personnel Specialists — Identify personnel with specific skills, processes consultants, review job descriptions and labor categories, recruit personnel for the proposal team or design team.

Facility Managers — Acquire special facilities or equipment needed for the proposal, evaluate facilities for use in contract performance, and negotiate options for facilities to be used in the contract.

Accounting Specialists — Ensure that visiting corporate personnel receive pay checks, issue money for travel and per diem, prepare financial expenditure reports, provide petty cash funds.

Travel Specialists — Make the travel arrangements, provide local transportation means, procure tickets.

Office Service Specialists — Provide offices supplies, acquire office furniture, handle moving and relocation of proposal personnel.

Computer Technicians Install local area networks, check out rental computers, install software, and maintain computer-related hardware.

It is noted that most of these proposal support activities and resources are provided by personnel, organizations, and facilities belonging to the corporation and do not require the Proposal Manager to pay for them. These capabilities and organizations are paid for by the corporate general and administrative accounts. Of course, proposal-specific purchases or leases, such as computer rentals, airline tickets, and office rentals are not overhead charges and must be paid from the B & P charge account.

CHAPTER 4

ATTENDING TO IMPORTANT COST MATTERS

4.1 ENSURING THAT ADEQUATE FUNDING IS AVAILABLE

The Proposal Manager and the Proposal Planner are the ones responsible for estimating the costs associated with the proposal effort, and the Chief Engineer is responsible for estimating the costs associated with the system design. The Corporate Officer Responsible is in charge of obtaining the funding from Corporate or Group sources, based on the estimates provided by the Proposal Manager and the Chief Engineer.

The Proposal Manager, when preparing the estimate of proposal costs, is concurrently making a commitment to prepare a winning proposal for that amount of money. Likewise, the Chief Engineer, when preparing the estimate of design costs, makes a commitment to prepare a winning design for that amount of design money. The major costs, for which funding is definitely required, include those associated with personnel, facilities, equipment, supplies, and services.

4.2 DEFINING THE TOP-LEVEL PROPOSAL FINANCIAL MATTERS

4.2.1 SETTING UP THE CHARGE NUMBERS

One of the signs, perhaps the most important sign, of a corporate commitment to a proposal is the establishment of charge numbers that will be used for time cards of the proposal team members and for accruing costs by the accounting department. It is critical that these charge numbers be easily identified as Bid and Proposal numbers and that they be used only by members of the proposal team and by personnel or organizations providing direct support to the proposal team.

Charge numbers normally include those for personnel costs, materials costs, consulting costs, travel costs, office costs, production costs, and special facilities or rentals. For major system development proposals, the personnel costs can be divided into those associated with the design team and the proposal team. Depending on the corporate disclosure statement on file with the DCAS office, indirect costs associated with the higher-level corporate managers and administrators are not charged directly to the Bid and Proposal number.

4.2.2 SETTING UP A MANAGEMENT RESERVE

The Proposal Manager must retain a management reserve that will be committed to overcome problems, to get the proposal back on schedule, or to add value to the proposal. Just like in normal project management, the Proposal Manager must set aside about 6 to 7 percent of the total proposal funding and ensure that it is not allocated to any of the design or proposal team activities. The management reserve is released only upon the written approval of the Proposal Manager and is used only under the direst of circumstances. A skillful Proposal Manager knows where and how to hide the management reserve from the rest of the team members.

4.3 ESTIMATING THE PROPOSAL COSTS

4.3.1 MAJOR TYPES OF PROPOSAL COSTS

Proposal Management Costs - for the Proposal Management Staff, which includes the Proposal Manager, Proposal Planner, Subcontractor Specialist, Financial Assistant and Costing Specialist

Proposal Volume Personnel Costs - for the Volume Leaders, Plan Leaders, Proposal Writers, and Plan Writers

Proposal Production Costs - for the Production Coordinator, artists, graphics specialists, editors, proofreaders, word processing specialists, and printing and binding specialists

Proposal Facilities and Other Costs - for the office services, office supplies, office space, office equipment, micro-computers, facsimile machines, XEROX machines, etc.

4.3.2 MAJOR TYPES OF DESIGN COSTS

Design Team Personnel - includes the Chief Engineer, Lead Engineers and Designers, System Engineers, Design Engineers/specialists, System Engineering Specialists, Draftsmen, Software Specialists, and Hardware Specialists

Design Team Volume Leaders - includes those supervisory personnel responsible for preparation of the Technical Volume, Engineering Plans, Software Capability Evaluation, Facility Design Document, and Facility Demonstration Plan

Special Design Facilities and Equipment - includes costs associated with: the micro-computers, automated design and drafting systems, computer centers, laboratories, and system demonstration facilities needed by the Design Team

Design Production Costs – includes the artists, graphics specialists, editors, proofreaders, word processing specialists, and printing and binding specialists needed for the technical plans, drawings, and documentation prepared by the Design Team

Other Design Costs - includes office services, office supplies, office space, office equipment, facsimile machines, and XEROX machines

4.3.3 ESTIMATING THE PROPOSAL COSTS

Estimating the Proposal Personnel Costs - Personnel costs are the single most important costs associated with the preparation of a competitive proposal, so the preparation of a cost forecast by the Proposal Manager or the Proposal Planner is a critical activity. As a first effort to produce a ball-park estimate of the proposal personnel costs, use the proposal outline and page budget. Multiply the number of pages by 2 to obtain a reasonable estimate of the man-days needed to prepare the proposal; multiply the number of pages by 1 to 1.2 to obtain an estimate of the minimum number of days needed to prepare the proposal and the supporting plans.

It is important to note that the number of days needed to prepare the technical and management volumes and the associated plans include only the full-time writers assigned to the proposal team, the proposal management team, and the production personnel. It is equally, if not more, important to understand that this estimating process does not include the personnel costs associated with the Gold and Red Team reviews, the contracts and subcontracts personnel, the design team, the Corporate Officer Responsible, and the Green Team reviews.

Estimating the Proposal Design Team Related Costs - Estimating the costs associated with the design team is truly a black art and it always seems that design costs exceed any initial cost estimates by a wide margin. In estimating design team costs, the Chief Engineer must consider the personnel costs for the engineers on the design team, the special facilities required by the design effort, the special activities needed to support and to validate designs, the costs for computer main-frame operations, and the expenses associated with the engineering drawings. In addition to these costs, the Chief Engineer must consider the complexity of the system being designed, the need for travel by the design engineers, the special security requirements, and the use of consultants and contract personnel.

The methods used for estimating the design team costs include such diversity as using:
- An algorithm based on the type and number of drawings needed
- Costs associated with the design of a system of similar complexity
- A computerized cost estimating method such as COCOMO or RCA Price
- Standard construction estimating handbooks for man-hours
- Corporate cost estimating handbooks or commercially-available handbooks
- Detailed estimates based on time-motion studies
- Planning factors based on the estimated cost of the total system or facility

It is not intended that this listing is all-comprehensive, because the cost estimating effort for system design varies depending on many factors such as system complexity, security requirements, customer-generated requirements (like system demonstrations), risk mitigation efforts, and number of design team reviews. In conclusion, the design team costs can be estimated only when a system- specific design plan or development plan has been prepared by the Chief Engineer and his senior technical personnel.

Estimating the Proposal Facility-Related Costs - As a general rule, most of the facility costs associated with the proposal team and with design team is included in the direct overhead for the employee. But the direct overhead seldom covers the costs for the facilities used by the proposal team or the design team. So these proposal facility costs must be addressed. For the proposal team, the facility costs can be computed as a simple function of the number of personnel working on the proposal. Normally, the Proposal Center has a fixed price for offices, office furniture, office supplies and services, and administrative support. The Center's variable costs include items such as the rental of microcomputers for writers and the purchase of specific software. The Proposal Center can provide accurate and timely estimates for the proposal-related facility costs without any problem.

Estimating the Special Activity Costs - While very few proposals entail costs for exotic systems or facilities. Inevitably, there will be instances when the proposal effort will incur special activity costs, such as:

- The need to work in a Tempest-approved location
- The need to obtain security clearances for additional personnel
- The need to provide special services and facilities to subcontractors
- The need to use STU-III equipment for classified transmissions
- The need to obtain special training for design or proposal personnel
- The need to provide facilities and services to customer personnel
- The need to conduct system demonstrations

All that I can say about these special activities is that they all require more time and attention than they should and that when they occur, the proposal design and writing efforts are impacted.

Estimating the Proposal Production Costs - The department responsible for providing the proposal production support will submit a fairly accurate estimate of the costs, including both personnel, supplies, and other items in a relatively short time. Provided that the proposal manager can provide a reasonably accurate estimate of the proposals needs for art, graphics, word processing, printing, binding, coordination, editing, and proofreading. Basically, the Proposal Manager or Proposal Planner must provide early estimates of:

- Number of pages in the final proposal
- Number and type of graphics or artwork in the final proposal
- Level of editing and proofreading required
- Number of review or working draft copies needed
- Number of shipments required

4.3.4 Quick and Dirty Methods of Estimating Proposal Costs

Several nationally recognized proposal authorities have presented several methods for estimating proposal costs, with the methods based on two general planning factors:

First. The total costs for a proposal can be estimated as a percentage of the total value of the contract resulting from a winning proposal. I have prepared the following table from material that the authorities presented at symposia.

Type of Proposal	Value of Contract	Proposal Cost
Small studies and technical services	$500,000 or less	seven (7) percent.
Large technical services/studies	$ 2,000,000	five (five) percent
Major system development proposals	$50 million or more,	two (2) percent+
+ plus the extensive costs associated with the design effort		

Second. The total costs for a proposal can be estimated from the number of pages in the proposal. The planning factor of one-half page per writer per day can be used to estimate the probable highest cost for the proposal. In this method, multiply the number of pages by two, then multiply that resultant by the average daily cost, fully burdened, of the proposal team members. Then the costs for other support and services are added to those costs.

Example: For a 100 page proposal, 200 man days by writers and manager/leaders will be required. At a direct labor rate of $250 per man-day, the direct labor costs will total about $50,000 for the writers and the managers/leaders. If production, facility, and other costs are 30 percent of the direct labor costs for writing and managing, the total direct labor cost for that proposal is calculated to be about $65,000. Of course, when the taxes, fringe benefits, direct overhead, indirect overhead, and general and administrative costs for the personnel are added, the total labor costs will increase by about $ 125,000, driving the total proposal costs to over $190,000.

Notes: (1) The costing algorithm above (which is based on pages) is not suitable for estimating the costs associated with a major system design and development proposal which requires matters such as a major engineering design effort, a system demonstration facility, and development of software. (2) The costing algorithm (based on pages) above can be used for estimating the costs for preparing the supporting plans and other similar documentation.

4.4 SETTING UP A COST MANAGEMENT SYSTEM

The Proposal Manager is responsible for the cost performance of the proposal team and the Chief Engineer is responsible for the cost performance of the design team. In this dual responsibility arrangement, these managers are responsible for:

- Preparing cost estimates for the proposal team and the design team
- Preparing a time-phased budget or estimate for funds expenditure
- Comparing the actual costs with the budgets/estimates on a weekly or biweekly basis
- Identifying the activities or phases where the budgets and actual costs differ
- Determining the causes for cost variances
- Implementing cost get-well plans and committing management reserve
- Reporting cost problems to higher management (Corporate Officer Responsible)

4.5 SPECIAL SUBCONTRACTOR-RELATED COST MATTERS

Costs for Subcontractors Working at Your Facilities - When your corporation is the prime contractor, you should require the subcontractors to work at your facility; where you will provide their equipment, software, offices, supplies, and office services. This means that you will be subsidizing your subcontractors in these matters, but rest assured that such instances will be money well spent because subcontractor productivity is always much greater when they work closely with the Proposal Team or the Design Team at a common facility.

Costs When Working as a Subcontractor at a Prime Contractor Facility - When your design team members or proposal team members must work on-site at the prime contractor's facility, the prime contractor must provide your equipment, software, offices, office furniture, office supplies, and office services. You will be required to pay the travel and per diem expenses of your personnel when working on-site at the prime contractor facility. The number and type of personnel to be provided to the prime contractor and the duration of their assignment is negotiated by the Corporate Officer Responsible, as a general rule.

When working on a proposal as a subcontractor to Martin Marietta in Denver, CO, we provided five full-time technical personnel for over four weeks to participate in the system design effort. When working as a subcontractor to the Flour Corporation in Irvine, CA, we provided four full-time analysts and proposal specialists (me) to the Flour proposal team for a period of two weeks. When a subcontractor to Dynalectron, in Albuquerque, NM, we provided two laser technologists and one proposal specialist (me) to work for three weeks on the technical and management volumes of the proposal.

4.6 AVOIDING FINANCIAL FIASCOS

The major causes for financial disasters during the preparation of a proposal can be summarized in the following simple statements:

The Proposal Manager overestimated the productivity of the proposal writers, underestimated the level of effort needed to write a winning proposal, or failed to motivate the writers to an acceptable level of productivity.

The higher level corporate managers who control the Bid and Proposal budget did not allocate enough money to prepare a winning proposal, did not assign the resources needed by the proposal team, or assumed indefensible levels or productivity.

The proposal writers did not commit themselves to being productive, to meeting schedules, or to meeting the proposal working conditions.

The Proposal Manager or the Design Manager did not control the travel and per diem costs for staff members coming in from remote offices.

As an example: When West Coast personnel were assigned to my East Coast proposal effort, they wanted to leave California on Monday morning and to return to California on Friday morning. Because of this travel agenda, they were available three days a week but wanted to charge for five days of their time. I refused to pay for their travel time and I paid for only one trip to the East Coast and one trip to the West

Coast. And we had a minor crisis with much wailing. But since I approved the time sheets, I won. Any proposal manager who does not control these types of costs is not doing his job. When I worked in San Diego on a proposal, I was allowed one round-trip flight home during a ten week assignment.

4.7 BUY OR LEASE DECISIONS ON PROPOSAL PROCUREMENTS

The acquisition of hardware, software, facilities, publications, and special equipment for the proposal team and the design team can be through outright purchase or through leasing or rental. The Proposal Manager and the Corporate Officer Responsible must decide on the method for acquiring these essential resources. While each proposal presents a special set of circumstances, the following guidelines are suggested:

1. Lease facilities from other organizations within the corporation that meet the space, security, and other requirements of the design and proposal teams. Go outside of the corporation only when absolutely necessary.
2. Lease facilities from a third party when the facilities are not available within the corporation. Avoid using facilities of major subcontractors who will become deadly competitors on other procurements in the future.
3. Lease computers, servers, reproduction machines, facsimile equipment, and other high-value equipment whenever possible.
4. Buy applications software and software tools with the rights to use them on many computers and to use them in other competitions and during contract performance.
5. Buy books, references, publications, and other commercially available material needed by the staff.

Note: It is always wise to use the Purchasing Department to handle all procurements and to use the proposal and design teams to prepare the specifications for the procurement.

4.8 SECURING HIGH LEVEL APPROVAL OF CORPORATE COMMITMENTS

During the analysis of the Request for Proposal and after review of the marketing intelligence, the Proposal Manager, Proposal Planner, and the Volume Leaders will develop the win themes and discriminators for the proposal. It is likely that some of the win themes and discriminators will require the corporation to make major, costly commitments to the customer. Such commitments can include:

- Key project personnel for the duration of the contract
- Providing proprietary software at no cost to the customer
- Locating special facilities close to the customer
- Granting data rights to corporate data bases and publications
- Acquiring upgraded computers for work on the contract
- Providing office space and conference facilities to customer personnel
- Granting customer personnel the privilege of attending corporate functions

Since these commitments cost money, sometimes a lot of money, the Proposal Manager must obtain high-level corporate agreement and support. Under no circumstances does any person on the proposal team or the design team make any statement that implies an unrestricted corporate commitment, particularly one that will cost the corporation. Normally, the Corporate Officer Responsible handles this matter.

4.9 DEALING WITH SUBCONTRACTOR COST PROPOSALS

4.9.1 DEALING WITH SUBCONTRACTOR PRIVILEGED COST INFORMATION

In every competition, our corporation shielded its cost information from the subcontractors and our subcontractors denied us access to their detailed cost data. Both the subcontractors and our management were concerned about the compromise of their respective cost data, which included information such as employee salaries, fringe benefit and tax rates, overhead, and general and administrative costs. We could not demand such privileged cost data, so a compromise was necessary when the RFP issued by the Government required detailed cost data.

The only viable compromise in the matter has proven to be: The subcontractor would submit fully-burdened labor rates to our corporation for inclusion in our cost proposal and would submit the detailed cost data to the Government Contract Officer. This compromise proved valuable when our corporation was bidding as a subcontractor.

4.9.2 Providing Cost Proposal Instructions to the Subcontractor

The prime contractor is obligated to provide detailed instructions to the subcontractor for the preparation of their cost proposal, which will be included with or incorporated into the cost proposal submitted by the prime contractor. These instructions which are directly related to the specific deliverables and specific activities of the subcontractor should include the full range of information that they need for the preparation of their cost proposal. These instructions should include the following:

- Project Work Breakdown Structure with specific work packages to be accomplished by the subcontractor
- Position descriptions for labor categories to be provided by the subcontractor
- Descriptions of the deliverables to be prepared and the services to be provided by the subcontractor
- Schedules and milestones associated with the project and with the subcontractor part of the work

- Recommendations for the preparation of the subcontractor's Cost Realism inputs
- Directions regarding the costs for supplies, materials, equipment, services, and for the leasing of facilities and other resources
- Instructions regarding subcontractor personnel that must work at the facilities of your corporation (duration, other factors)

It has been my experience that small businesses need assistance in the preparation of their cost proposals. Small businesses seldom have experience in Work Breakdown Structures, cost realism, cost estimating algorithms, cost documentation, and many other aspects of preparing a cost proposal to a large business submitting a proposal for the design and development of a major system. Invariably, the small businesses have needed assistance in these matters.

4.9.3 Defining Costing Guidelines and Restraints with Subcontractors

The Corporate Officer Responsible must have early discussions with managers from the subcontractors regarding their costs, most importantly their labor costs, when bidding a technical services contract. This discussion is critical when providing skilled personnel to work on Government-specified assignments under SETA-type contracts. On such proposal efforts, where labor costs comprise the overwhelming amount of the total contract value, the corporation has decided the maximum labor rates that will be bid.

If the subcontractor labor rates are significantly lower than your corporation's rates, this matter becomes a non-issue. If the subcontractor labor rates are significantly higher than your corporation's rates, perhaps the Corporate Officer Responsible can negotiate a special rate. This matter is very sensitive, so deal with it with tact and resolve.

4.10 BECOMING SERIOUS ABOUT COST PROPOSALS

When I attended a two-day cost proposal seminar taught by Doug Leffler, it was very obvious that none of our 17,000 employees knew much, if anything, about the art and science of preparing winning cost proposals for major system development projects. I was stunned by the amount of knowledge that was absolutely necessary for a major system proposal. And now I state, without any reservations, that every Cost Volume Leader for system development proposals should attend a cost proposal seminar before attempting to prepare such a volume.

The Cost Specialist must know about cost estimating systems, cost data bases, cost relationships, cost realism, cost strategies, approaches to costing, should-cost methods, customer costing models, cost documentation, and many other subjects.

CHAPTER **5**

SPECIAL AND CRITICAL CONSIDERATIONS

5.1 PROPOSAL SECURITY REQUIREMENTS

5.1.1 PERSONNEL SECURITY

Proposal personnel must meet the security requirements of the Government or the customer when working on classified or sensitive proposals. These requirements include:

- Personnel security clearances and need-to-know are required for work on proposals in which the RFP and the proposal are classified. They must meet the provisions of the Industrial Security Manual published by the Government
- Specific approval of proposal personnel for the handling of customer proprietary data and information must be in accordance with the customer instructions
- Unclassified, but sensitive and proprietary, corporate matters are restricted to those personnel who have a need-to-know
- All proposal and design personnel must attend presentations by security specialists on classified matters and briefings by the Proposal Manager on sensitive, unclassified matters

5.1.2 PHYSICAL SECURITY

The physical security requirements of the proposal effort include those needed to safeguard classified and proprietary data, information, and publications. These requirements include, use of physical assets such as safes, vaults, and controlled areas, procedures such as the proper destruction of material (paper, magnetic media, CDs), controls on the reproduction of classified or proprietary matter, and use of badges that denote access levels, high technology applications such as the use of special locks and ciphers to control access to work areas and the masking of windows to prevent high technology monitoring. Visitor access and control, defining need to know, and working in pairs are techniques used in some proposals.

5.1.3 DATA SECURITY

Data security encompasses all systems, procedures, and controls needed to safeguard data that is important to the corporation and to the proposal. Data can include such diversity as: data bases, marketing reports, costing algorithms, cost data, tabulated information, publications, resumes, proposal text, design papers, plans and procedures, personnel rosters, names of proposal personnel, win themes and discriminators, estimating tools, quality assurance reports, configuration management documents, and many more such items.

During major and small proposal efforts, every member of the proposal and design teams must guard against the loss of data to potential competitors and to employees who are not loyal to the corporation. This is not a simple undertaking because of the widespread use of microcomputers, local area networks, wide area networks, and computerized data sources. The corporation spends a great deal of money on data that would be extremely valuable to other companies and unscrupulous individuals.

5.1.4 Computer/Telecommunications Security

Computer and telecommunications security should be a major concern now that most employees and even a few outsiders can enter the corporate networks and gain access to the servers and computers of the design and proposal teams. One may wonder about my concern over the employees having access to the proposal, but in one proposal effort, it was apparent that someone in a remote office gained access to the server and to some of the computers used by the proposal team. Perhaps the intruder-hacker was harmless, but we did lose that competition in which we were the incumbent contractor.

Ensure that your computer systems and servers use state-of-the-art security approaches to prevent entry to the proposal files. Use of simple code assigned to certain individuals concerned with the proposal will not delay an experienced hacker very long. The use of firewalls and other more-advanced techniques are recommended to make entry into the proposal servers and individual computers much more difficult. As part of the security briefing to the proposal and design teams, this type of security must be discussed.

5.1.5 Other Proposal Security Initiatives

The Proposal Manager is required to state the security policies, practices, systems, and procedures that will be observed by the proposal team. As a general rule, the Chief Engineer will issue instructions to the Design Team that the same security requirements apply to all members of the design team. The purpose of the proposal security effort is to ensure that vital information about the proposal, the design, the costing are not inadvertently disclosed to unauthorized personnel.

The key features of the proposal security initiatives by the proposal and design teams include these activities:

- The Proposal Manager publishes a Proposal Security Policy that is distributed to members of the proposal and design teams
- Code Names, such as Quicksilver, will be used for all proposals so that design and proposal personnel can refer to an ongoing effort without disclosing the actual title
- o Conversations between the proposal and design team members with consultants or vendors are very restricted, if not prohibited, in the matter of the proposal and the design
- Proposal and design papers that have been discarded or replaced should be destroyed by shredding and incineration like classified material. No normal office trash pickup
- All copies of volumes and drafts provided to the proposal, design, and review teams are controlled by the Production Coordinator
- Draft material, draft proposal copies, proposal planning documentation, and corporate data base material cannot be removed by subcontractors or consultants for any reason

5.2 SPECIAL SECURITY CLEARANCES

Many proposals involve highly classified or very sensitive matters, which mean that the design team and the proposal team members, must have special personnel clearances and that the work must be performed in a specially cleared facility. In such facilities, the computers must be TEMPEST- approved; hard drives must be removed, and placed in safes when not in use. Working spaces must never be left unguarded and unoccupied. In such instances, the corporate Special Security Officer, not the normal Security Officer, controls access to these proposals that may involve Cryptographic, Code Word, or Special Compartmented Information. As a general rule, the corporation is allowed very few billets for cleared personnel and the design and proposal work must be accomplished by a few cleared personnel.

While normal security clearances (Secret and Top Secret) are handled by the Corporate Security Officer that everyone knows, there are always special personnel security problems when working on proposals to the Federal Bureau of Investigation. The FBI does not have: Confidential, Secret, or Top Secret levels, does not have publications that specify the requirements, or provide any information on its process. How they approve people, even those with Top Secret clearances from the Defense Industrial Security Clearance Office, is a black art, in my opinion. I had some problems being cleared to work on a proposal for an unclassified FBI project, even though I had Top Secret, Code Word, SCI, and Crypto clearances.

The only thing that I can say strongly and definitely about the matter of Special Security Clearances is that: (1) your options in staffing the proposal and design teams become very stressing, (2) the number of personnel approved for work on the proposal and design teams will be very limited, and (3) you will be introduced to the Special Security Officer, an important person you never knew about before.

5.3 CORPORATE AND SUBCONTRACTOR TEAMING AGREEMENTS

5.3.1 CORPORATE TEAMING AGREEMENTS

In many proposals, the most stressful activity turns out to be the negotiation of teaming agreements that specify how the contract work will be divided between the various corporate entities after contract award. Some corporate entities appear to have an unstated policy of drawing upon the resources, resumes, and contract experience of other organizational elements within the corporation in order to win a competition without any intention of sharing a contract. Some corporate entities will sign teaming agreements with other parts of the corporation to get their assistance on the proposals, without ever intending to share the contract after award.

The only advice that I can offer in this matter is to deal only with those managers who have a reputation for dealing honestly with other managers and who have a record of sharing contracts with other divisions. You will find that corporate agreements, even written ones, are difficult to enforce. In my college course on contracts, the instructor said, "a contract is valid and will be observed only when both parties wish it so". So, deal with honest managers.

5.3.2 SUBCONTRACTOR TEAMING AGREEMENTS

Every subcontractor will request a teaming agreement that describes the type and amount of work that it will perform after contract award. Such a teaming agreement is comprised of five pages of "boilerplate" statements, such as "award of work is contingent upon the winning of the contract". One page will describe the work to be performed by the subcontractor, essentially a micro Statement of Work. Such teaming agreements will not specify the dollar amount of the subcontract, but the subcontractor data package may define an upper limit on the dollar amount.

These teaming agreements are very important to the subcontractor for several important reasons, such as:
- Determining the amount of money to be expended by the subcontractor in its proposal support effort
- Estimating the probable sales that could result from its investment in the proposal effort
- Focusing the subcontractors attention on specific proposal support requirements, such as skilled writers and facilities

I have usually found that most corporations honor their subcontractor teaming agreements because subcontractors have a way of spreading information about their experience with your corporation. I dealt with a firm in Florida that had supported my corporation during two proposals to a military client without ever having any work assigned to it. That firm had also talked with Government contract officers about the way that my corporation dealt with them which made me recall an old western expression: poisoning the wells.

5.4 SUBCONTRACTING GOALS AND ROLES

Virtually every Government agency will require prime contractors to employ subcontractors during its contract performance. The Request for Proposal may specify the subcontracting goals for small businesses, small disadvantaged businesses, and woman-owned small businesses that the prime contractor must meet. These contract goals are based on the small business goals of the Government agency issuing the contract, and the prime contractor must agree to meet or exceed specific goals.

While there appears to be no universal guidelines for subcontracting goals, the following instances demonstrate the range of such goals.

- Construction contracts will frequently have small business subcontracting goals in excess of 50 percent, with some contracts requiring 66 percent subcontracted
- System development contracts for major military systems will usually have small business subcontracting goals in the 10 to 15 percent range
- Subcontracts to large and small businesses should not reduce the work performed by prime contractors to less than 60 percent in most military procurements
- Small business subcontracts frequently include small businesses, small disadvantaged businesses, and woman-owned small businesses in the following ratios: SB - 10 SDB - 4 WOSB - 2

Every proposal should cite the corporation's small business subcontracting goals in recent years and the success that the corporation has realized in meeting these goals. Do not worry that the RFP does not specify such a proposal requirements, do it always. If you do not address this matter, the Government Contract Officer is most likely to assume that you do not have goals or that you do not meet your goals. It would be great if the current proposal could cite a prior contract with the customer for whom the proposal is being prepared in which the small business subcontracting goal was met or exceeded.

5.5 USING CONSULTANTS TO AUGMENT THE DESIGN AND PROPOSAL PERSONNEL

The cardinal rule in the employment of consultants, whether for the design team or the proposal team, is to ensure that the consultants are working exclusively for your corporation. Consultants must disclose their customer list and their relationships with those customers. They must sign a statement that they are providing services exclusively with your corporation in regard to the specific procurement. Only then can consultants be used with confidence on technical or management matters. Note: under no conditions are technical or management consultants used in the planning and preparation of cost proposals; however, experts in costing should be employed on major system development proposals.

This harsh concern over the use of consultants in the preparation of designs and proposals does not mean that consultants do not have a role in the proposal process. Consultants are valuable in areas such as competition intelligence, status of technologies, Government procurement objectives, and development of win strategies. In these matters, the consultants do the talking and answering while your corporate personnel do the listening and questioning. Always assume that consultants will, deliberately or accidentally, reveal your privileged information to a competitor.

5.6 MONITORING THE PRODUCTIVITY OF THE PROPOSAL PERSONNEL

The Proposal Manager must issue instructions to the Volume Leaders and Plan Leaders governing the process by which the productivity of each proposal writer is assessed on a continuing basis. If the Proposal Manager does not know how to monitor the productivity of the proposal writers, hopefully the Volume Leaders and Plan Leaders know how to monitor and measure the productivity of the writers. If no member of the proposal management team has an idea on this subject, the proposal is in serious trouble.

The most effective and fairest method for monitoring and measuring the productivity of each proposal writer by the Volume-Plan Leaders is:

1. Assign work to the writers in one, two, or three-page units with a very short time in which to submit the finished proposal material to the Leader.
2. Require the writer to prepare a page layout for the unit, denoting the type and size of graphics and the topics of each paragraph.
3. Review the page layouts, graphics designs, and paragraph themes as quickly as possible and provide comments within minutes.
4. Conduct very brief (usually less than 20 minutes duration) status meetings each morning and each afternoon to identify problems and assess productivity.

It is highly recommended that the Volume Leader or Plan Leader consider replacing any proposal writer who does not meet the deadline for the delivery of his/her first writing assignment. If any writer misses two deadlines, that writer is not productive and must be replaced quickly. There is no time or money to support unproductive proposal personnel.

Part II

CRITICAL UNDERSTANDINGS NEEDED TO WIN

CHAPTER 6

UNDERSTANDING THE PROCUREMENT PROCESS

6.1 THE MAJOR TYPES OF GOVERNMENT PROCUREMENTS

This book is directed to the competitive procurements in which organizations must compete for a contract through competitive proposals. Of course, much of this book can be used in the preparation of unsolicited proposals for the sole-source procurements. Just remember that sole-source procurements do not involve companies in a competition for a contract and that competitive procurements mean that other organizations will be preparing proposals and competing against your corporation. Note: your proposal to the Government is an offer and when you submit a proposal your company is an offeror.

The Government will procure goods and services through cost reimbursable, fixed price, and cost sharing contracts. The major features and types of contracts within these categories include:

Cost Reimbursable Contracts - In which the Government reimburses the Contractor for all costs incurred in a contract, plus either a fee (profit), an incentive, or award fee. Incentive and award fee contracts are usually associated with programs that involve emerging technologies, major uncertainties, or high risks. The key features of these types of contracts include:

Cost plus Fixed Fee - The Government will pay costs, including cost over- runs associated with the contract work, but the fee (profit) will not increase as the contract costs increase. Basically, the contractor cannot lose money on these contracts, but the profit percentage drops as the cost overrun increases.

Cost plus Incentive Fee - The Government will pay all costs, plus an incentive fee (or variable profit) will be contingent upon the degree of success the contractor achieves in the required technical, quality, or schedule performance. The incentive fee is in addition to the base fee.

Cost plus Award Fee - The Government will pay all costs, but the award fee will be contingent upon the Government's evaluation of Contractor performance in many different areas. Frequently, the Government does not pay a base fee, and all profit to the contractor is from award fees.

Fixed Price Contracts - In which the Government agrees to pay a fixed price for a product or a service, although there are incentive and escalation clauses in many such contracts. The key features of these types of contract include:

Firm Fixed Price - In which the contractor or supplier agrees to provide a well-defined product or service to the Government; in this type of contract, the product or service is very well defined and both parties agree. The risk is entirely on the part of the contractor.

Fixed Price Incentive - In which the contractor agrees to deliver a product or service that meets the specifications of the Government for a fixed price. The Government agrees to pay an incentive fee to the Contractor for contract performance well above some norm with the incentive fee being in addition to the profit bid on the contract. Again, the contractor assumes all risks.

Fixed Price with Escalation - In which the contractor proposes to perform work or deliver a product at a fixed price, except there is a possible escalation of the contract value due to factors beyond the control of the contractor and the Government. An example is the increase in the cost of steel due to labor settlements between the steel industry and its unions. Any profit on the increased cost of materials is subject to negotiations.

Cost Sharing Contracts - In which the Government and the contractor share the costs, usually equally. The contractor does not receive any profit or fee in these contracts, but the contractor will not lose any money on the contracts. These contracts are associated principally with research and development studies and most of these contracts place the contractor entirely at risk for any cost overruns.

Indefinite Delivery-Indefinite Quantity Contracts - In which the Government executes a contract with a bidder that does not include a specific amount of money or a specific statement of work. Usually proposals in response to ID-IQ solicitations are more like very high-powered qualification statements with examples of how the contractor would perform a series of tasks. After the contract has been awarded, the Government will issue task orders or delivery orders to the contractor for work of a very limited scope in essence a miniature contract. In this type of procurement, the Request for Proposal, its attachments, and its references and citations become a major part of the ID-IQ contract; your proposal becomes part of that contract also.

Delivery Order Contracts - In which the Government intends to issue delivery orders (or task orders) for specific work of a limited duration to be accomplished during the contract. These contracts are very close to the ID-IQ contracts described above, but they can be quite different in some respects. For example, the contractor may agree to provide an agreed-upon number of labor hours to the Government and the Government issues enough delivery (or task) orders to fully utilize those labor hours. Basically each delivery order is like a miniature contract but the contractual requirements are less than for an ID-IQ contract.

Invitation For A Bid Contracts - In which the Government intends to procure items that are in existence, whose characteristics are well-know and are virtually always readily available from commercial sources. In these IFB contracts, the Government issues a very detailed specification for material and items known to currently exist. The suppliers do not prepare a proposal in these procurements, they only need to submit a cost quote and a delivery schedule. This book recognizes these procurements but does not address this type of procurement.

Descriptions of These Contracts - The key features of these types of contracts and procurements are described in the Federal Acquisition Regulations and in the supplementary regulations of the various Government Departments or Agencies. For example, the Department of Defense has issued its Defense Acquisition Regulations (DARs), and the Department of Transportation has issued Transportation Acquisition Regulations (TARs). Every true proposal specialist is encouraged to obtain their own copies of these publications and to know them well.

6.2 THE PROCUREMENT DOCUMENTS ISSUED BY THE GOVERNMENT

The Request for Proposal is the most important document

governing the proposal to be prepared and submitted by the contractor. The RFP is organized into sections identified by the alphabetical letters from A to Z, with each section including clauses that address a proposal or contract requirement. The RFP virtually always cites references and frequently contains a series of attachments and enclosures. The RFP references sections of the Federal Acquisition Regulations related to the procurement, and cites the specifications governing the work and the product. A Contract Data Requirements List (CDRL) specifies all of the documentation to be submitted by the contractor during the period of performance.

After the initial RFP has been issued, the Government will issue a series of other, equally important documents to potential bidders. Typically, this documentation includes: changes to the RFP, changes or clarifications to the specifications, list of questions from potential bidders, and the Government response to the questions. Sometimes, but not often, the Government may include material from its Advanced Procurement Briefing to Industry, may provide a listing of all interested bidders, and may list the attendees (name and company) at Bidders Conferences. Rarely, some Government offices list the people on the Source Selection Evaluation Board and their qualifications.

In summary, the procurement documents issued by the Government procuring office that are probably most critical to the development of a complete, compliant, winning proposal include:

- Request for Proposal
- Attachments
- Contract Clause References
- Covering Letter
- DD-254 Security Form
- Contract Data Requirements List
- Specifications
- Acquisition Regulations
- RFP Changes-Amendments
- Questions/Answers

* Note: Attachments can include position descriptions for key personnel, detailed descriptions of facility requirements, and special security requirements.

6.3 REGULATIONS AND REFERENCES GOVERNING PROCUREMENTS

The principal publications regarding the procurement regulations, procurement processes, and procurement systems include:

Federal Acquisition Regulations

Department Acquisition Regulations

Department Instructions, Regulations, and Handbooks

Defense Systems Management Center Publications and Course Material

Army, Navy, Air Force Regulations, Instructions, and Handbooks

Every Proposal Manager, Proposal Planner, and Responsible Corporate Officer should be conversant with the above publications and have current copies available for quick reference. It is not enough to read a short title or, a short paragraph in the Request for Proposal; it is imperative to read the complete text of the paragraphs in the publications cited in the RFP. Do not assume that someone else is knowledgeable in all such matters. Read the material yourself. **Note:** the References section of this book includes the full titles and other identification information so that you can acquire these publications for your own library.

Several commercial organizations publish up-to-date material related to procurement regulations and codes, like the Commerce Clearing House. The Naval Publications Center in Philadelphia is the source of all items listed in the Contract Data Requirement List. The Defense Systems Management Center is the source of many references governing activities that are essential in most contract work. The Government Printing Office publishes and sells most procurement related publications, with many being in both hard copy and on CD-ROM disks.

Every leading proposal center and every winning Proposal Manager should have these references and should use them during every major proposal effort. Some of the references, such as the Defense Acquisition Regulations, are critical to the preparation of a winning proposal. For example, the RFP may not state a requirement for information on the quality program of the contractor, but the DARs state that quality is evaluated in every proposal. The RFP may not address the particular requirements for a Cost Schedule Control System, but the DARs describe the conditions under which such a massive effort is required. These are major proposal requirements.

6.4 THE GOVERNMENT PROCUREMENT ORGANIZATIONS

6.4.1 AN INTRODUCTION TO PROCUREMENT ROLES AND ORGANIZATIONS

The procuring agency designates specific personnel who are responsible for the development of procurement documents, the evaluation of proposals, and the award of contracts. The procurement personnel include such diversity as: specialists from the contracting office, technical personnel from line organizations, management specialists, small business advocates, compliance specialists, cost analysts, and data management specialists. Such diversity in the procurement-related personnel usually ensures that all applicable requirements, legal and contractual, are considered in Government procurements.

6.4.2 KEY PERSONNEL ROLES IN THE GOVERNMENT'S PROCUREMENT PROCESS

Source Selection Authority - Is the very high level person who has the authority to make the final selection of the contractor and to sign the contract. The SSA has the ultimate authority to commit the Government to a contract, but it is noted that this authority can be delegated to a Contracting Officer for smaller procurements. As a general rule, but not a universal rule, the SSA executes the contract with the contractor recommended by the Source Selection Advisory Council but that is not a certainty in all procurements.

Head, Source Selection Advisory Council - Is the manager of very senior technical and management experts who review the evaluation factors-sub factors-standards and assign weights to those items. When the Council receives the evaluation results from the Source Selection Evaluation Board, it assigns these weights to those evaluation results and identifies the contractor with the highest rating. The Council submits a recommendation to the Source Selection Authority regarding the contractor to be awarded the contract. The Council also provides the relative rankings of the other proposals submitted by other bidders.

Leader, Source Selection Evaluation Board - Is the manager of the technical, management, and administrative personnel assigned to the Board and the special personnel who work on the special teams supporting the evaluation effort. The Leader-SSEB is responsible for determining if the offeror has submitted a compliant and complete proposal. When a proposal is judged to be non-compliant or incomplete, he/she can eliminate that proposal from further consideration, unless it is determined that the proposal can be made compliant. The Leader-SSEB assigns personnel to the evaluation of specific portions of the proposal, schedules the activities of those personnel, and monitors their progress and performance. The Leader-SSEB prepares the documentation for the Source Selection Advisory Council.

Contracting Officer - Is the individual responsible for the overall procurement, beginning with the notice to potential offerors, continuing through to the completion and approval of all work at the completion of the contract. The Contracting Officer has been designated and approved by the head of the agency and cannot be overruled in contractual matters by any other person or organization. The Contract Officer receives the proposals from the contractors and determines if they are competent bidders. During the lifetime of the contract, the Contracting Officer or his alternate the Contracting Officer Representative, receives all contract deliverables and monitors contract performance on a continuing basis. Changes or modifications to the RFP or to the contract are prepared by and signed by the Contracting Officer. Talk about power.

Contracting Officer Technical Representative - Is a technical Government employee who is assigned to work with the Contract Officer as a subordinate. The COTR is a prime contributor to the technical specifications of the RFP, is completely knowledgeable on all technical issues, and serves on the contract reviews as a lead member. The COTR answers the technical questions during the pre-award phase, deals with the technical staff of the contractor after award of contract, and assesses the technical performance of the contractor. The COTR integrates the many technical inputs to the proposal, including the statement of work, the specifications, and the special instructions.

Cost Specialist - Is responsible for preparing the should-cost estimates for the Government, evaluating the cost proposals of the offerors, and assessing the cost risks associated with the procurement. The Cost Specialist uses approved models, algorithms, and data bases to prepare the cost-to-the-Government estimate and to check the costing information provided by the offerors. The specialist also reviews the Cost Realism material prepared by and submitted by the offerors to assess its credibility and relevance.

Legal Officer - Is responsible for ensuring that the procurement complies with all of the Government's legal obligations and, in particular, the Code of Federal Regulations (the regulations) and the U. S. Code (the law). The Legal Officer ensures that the offerors meet the legal standards for a responsible offeror and that the procurement documents (such as the RFP) do not infringe on any federal or state laws or regulations.

Small Business Advocate - Is initially responsible for reviewing the procurement documents to determine if the contract should be restricted to a small business. If the procurement is determined to be unrestricted, the Small Business Advocate reviews the proposals to determine if the offeror is aiding the procuring authority in meeting its goals for subcontracting with small businesses. The Advocate can cause unrestricted competitions to be designed as small business set-asides and can judge offerors' proposals to be unacceptable because of lack of subcontracts with small businesses.

6.4.3 IMPORTANT GOVERNMENT ORGANIZATIONS IN ITS PROCUREMENT PROCESS

Source Selection Evaluation Board - The evaluation of the proposal is a most demanding activity by the Government, in that the Board must review and evaluate the proposals of all compliant offerors within a relatively short time. The Board is responsible for evaluating the contractor proposals against the evaluation standards approved by the Source Selection Advisory Council. The Board submits its evaluation results to the Source Selection Advisory Council.

The Source Selection Evaluation Board includes technical, management, contracts personnel, and part-time specialists from a number of procurement-related organizations. The Board is usually divided into teams that evaluate specific sections of the proposal; normally, one team will evaluate all proposals in their specific area of responsibility. Note: contract experience and past performance are two examples of specific areas of responsibility for an evaluation team.

Source Selection Advisory Council - This organization is a high-level group of technical and management specialists that are responsible for planning the evaluation of proposals and for the identification of the winning contractor. The Council is the principal advisor to the Source Selection Authority and to the Contracting Officer; accordingly, it reports directly to the these decision makers. The Council frequently is tasked to make risk assessments, identify management problems, and participate in the Gray Beards Group.

Basically, the Source Selection Advisory Council takes the quantitative or qualitative results from the Source Selection Evaluation Board and applies weights to those evaluation results. The Council also examines major risks associated with each offeror and then determines which offeror represents the "Best Buy" for the Government.

Special Evaluation Teams - The Government will organize member of its SSEB into teams to handle special assignments during the proposal evaluation effort. Some of these teams work in areas as diverse as:

Past Performance Verification - in which team members contact Government contract and technical personnel to verify the contractors performance on contracts. They telephone the points of contact cited in the Past Performance Volume and discuss the successes and failures of the contractors with other Government personnel.

Risk Management Assessments - in which specialists in risk identification, risk analysis, risk mitigation, and risk management review the proposal to determine the risks associated with the proposed work programs. They review the contractor's risk management plans and policies and the qualification of the project staff to handle risks.

<u>Cost Reviews</u> - in which experienced cost analysts review the costing data presented in the contractor's cost proposal, focusing on the Cost Realism section particularly. They make recommendations as to the amount of contingency funds the government should establish to handle the cost risks.

Gray Beards Group - On major procurements, the Government usually convenes a panel of experts, known as the Gray Beards, with major credentials in critical technical and management matters. This panel, interviews and questions key personnel from the contractor, in a session that brings an understanding of the word "inquisition". The Gray Beards may include six or seven members, but usually the group will have a lesser number of members. Most members of the Gray Beards Group have worked in similar assignments on earlier procurements and probably have already met with one or more of your competitors in the current procurement.

Major emphasis in the questioning by the Gray Beards is placed on the understanding of and technical approaches to critical issues. The Project Manager, Chief Engineer, and other key technical personnel are expected to respond to the questions, to discuss technologies, to elaborate on the key issues without a caucus. In many instances, the Gray Beards may direct questions to matters such as: workaround plans, contingency planning, risk management, and other topics not included in the proposal.

It is noted that very few contractor personnel who have endured a Gray Beards session, which is usually an all-day affair, at the minimum, look forward to such an experience again.

FCRCs, Technical Advisors, and Consultants - Frequently, the Government will assign technical personnel for Federal Contract Research Centers, specialists from SETA contractors, and consultants to assist in certain aspects of the procurement process. These people will assist in the preparation of the RFP, the system specifications, and other technical matters. In special issues and technologies, they will assist in the evaluation of the technical proposal, and they review and comment on documents such as the offeror's description of its Cost Schedule Control System.

It seems to be an almost universal rule that these outsiders do not assist in defining the evaluation process or in the development of the evaluation standards. Further these non-government personnel sign very stringent non-disclosure statements, agreeing to never divulge their work on the procurement. Personally, I regard these specialists who work in limited assignments to be a major asset to the Government and I welcome them.

6.5 THE MAJOR PROCUREMENT ACTIVITIES AND TIMELINES

6.5.1 ACTIVITIES THAT CREATE A NEED FOR PROCUREMENTS

Military R & D Procurements - In some military procurements, the acquisition process begins when an operational requirement is identified, a need that is stated in high-level documents such as the Five Year Defense Plan. In this situation, one of the military services prepare a series of planning documents, such as a Required Operational Capability for a procurement in the near future, using technology currently available. In long-term matters, the military services may prepare an Exploratory Development Requirement that will start a research program to stimulate the development of new and innovative technologies.

Other R & D Procurements - In other Government agencies and departments, the acquisition process frequently begins when Congress dictates the development of new systems or the acquisition of existing systems. The Congressionally-mandated procurements are usually directed to near-term systems using existing technologies. Congress may influence the long-range development of systems in many of the Government agencies and departments by directing funds to new technologies.

Construction and Maintenance Procurements - The Government funds many types of procurements, most of which are not research and development oriented. For example, the acquisition of aircraft, ships, fighting vehicles, engineer equipment, logistics systems, spacecraft, weapons, and ammunition are production procurements. The construction of buildings, roads, airports, storage facilities, embassies, port facilities, offices, and bases are engineering procurements.

Services and Support Procurements - The acquisition of services for the operation and maintenance (O&M) of airfields, harbors, inland waterways, highways, petroleum reserves, and communications systems are major areas of procurement. The acquisition of Architect and Engineering services, SETA support services, and consulting services is a wide-spread procurement activity. So, the number and type of procurements is extensive, but all depend on how a need is being defined and funded.

6.5.2 ORGANIZATIONS ASSOCIATED WITH THE PROCUREMENT DOCUMENTATION

The development of a Request for Proposal and it supporting documentation is the result of a major effort in which the activities of many Governmental organizations are integrated into a single, focused program. Some of the organizations and sources of important procurement support personnel in the preparation of procurement documents include:

Field and line personnel (the users) define the operational requirements for hardware, software, and services

Engineering and scientific specialists define the design requirements and design specifications for hardware and software systems

Systems management and logistics specialists define the operational and maintenance requirements for hardware and software

Cost specialists define the should-costs, cost risks, cost planning factors, cost models, and cost estimating systems for hardware and software

Contracts specialists define the type of procurement, coordinate work by other organizations, and prepare the final set of solicitation documentation

Budgeting specialists define the budgeting constraints, the availability of funding over the life of the contract, and the funding profiles

6.5.3 THE MAJOR PROCUREMENT TIMELINES AND MILESTONES

Procurements are different, so the procurement schedules and milestones are quite different, but some general guidance in these matters can be formulated from experience in many Government procurements. The following planning factors can be used for general planning by a contractor:

For Non-System Development Procurements

1. The time between when an operational requirement or user need has been established and procurement has been approved and the time at which a Request for Proposal and its attachments are ready for issuance to potential offerors should average about five to six months.

2. The time from a notice to offerors to submit qualifications and the issuance of the Request for Proposal should average about 30-40 days.

3. The time from the issuance of the Request for Proposal to the submission of the proposal can range from a minimum of 30 days to a maximum of 60 days.

4. The time from the submission of the proposal to the time at which questions are submitted by the Government to offerors in the competitive range can vary from 20 days to 30 days. Offerors are typically allowed 10-20 days to submit their answers.

5. The time at which the post-submittal activities occur is quite difficult to predict, but the following planning factors may be useful: Site Surveys 30-40 days after proposal submittal, for Gray Beards reviews 40-45 days after proposal submittal, for Best and Final Offers after 60-75 days after proposal submittal.

For System Development Procurements

1. The time between the approval of the procurement (and its funding) and the start for the preparation of the procurement documentation by the Government should average five to six months.

2. The time required preparing the performance specifications, the design specifications and the Request for Proposal should average about six months.

3. The time between the issuance of the first procurement documentation to the offerors and the submittal of a proposal accompanied by the cost proposal, the engineering design,

and associated plans should range from four months to five months.

4. The time from the submission of the proposal to the time at which questions are submitted by the Government to offerors in the competitive range can vary from 30 days to 50 days. Offerors are typically allowed 10 to 20 days to respond to the questions.

5. The time at which the post-submittal activities occur is quite difficult to predict, but the following planning factors may be useful: Site Surveys-30 to 40 days after proposal submittal, Gray Beards reviews 40 to 45 days after proposal submittal, Best and Final Offers 60 to 75 days after proposal submittal.

For Procurements under Existing ID-IQ and Delivery Order Contracts

1. The time between a Government agency deciding to procure a product or services under a Delivery Order contract and the issuance of the procurement documentation is probably in the order of 30 to 60 days.

2. The time between receipt of a sole source Delivery Order (or Task Order) and the submission of a Work Plan and Cost Proposal is normally less than 30 days.

3. The time between the issuance of contract documentation for a major Delivery Order and the submission of Work Plans and Cost Proposal by several competing contractors is normally less than 30 days.

4. The time between the receipt of a sole source proposal or a number of competitive Work Plans under Delivery Order procurements and the issuance of a Work Order will normally be less than 30 days, usually less than 20 days.

CHAPTER 7

UNDERSTANDING THE REQUEST FOR PROPOSAL

7.1 CONTENTS OF THE REQUEST FOR PROPOSAL

THE FEDERAL ACQUISITION Regulations and Department Acquisition Regulations describe the contents of a Request for Proposal (RFP) and for a Request for Quote (RFQ). The Government has specified the contents of such procurement documents in CFR 15.406 to include the following sections:

Covering Letter - is issued by the Contracting Officer and provides the highlights of the Request for Proposal. Presents the topics of great importance to the contractor and, sometimes, will have one or more proposal requirements in the text.

Section A - includes the Standard Form 33 for RFPs and Standard Form 18 for RFQs Includes the Solicitation number, the name and address of the Contracting Officer, and a place for submittal of the proposal. Describes the type of procurement, the date and time for submission of proposals; contains brief description of the procurement.

Section B - includes the listing of supplies or services and the price/costs for these items and for major contract activities, deliverables, and items supplied to the Government.

Section C Statement of Work - describes the services, products, or materials that the Government is procuring. Specifies the major tasks and activities to be performed and the general process or schedule for performing the work. Describes the objectives of the procurement and the general requirements governing contract performance and the role that the Government will assume in its control of contractor work.

Section D - provides packaging, packing, preservation, and marking requirements for contract deliverables.

Section E - describes inspection, acceptance, quality assurance, and reliability requirements for contract deliverables.

Section F - specifies the requirements for time, place and method of delivery or performance.

Section G - includes any required accounting and appropriation data, any required contract administration information, and instructions other than those on the solicitation form.

Section H - contains the special contract requirements, including a clear statement of any special requirements that are not included elsewhere in the clauses and sections.

Section I - contains the contract clauses required by law or by the CFR, includes clauses expected to be included in the final contract.

Section J - includes a listing of all attachments including the title, date, and number of pages.

Section K - contains the representations, certifications and other statements of offerors or quoters. Includes those solicitation provisions that require certifications, representations, or submission of other information.

Section L Proposal Instructions - describe the form and content of the proposal, provide preparation instructions to offerors, specify page limitations, define critical editorial matters, specify topics to be included in the proposal, list and names the required volumes, specify the number of volumes to be submitted.

Section M Evaluation Factors - describe how the Government will evaluate the proposal, defines the factors and sub-factors considered in the evaluation of the proposal, indicates the relative importance of the evaluation factors and sub factors, and provides guidance on subjects of importance not included in Section L.

Attachment: Contract Data Requirements List - specifies the number and type of deliverables from the contractor to the Government, cites the references governing the contents of the deliverables, specifies the schedule for the submission of deliverable, and provides special instructions for certain deliverables.

Attachment: Technical Specifications - defines the technical aspects of the hardware, software, or firmware to be developed by the contractor; describe the performance, design, and technical requirements; provide specific information on materials and supplies to be used by the contractor; specify the testing, IV&V, and documentation requirements.

Attachment: Form DD-254 Security Requirements - defines the classification of the proposal and the work program, provides instructions on handling of classified hardware and software, the need for personnel and facility clearances, the need for special security measures, and the level of access granted for additional information.

It is recommended that the Code of Federal Regulations, part 15.406, become an essential item for every proposal specialist to know well.

7.2 MANDATORY REQUIREMENTS FOR THE PROPOSAL

The RFP and other Government documents specify a series of mandatory requirements that are critical to the success of a proposal effort. If you ignore these mandatory requirements, you will lose in a most miserable manner. Some of the more common mandatory requirements include:

1. You must meet the **security requirements** (facility, personnel, cryptographic, special, other) in order to be awarded the contract. If the DD-254 form specifies a facility clearance of Top Secret, and your corporation has a Secret facility clearance, you cannot win the contract. You may promise to obtain a Top Secret facility clearance, but Government personnel know all too well that the clearance process will require three to six months. Remember, you cannot have personnel cleared at the Top Secret level unless you have a Top Secret facility clearance.

2. You must meet the **financial requirements** in order to be awarded the contract. This means that you must prove that you have the financial resources needed to finance the contract work, to acquire the needed facilities, and to purchase the required materials and supplies. Financial resources can be either cash, cash equivalents, or they can be access to banks for guaranteed loans. If you do not have the ability to fund the contract, you will not be awarded the contract. The Contracting Officer will make the decision that you are not a competent offeror.

3. You must meet the **location requirements** when the customer specifies the proximity of the work sites to the customer sites. You must respond to the RFP paragraph that requires the bidder to state Place of Performance. If your employees must work at Government sites, then your response must acknowledge and demonstrate compliance with this requirement.

4. You must meet the **plans requirements** when the customer specifies the plans to be included with the proposal. These plans can be directed to many different topics such as Security Plan, Staffing Plan, Build-Up Plan, Work Plan, Management Plan, and Drug-Free Workplace Plan. When required by the RFP, you must prepare and submit these mandatory items.

5. You must not take **exception to the RFP**. You must state your concurrence with and acceptance of the RFP, including all terms and conditions, all specifications and statement of work, all deliverables, and all governing regulations and instructions. Do not omit this statement from your proposal. I have never known a firm that took exception to a RFP that won the contract.

6. You must have an **accounting system** that meets the Government's Cost Accounting Standards, which means that you must accrue all costs, allocate costs to cost accounts, and have a viable cost auditing system. Your cost accounting system must support the Cost Schedule Status Report requirements, and possibly the Cost Schedule Control System Requirements, if they are required by the Government.

7. You may be required to have a **Cost Schedule Control System** for projects that require major research and development efforts and significant production-fabrication efforts. Traditionally, projects leading to the production of a system required a CSCS when the R & D costs exceed $50 million and production costs exceed $200 million.

8. You must not have any **Organizational Conflicts of Interest** as defined by the Government regulations. These OCI matters

may include projects within your own corporation and within your subcontractors, matters that give your corporation an unfair advantage in the competition. You must investigate and prepare a response in virtually all proposals.

9. You may be required to submit annual **financial statements** for previous years to establish your ability to perform the work from a financial viewpoint. The financial reports must meet the Government standards for such information, which will include the full suite of explanation and clarification statements.

10. You may be required to submit information about **recent, ongoing, or pending legal matters,** including subjects such as outstanding law suits, pending fines, judicial restraints and injunctions, recent fines and admonishments, and Government contract prohibitions.

11. You must satisfy the requirements for the use of **small business subcontractors** during the contract performance. This means that when the Government dictates that percentage of subcontracting you must comply with the matter, without exception.

7.3 PROPOSAL REQUIREMENTS IN NON-RFP DOCUMENTS

7.3.1 THE FEDERAL ACQUISITION REGULATIONS

The Federal Acquisition Regulations govern all procurements by the Federal Government, and all of acquisition regulations of all federal agencies and departments must be consistent with the top-level Federal Acquisition Regulations. The Federal Acquisition Regulations, commonly called the FARs, are published in the Code of Federal Regulations, Part 48. Other parts of the CFR contain the department acquisition regulations. Every proposal center, every Proposal Manager, and every Proposal Planner should have a copy or access to a copy.

The FARs specifies a number of proposal requirements that must be the subjects of responses in the proposal, preferably meriting a title. The most important of the FAR proposal requirements is a statement that "quality is evaluated in competitive procurements". Other sections of the FARs dictate the conditions and format under which cost reporting is required in the ensuing contract. Every proposal must have a response to these and other FAR requirements.

As a general rule, the Requests for Proposal seldom list the proposal requirements that are listed in the FARs. The offeror is assumed to know what the FARs require.

7.3.2 DEPARTMENT REGULATIONS, INSTRUCTIONS, HANDBOOKS

The various departments and agencies of the Government has published their acquisition regulations, such as: DARs, Defense Acquisition Regulations and TARS, Transportation Acquisition Regulations. In addition, many departments within the federal Government have published Instructions and Handbooks that specify the procedures, processes, and requirements of their department. One handbook of importance is MIL-HNBK-245, Preparation of Statements of Work. They can be ordered from the Navy Publications Center, Philadelphia, PA.

The Defense Systems Management Center, located in the Metropolitan Washington, DC, area, has published a series of handbooks that are directly related to the acquisition of major systems, and every good proposal center will have current editions of them. The most important of the DSMC handbooks are entitled Acquisition Management. The Government Printing Office has these handbooks for sale off-the-shelf or by mail.

7.3.3 Sections of the U. S. Code

Section 10 of the U. S. Code does not have any proposal requirements as such, but this part of Federal criminal code does specify harsh penalties for criminal actions during the acquisition process. It covers both federal employees and contractor personnel. Just be warned that you cannot think up a sneaky way to do something that has not been thought about before and has been the subject of judicial proceedings.

7.4 EXCLUSION FACTORS AND OTHER POISON PILLS IN THE RFP

7.4.1 Hiring of Government Procurement Personnel

The Federal Regulations prohibits contractors from submitting proposals for government contracts when the contractor has hired personnel who have worked on the Request for Proposal. These personnel, includes Government employees, FCRC personnel, and employees of special non-Government support organizations (SETA Contractors), are considered to be "procurement officials". This legal requirement presents a major problem to large corporations with many different office locations, because the average Proposal Manager does not know if such personnel have been hired elsewhere in the corporation.

The Government requires a corporate representative to sign a statement to the fact that the corporation has not hired any procurement personnel and to submit this statement with the proposal. In effect, the Government is asking which corporate employee will be prosecuted and jailed when it is found that the corporation has hired a procurement official. I always advised all Proposal Managers not to sign this form, forcing a higher level corporate officer to sign the form. Let the people earning the big salaries sign this form.

7.4.2 Conflicts of Interest Because of SETA Work

One of the major problems in organizing a team for bidding on Government procurement is the presence of corporate personnel or subcontractor personnel who have worked in a SETA role for the Government office issuing the Request for Proposal. SETA support personnel have great access to many documents of the Government when working closely with Government Personnel, and any Government prosecutor will have no problem proving that the personnel could have had access to procurement documents. Note: SETA means System Engineering and Technical Assistance.

The approaches to avoiding legal problems associated with having access to procurement officials and procurement documentation is rather limited. The best approach is to make a No Bid decision in regard to any procurement in which corporate entities have worked as a SETA for the Government organization issuing the RFP. The second best approach is to deny subcontractors with procurement official problems the opportunity to work on the proposal and in the work after contract award

7.4.3 Need for Cost Schedule Systems

As a near-universal rule, proposals for contracts in which research and development will exceed over $ 50 million or for contracts in which production will exceed $ 200 million require the bidders to have a validated Cost Schedule Control System (CSCS). Very few contractors have a validated CSCS because of the costs and the time delays associated with the development and validation of the system. Rest assured, the CSCS requires an very large corporate investment (probably in excess of $ 10 million) and a very long time (probably greater than three years) for validation by Government personnel.

If the RFP requires the winning contractor to have a validated CSCS, a offeror without this cost accounting and forecasting system has only three viable alternatives. **First**, convince the Government Contract Officer to accept a Cost Schedule Status Reporting system instead of the CSCS. **Second**, employ a company with a validated CSCS as a subcontractor and employ that subcontractor as the CSCS worker on the contract provided the Government will accept this arrangement. **Third**, make a No Bid Decision.

7.4.4 REQUIREMENTS FOR DATA RIGHTS

If you ever had to provide one example of a poison pill in a RFP, the government's requirements for data rights are the number one candidate. Basically, the Government may require the bidder to provide rights to all information, data, and software used and cited in the proposal after award of contract. The Government interprets this right to include providing the data to other contractors. Consider the following:

- Your company used a software development tool to design, develop, and test the software system that you are proposing. The RFP says that you must provide rights to that tool. But the tool belongs to another company that leased or sold the tool with legally-enforced restrictions.
- Your company has invested a great deal of money on an Independent Research and Development project to gain an edge in future technologies. The RFP says that you must provide the Government with full rights to use that system or tool as it sees fit.
- Your company has invested much money in the compilation of an extensive data base in some technical area. The RFP says that you must provide the government with the right to use and distribute this data base even though you consider it to be proprietary.

7.4.5 DRUG-FREE WORKPLACE

Virtually every Government Request for Proposal requires the offeror to provide information on its Drug-Free Workplace Program or its Drug-Free Workplace Plan. Be forewarned that the difference between a "Program" and a "Plan" in regard to a Drug-Free Workplace is almost as great as the difference between paying homage to do-gooders and firing the offenders. Check the difference in the Federal Acquisition Regulations before preparing a reply to the RFP requirement, because this matter is a poison pill which will kill you. Ensure that you have full corporate support for any Drug-Free Workplace Plan that you may have to include with your proposal.

7.4.6 ORGANIZATIONAL CONFLICT OF INTEREST WITHIN YOUR TEAM

Most proposal efforts will not be endangered by the organizational conflict of interest clauses in the RFP, but the Proposal Manager and the Proposal Planner should analyze every paragraph and every sentence to identify possible OCI problems. Require all subcontractors to sign OCI statements before making them members of your team. Take special care when employing senior retirees from Government organizations as consultants to ensure that they do not bring OCI problems to you. If you appear to have a possible conflict of interest, discuss the matter with the Government Contracting Officer at an early date and get an opinion on the matter.

7.4.7 PRIVACY ACT RESTRICTIONS

The Government may request very personal information about personnel who have been designated as key personnel. But the corporation may not be able to legally provide this information due to a federal law, entitled The Privacy Act. In these instances, the Proposal Manager must point out to the Government's

Contracting Officer that such a response in the proposal will violate federal law. I advise all Proposal Managers to decline to provide the personal information, but not cite this action as an exception to the RFP. Consider your action to be a clarification and the Contracting Officer will understand. REMEMBER, it is not against the law for the Government to request personal information covered by the Privacy Act, but it is against the law for the corporation to provide such information. Do not violate the law because of this RFP requirement.

7.4.8 DISCLOSURE OF DETRIMENTAL INFORMATION

Some RFPs require the bidders to list all instances in which they have been: (1) barred from Government contracting, (2) convicted of fraud, (3) prosecuted in state and federal courts, (4) cited for filing false claims, (5) denied a facility security clearance or lost an existing facility clearance, (6) the subject of major law suits, (7) subjected to contract termination for cause, (8) cited for violation of environmental standards. If your company has been in such legal trouble, you must admit the fact; to certify that your corporation has not had any of these legal problems is in itself a fraudulent statement. It is strongly recommended that when admitting to any of the above matters that you explain the circumstances and provide an explanation of the corrective actions taken.

7.4.9 WARRANTIES

The RFP states that you must provide warranties on the systems, hardware, software, and equipment delivered to the Government. This could mean that your corporation must provide warranties on purchased material, unless you seek clarification in the matter. It is strongly recommended that you should have a written agreement that the manufacturers or developers of items that you purchased and delivered to the Government are liable for warranties on their items. It is also strongly recommended that the Government accept the warranties from these sources in lieu of a warranty from your corporation.

7.4.10 FEDERAL COST ACCOUNTING STANDARDS

The RFP usually states that the offeror must have the capability to meet the Federal Cost Accounting Standards, as established by the Government's board. This requirement means that the offeror must have a proven cost accounting system that accrues costs on a contract by contract basis and allocates major overhead costs (which are pooled) to the individual contracts. Clearly, the offeror must be capable of meeting high standards for cost accounting. It is strongly recommended that a competent CPA determine if your accounting system meets the Government's standards before you sign the certification included in most RFPs.

7.4.11 SUBCONTRACTING GOALS

Every Government agency has subcontracting goals that specify the percentage of contract dollars that must be allocated to small businesses, small disadvantaged businesses, small woman-owned businesses, and minority-owned businesses. The goals also extend to Historically Black Colleges and Universities and Minority Institutions. It is critical to the winning of a contract that you know these goals and that your proposal meets these agency goals. Usually the agency is quite willing to provide information on its subcontracting goals, so you are not considered as being illegal to inquire about this matter.

7.4.12 PASSING DOWN TERMS AND CONDITIONS TO SUBCONTRACTORS

Most RFPs require that the prime contractor pass down all of the terms and conditions of the RFP to the subcontractors. While this is not a problem with large companies that are subcontractors, small businesses will have problems in most instances. Small businesses do not really have the paperwork required of most offerors. This RFP requirement means that very few small business subcontractors cannot meet the terms and conditions. It is highly recommended that specialists from the prime contractor assist the small businesses in the preparation of plans, policies, and procedures that meet the Government's requirements.

7.4.13 BONDS AND LETTERS OF CREDIT

During design and construction contracts, the Government may require the offeror to provide documentation on the three major types of bonds being satisfied. These requirements can include Bid Bonds, Performance Bonds, and Payment Bonds. The Government may also require the offeror to submit a Letter of Credit and/or an Irrevocable Letter of Credit. Read theses contract clauses carefully and reply to the clauses in the proposal. These matters are important.

7.4.14 MATERIALS, SUPPLIES, OTHER COSTS

Most RFPs use the terms "materials" and "supplies". Materials, as defined in the DARs and FARs are those items purchased directly by the contractor and consumed during contract performance. Supplies, as defined in acquisition regulations, also are those items purchased directly by the Government and provided to the contractor during contract performance. Other costs separately listed can include those associated with: transportation, duties and tariffs, packaging and shipping, storage, and safeguarding. Do not confuse or overlook these cost items or these terms, because the Government auditors know their meanings.

7.4.15 OTHER MATTERS OF IMPORTANCE

Other matters of importance in the terms and conditions of the solicitation include the following items:

Buy American Act - this can be a problem when working in a foreign country

Davis Bacon Act - this defines minimum wages in the area of the place of performance

Insurance - this includes liability insurance for your employees working on government sites

Price Adjustments for Small Disadvantaged Businesses - a 10% surcharge to bid prices

Adverse Weather Conditions - this provides guidance on weather-caused no-work days

Affirmative Action Program - this requires the offeror to have an approved plan

NAFTA and other Treaties - which specify conditions for work in foreign countries

State and Local Taxes - which specify if these taxes are billable to the federal Government

It would be wise to have an attorney with experience in Government contracting law to review these matters and to assist you in preparing a response. Most of the responses to these RFP requirements are simple, but some require plans and policies to be prepared by the offeror that will be available to auditors.

7.5 PREPARING QUESTIONS ABOUT THE RFP

In procurements, potential bidders can ask the Government to clarify the RFP and the Specifications. In all procurements, the Government actually specifies the process and schedule for submitting questions. When any bidder asks a question formally, the Government is obligated to publish the answers and to provide all answers to all potential bidders. Typically, the questions are directed to matters such as: developing a better understanding of the technical requirements, clarifying inconsistencies in the RFP, correcting obvious mistakes in the procurement documents, and eliminating "poison pills" inserted by the competition.

The importance of asking questions related to the procurement documents can be illustrated by two competitions with which I had experience:

> **First**, in a competition to develop a computer-based system for the Atlantic Missile Range the RFP specified that the conversion of digital data to decimal data would be accomplished by hardware. Our team member, AT&T, whose equipment we planned to use, performed that conversion by software. The Government refused to change this apparently minor specification. Since we did not have the hardware capability, we withdrew from the competition. In this case, the answer to our question meant that we were not compliant so we made a No-Bid decision immediately.

> **Second**, in a competition for a technical services contract with the Navy, the RFP provided no guidance on the matter of office location. Our Department Manager refused my request to ask a question on this matter, stating that the answer would assist the competition. Since we did not know the answer to that question, I made a guess in the matter. I was wrong and we lost the competition. In this case, we did not ask an important question. I just wished that the high-level corporate officer who decided not to ask the question had the guts to step forward and accept blame in this matter.

My philosophy in the matter of asking important questions about the RFP is that if we do not know the answer to the questions, our proposal may be non-compliant or irrelevant. I believe that if we need the answer, it is not important if it also helps the competition. I never ask questions or make observations about editorial matters and I never reveal our corporation's strategy or strengths.

CHAPTER 8

UNDERSTANDING THE CUSTOMER

8.1 UNDERSTANDING THE REASON FOR THE PROCUREMENT

Some proposal specialists do not think that the reason for a procurement is important, because whatever the driving factors, they are only concerned with the Request for Proposal. The reason for the Government procuring products, supplies, and services can be important, although no imperative. In some of my competitions, the reasons for the procurement were as diverse as:

- Congress had mandated that a program be conducted and a report prepared
- Military forces had identified a need for a new system to counter a new threat
- Weapon systems upgrades were needed to meet the upgraded threat systems
- Computer systems using old hardware needed to be replaced
- Commercial clients demanded new services and systems to meet the competition
- Emerging technologies were needed for systems being developed
- Clients needed new, innovative technologies to be integrated into their systems

- Basic research was needed to solve complex problems with materials
- New commercial hardware and software was needed for new client services
- Cost estimating systems, cost data bases, and cost models needed development
- Military services needed automated systems to support reserve forces
- Hospitals needed automated systems to upgrade patient treatment
- International treaties required the US to develop a chemical weapon destruction system
- Warehousing and logistics operations needed a robot for handling materials
- Foreign military forces needed operational training for a new command system
- A major law enforcement organization needed a national crime information system
- Military services needed automated systems to support their logistics operations
- A military services needed a modern automated world-wide command and control system
- Law enforcement agencies needed an automated intelligence system for drug interdiction

Knowing the reason for the procurement usually means that you understand what the contract will produce, in what environment the products or services be used, and the urgency and priorities associated with the procurement. In addition, you will probably have a better understanding of the organizations that will employ the products and services, the skill levels of the operating and maintenance personnel, and the associated facility requirements. Hopefully, the Acquisition Manager will assemble this information and provide it to the Proposal Team.

A second set of customer understandings, different but equally important to the Proposal Manager and the Proposal Planner are such important issues as:

Risk Tolerance - The Advanced Research Projects Agency is willing to accept very high risks in programs with potentially high payoffs because they have a very long range view of the development business. The Army Missile Command does not want any risks associated with the software needed to handle fire direction at the battalion or regiment level because they may have to fight tomorrow; two customers, two different risk levels.

System Upgrade Capability - The hardware and software systems for a hospital information system for DOD had to be capable of expansion through the acquisition of commercially-available assets. The hardware and software developed for military aircraft radar systems were procured for a specific application and had to meet military standards.

Operational Constraints - Major computer centers operated by contractors can rely on commercial hardware and software that is operated in a friendly environment. Computer-based system for military organizations must operate in extreme environments, i.e., survive on the nuclear battlefield. Non-military computer centers usually employ civilians and military centers employ military personnel.

Phase-In Operations - Most commercial organizations can afford some degree of down time when a new system is being installed, so the phase-in plan seldom includes operating the new system and the old system in a parallel operation at first. Very few, if any, military combat organizations can tolerate any operational downtime while a new system is being installed, checked out, and tested.

I have always believed that the more that I knew about the reasons for the procurement and the operational environment, the better I understood the many issues that must be addressed in the proposal.

8.2 UNDERSTANDING THE CUSTOMER'S UNSTATED NEEDS

The customer will always have some requirements that will be fully satisfied by the corporation with the winning proposal but which are not included in the procurement documents. Some of these unstated requirements that I have learned from discussions with Government personnel who knew the procurement include:

- The SETA contractor must have an office with virtually all of the support contractor personnel within a ten minute walk from the customer's technical facility.

- The contractor must be able to provide offices and conference rooms with a video- conferencing system for Government personnel working at the contractor site.

- The contractor must give the Government the right to interview and approve/disapprove the assignment of any new personnel to a technical services contract.

- The incoming contractor must agree to hire those personnel working for the incumbent contractor that the Government has designated as key to its program.

- The contractor must replace all employees assigned to sensitive work immediately after they fail the drug testing program.

- The contractor must use word processing and graphics software compatible with the PC-based computer systems used by the Government.

- The contractor that has the least impact on the operations of a maintenance facility during its on-site work will be the winner.

- The contractor work force must not have more than 15 percent of its staff comprised of retired military personnel.

8.3 UNDERSTANDING THE CUSTOMER'S SECURITY REQUIREMENTS

8.3.1 NORMAL SECURITY FOR DOD CLASSIFIED MATERIAL.

Government contracting activities issues classified RFPs and provides classified material to the bidders, and those bidders must meet the DOD requirements for the receipt, handling, access, storage, accountability, destruction, and return of classified material. Personnel must have security clearances at the level associated with that material, security containers must be approved by DIS, and access must be restricted to those personnel with need-to-know.

8.3.2 SPECIAL SECURITY FOR SPECIAL CLASSIFIED MATERIAL

Government contracting activities frequently issue special RFPs (and supporting documentation) only to a select group of contractors who are known to have the required special security clearances. These Code Word, Black, and SCI documents can be handled only by the Special Security Officer and by a proposal staff that have the required special clearances. As a rule, these special clearances are restricted to a limited number of people and the proposal team must be comprised of those people who already have the special clearances.

The FBI has its own restrictions on the handling of its sensitive material, and every member of the design team and the proposal team must be cleared by the FBI. It is unfortunate that the FBI does not have the equivalent of the DOD Industrial Security Manual because one never knows who will be approved for work on FBI projects or why people with Top Secret clearances cannot receive FBI clearances.

8.3.3 Special Handling of Proprietary Material

Frequently, proposals must be prepared for commercial or industrial clients that have designed their RFP and the supporting documentation to be Proprietary. This customer designation means that their material must be treated as if it were DOD classified, meaning restricted access, approved personnel, and secure storage. As a rule, the Acquisition Manager or Corporate Officer Responsible reaches an agreement with the client on the procedures and systems to be used to safeguard their material.

8.3.4 Preparing the Proposal Security Plan

It is always wise to prepare a security plan for classified proposals and to have a Security Officer present a briefing on the specific requirements of that plan at the start of the design and proposal efforts. All personnel should be required to sign a non-disclosure agreement when working on or using proprietary material.

8.4 KNOWING THE SSA, SSAC, SSEB, CO, ACO, COTR

Knowing the key personnel in the Government's acquisition team can be a major asset in procurements. You will know the Contracting Officer (CO) for the procurement immediately after receipt of the RFP, because his/her name is on the SF-33 form. Frequently the name of the Administrative Contract Officer (ACO) and the Contracting Officer's Technical Representative (COTR) are included in the RFP. If their names, ACO and COTR, are not stated in the RFP, ninety percent of the time they will be identified at the Pre-proposal Conference.

Your Marketing Specialist should know who the Source Selection Authority is, but if the individual's name is unknown, you may ask a question at the Pre-proposal Conference about that person. While the name of the SSA is not always critical, it is important to know the position of the SSA. Do not even bother to ask questions about the Source Selection Advisory Council, because it is seldom that the

Government provides the name of the members of the SSAC or the name of the head of the Council.

You should make an effort to learn the name of the Head of the Source Selection Evaluation Board and then to learn more about that individual. In major procurements by the Naval Air Systems Command, the Head of the SSEB was the same individual for many years, so his name was familiar to all competitors. Most agencies, however, do not use the same person to direct the SSEB on different procurements.

Once the names and titles of the key procurement personnel are known contact the Public Relations Office and obtain the biographical sketches of the personnel. They are free and available without subterfuge, in almost all instances. Why do this, you may ask. Well, you may want to know if the Head of the SSEB, is a technical, management, legal, contracts, or administrative person. This diversity in backgrounds means that different people look at proposals from differing views. Trust me, it is wise to know such things.

When preparing for a major Strategic Defense Initiative Office procurement, I was tasked to develop a quasi-resume for the Head of the SSEB. The Contracting Officer told me that it as General _____ and the Contracting Officer was pleased that I made this inquiry aboveboard. I obtained a cameo resume of the General from the Department of the Army. What was the value of this investigation, you may ask? Well, I found that the Head of the SSEB had a Ph.D. degree in engineering and had worked on many major technical programs. A company employee, who had worked on a SETA contract for that General, provided much data from which I built up a personal profile for this very highly qualified man. All from legal, open sources, mind you.

8.5 KNOWING THE KEY TECHNICAL CUSTOMER PERSONNEL

Encourage your technical leaders to make a major effort to meet the key technical personnel of the customer at the Pre-proposal

Conference and at the Advance Procurement Briefings for Industry. Learn as much about their educational qualifications, their work history, their current assignments, and their skills. Most Government technical personnel want to tell you about their interests and their programs, but they cannot volunteer the information. They can answer your technical questions and they want you to ask questions. Just pay them the respect that they deserve, let them do the talking, keep your own ego under control, and your technical questions will be answered.

Why is this activity desirable or even necessary? If the leading engineer is an electrical engineer, you will tailor your responses to that discipline. If the leading scientific person is a physicist, you will emphasize the physics of the problem. If the COTR is an active duty officer with a strong technical background, you will stress the importance of operational environments. If the technical personnel have developed an operational system, such as the NWC-Sidewinder effort, show your appreciation for such an effective weapon.

Try to have members of your technical/engineering staff talk with the technical personnel of the customer. Have them talk about technical matters. Do not send your technical people on a marketing mission.

8.6 KNOWING THE ROLE OF FCRC AND ASSOCIATE CONTRACTORS

Government procurements frequently draw upon the personnel skills of other contractors of the Federal Contract Research Centers during major procurements. In some of the competitions, these nongovernmental organizations provide the procurement authorities with in-depth expertise in key technologies and systems. This support has included such diversity as:

- for a major hardware procurement program, an FCRC cost analyst provided valuable assistance on cost risk assessments
- for a major software development procurement, several FCRC personnel served as members of the Gray Beards Group

- for a major shipbuilding project, a contractor with in-depth expertise in Cost Schedule Control Systems evaluated the offerors' CSCS systems
- for a high technology development contract, technical personnel from a Naval Laboratory performed evaluated offerors' approaches to technology infusion

It is definitely important to know which FCRCs, laboratories, and associate contractors will be involved in the evaluation of your proposal. People from sources outside of the procurement agency can have a major impact on your chances of winning if you do not ensure that their areas of expertise and concern are addressed in your proposal. If you can obtain the names of these outside supporting organizations, that are an important first step; if you can obtain the names of the technical personnel involved, that is great.

Your priorities in this matter are: (1) learn if outside organizations will be involved in the procurement on the side of the customer, (2) determine the role of those organizations, (3) determine the technical or management areas in which the organizations have expertise, and (4) learn the names and skills of the individuals who will provide the support.

8.7 KNOWING HOW THE GOVERNMENT ESTIMATES COSTS

The Government cost analysts use a variety of proven techniques to develop the "should- cost" estimates for procurements. These "should-costs' are used to budget money, develop cost profiles, and identify cost problems. The cost estimating techniques for upcoming procurements include such diversity as:

- For studies and analyses, labor costs are frequently based on the costs experienced in earlier procurements of a similar nature and similar complexity.
- For software development projects, man-hour estimates are usually based on outputs from computer models such as

COCOMO or RCA-Price. Man-hours are then converted to dollars using an average labor cost for each labor grade.

- For hardware development projects, costs are frequently based on the costs experienced with hardware of similar complexity, adjusted for inflation. Cost estimating relationships based on factors such as weight, technology, and speed are used in many instances.
- For basic research projects, costs are frequently estimated by the Government laboratories or Federal Contract Research Centers, based on some type of black magic.
- For technology development projects, costs are usually extrapolated from programs in which similar systems have been developed recently.
- For technical services contracts, labor costs are estimated from existing SETA-type contracts of a similar nature, and sometimes including an escalation factor.
- For projects stimulated by an unsolicited proposal, the cost proposal of the bidder is virtually always the basis of the cost estimate for the competitive procurement.

Question: Why is it important to know how the Government develops its "should-cost" estimates? Answer: your costs will be compared with the Government's own cost estimates, and you may be eliminated from the competition because of exceedingly high costs or unreasonably low costs. Solution: ensure that the Cost Realism response in your cost proposal proves that your costs are the only realistic set of costs.

8.8 KNOWING THE CUSTOMER'S RISK TOLERANCE

The government organization that has prepared the acquisition documentation never makes any statements about their concerns with risk and their tolerance of risks. This risk matter varies from Government office to Government office and there is no general rule that can be applied to all procurements. Certain general statements regarding technical, schedule, and cost risks can be made, like:

- When a Government organization must report the findings of a study contract to Congress by a certain date, that organization will not tolerate any schedule risk.
- When the Government organization is concerned with basic research, schedule risk is seldom a factor, but technical risks can become more important.
- When the military purchases hardware or software to update the capability of an existing weapon system, both technical risk and schedule risk are extremely important.
- When an international treaty requires a specific activity to be completed by a specific date, the Government organization is very concerned about schedule risk.
- When the government is purchasing two subsystems from two contractors to be integrated into a single system, both technical and schedule risks are a matter of great concern.

Other general statements can also be made regarding risks acceptable to certain types of customers or clients. For example, when a system must be installed and operational before an organization is deployed overseas, schedule risks are very critical. Or when an automated system for hospitals and health care clinics is used for matters such as prescriptions and treatment records, performance risks are super critical. It is suggested that the Acquisition Manager or Marketing Specialist discuss the matter of acceptable-unacceptable risks with customers whenever possible. I have found that this matter is freely discussed by Government and industrial clients who did not discuss risks in the RFP. Ask and you will be informed.

8.9 KNOWING ABOUT THE CUSTOMER'S CONTRACTING HISTORY

Sometimes it is important, if not absolutely essential, to know the customer's contracting history. Particularly if the current proposal that you are preparing is to be submitted to a agency with which you have no contract experience or acquisition information. Basically, you need to know details such as how the Contract Office deals with contractors or how closely the agency's technical personnel desire to monitor your work. If a small business, you may even want to know the time between submission of an invoice and receipt of a payment check.

It is wise to study the agency's contracting history to determine how much time they allow for completion on contracts or tasks. It is equally wise to learn about the types of contracts they issue, the average dollar value of their contracts, and it is very prudent to learn about their sophistication in matters such as "should-cost" estimates.

While employed by Braddock, Dunn, and MacDonald, I was tasked to assess the market potential of the Aberdeen Proving Grounds. In this effort I visited the Contracts Office, introduced myself, stated my objective, and asked for their assistance. They provided me with a listing of all contracts during the past five years, this information included: type of contract, value of the contract, and type of services or hardware involved. I learned that they had issued only one contract over $2 million in the past five years, that their average contract was less than $50,000, and that 90 percent of their contracts went to small businesses.

CHAPTER 9

UNDERSTANDING THE CUSTOMER'S PROBLEM

9.1 WHY THE PROBLEM UNDERSTANDING SECTION IS IMPORTANT

The most important matter to remember in the writing of the problem understanding section is that one must write about the customer's problem. It is the customer's problem, pure and simple, and the problem understanding section in the proposal must write about the problem from the customer's viewpoint. This may seem a very simple, obvious statement, but it is weird how often the Proposal Writer ends up writing about the problems that the contractor faces in solving the customer's problem. Remember this simple fact, the problem understanding section is about the customer's problem, not the contractor's.

The customer needs a study to be made, a design to be prepared, a service to be provided, a facility to be built, a hardware item to be developed, or a support effort to be provided. This need is usually the result of some outside stimulus, such as:

- A new law or regulation requires an agency to accomplish a certain task
- A military organization requires a new or improved capability

- An existing hardware system or facility has become obsolete and needs replacement
- An emerging technology must be examined to determine its potential capability
- A new and deadly threat to health or safety has arisen and must be countered
- A new system is required to meet the demands of a new operational requirement
- A new concept or phenomena requires basic and applied research
- A building must be modified, renovated, and modernized for continued usage
- A significant change in environmental conditions creates a need for new structures
- An existing system or structure costs too much to operate and maintain

The types of understandings associated with any procurement can fall into any of seven general understanding categories, these categories include: status of past and ongoing work, forces that make the procurement necessary, essential technologies, engineering challenges, associated organizations and their roles, the operational environments, and design and construction challenges. You must decide which type of understanding to be prepared at the earliest possible date during the proposal planning process.

My company was preparing a proposal to the Army's Harry Diamond Laboratory for experimental work and modeling in the field of Induced Electromagnetic Pulse Effects. I was the Proposal Manager for this effort, and I had a major disagreement with the Chief Scientist who was responsible for technical matters. I said that the problem understanding section must be directed to the customer's problem, which was the need for the communications systems of Army field forces to operate on the nuclear battlefield. The Chief Scientist argued that the real problem was that the existing EMP codes and models were not adequate for Army communication systems that were susceptible to EMP. Essentially, he had defined his problem to be the Army's problem. After a short ultimatum from me, he wrote about the Army's problem. And we won the competition.

It is so much easier to write about one's own problem than to write about the customer's problems, so many writers will drift from the real problem to their own problem. It is only human nature. So the Volume Leader and the Proposal Manager must be very diligent in monitoring the writers assigned to the Problem Understanding Section.

Note: it is important that the proposal describe the **problems** in the Problem Understanding section as **challenges**. The customer may have problems, but we must describe them as challenges.

9.2 DEMONSTRATING YOUR UNDERSTANDING OF THE CHALLENGES

In the proposal business, it is an axiom that when you cannot write about one type of problem understanding that you can write about a problem understanding that you know. For example, when you do not know the technologies associated with a program, consider writing about the history of the program or the operational environment. In this approach to problem understanding, you write about what you know well and state that your knowledge is crucial to the successful completion of the contract.

When working on our proposal to the Strategic Defense Initiatives Office for a System Architecture Study, my corporation was not qualified in the development of architecture for a major space-based defense system. We could not compete against the very large defense contractors in this type of work, so we decided to redefine the problem. We prepared a proposal in which our theme was that an understanding of the technologies needed for a space-based missile defense system was critical to defining that system's architecture. Since the procurement was based on multiple contracts, we won one of the contracts. And we ended up with over $ 100 million in SDI work because we won the first contract and each successive competition. With a marginally compliant proposal, I must point out.

Of course, if the customer is very specific in the RFP and one must compete for a contract directed to the development of a space-based X-ray laser, then you cannot write about other issues or aspects. The more specific the RFP in the Statement of Work, the less flexibility you have in preparing a responsive, winning proposal.

9.2.1 UNDERSTANDING THE FORCES OR NEEDS THAT CREATED THE PROBLEM

The contracting agency is well aware of the organizations, regulations, public laws, and government activities that have created a need for a problem to be resolved. The contracting agency is also quite aware of the pressure exerted upon them by the outside organizations, such as the user of a system. So, the customer may want you to demonstrate your appreciation for their problems. Be prepared to write about one or more of the following topics:

- New laws or regulations requires an agency to accomplish a certain task
- Military organizations require a new or improved capability
- Existing hardware systems or facilities have become obsolete and need replacement
- Significant changes in environmental conditions have created a need for a new capability
- A need to work or fight alongside allied forces dictates new systems

Example 9.4.1 is an example of an understanding of a legal requirement, specifically a federal law that created the need for a major health and safety program in underground coal mines.

9.2.2 UNDERSTANDING THE DESIGN AND CONSTRUCTION CHALLENGES

The Government contracting agency responsible for design efforts and construction efforts face many challenges that the typical Government contractor never encounters. These design and construction issues, problems, and requirements, which will have a serious impact on the contract work, can include matters as diverse as:

- An existing system or structure costs too much to operate and maintain
- A facility must be modified, renovated, and modernized for continued usage
- A significant change in environmental conditions creates a need for new structures
- Local and regional labor regulations creates employment challenges
- Use of foreign personnel to construct sensitive installations overseas is prohibited
- Construction activities and facilities must have minimal impact on ongoing operations
- An effort is needed to prevent foreign intelligence from compromising a US facility

Example 9.4.2 presents an understanding of the requirement to ensure that the construction project has minimal impact on the operations of the customer, the American embassy in Beijing.

9.2.3 UNDERSTANDING THE STATUS OF THE PROGRAM

The customer is fully aware of the status of its program and their need for contract support for the program. But it is important that the contractor fully understand the status, milestones, critical factors, risks, and challenges associated with their program, because such understandings are a critical input to the technical approach. Consequently, the proposal must address matters as diverse as:

- Much work has been performed to date in the program
- The program has migrated from advanced development to design and breadboard
- The contracting agency has been funding the program for many years
- Ongoing research work at Government Laboratories indicate major problems
- The program has achieved many of the DOD major milestones already

Example 9.4.3 is an example of an understanding of the military program to conduct tests related to the discharge of containers in an amphibious operation.

9.2.4 Understanding the Key Program Technologies

The Government may be concerned about issues such as technology infusion, technology risks, and technology development. These concerns may be the reason for the contract being issued and, consequently, are critical in their minds. A strong understanding of system technologies is critical in such matters because:

- The state of the art in key technologies is advancing rapidly
- Technology fusion will be necessary to meet new requirements
- A new concept or phenomena requires basic and applied research
- An emerging technology must be examined to determine its potential capability
- Technology roadmaps must be exploited as an essential element of technology infusion

Example 9.4.4 is an example of an understanding of a critical technology issue associated with an operational high energy laser weapon system.

9.2.5 UNDERSTANDING NEEDS AND CONDITIONS

When writing about the operating environments in the problem understanding part of the proposal, the proposal must address matters such as: the physical environment, threat environment, weather conditions, terrorist threats, man-machine issues, operator skills levels, degradation of equipment due to environmental factors, disease and other health-related issues. Some of the matters impacting on operational environments that may need to be addressed include:

- A major new and different set of needs have been identified
- A new operational environment has been recognized
- A new and different set of threats have emerged recently
- New systems have become available to meet the demands of new environments
- New and deadly threats to health or safety have arisen and must be countered

Example 9.4.5 is an example of an understanding of the needs for new approaches to providing air terminals to meet an expanded demand for air transportation.

9.2.6 UNDERSTANDING THE ASSOCIATED AND INVOLVED ORGANIZATIONS

Frequently, the customer requires the contractor to understand the role of many other organizations, government and non-government, that are associated with the contract work. These organizations, whose roles the contractor must understand and deal with during the period of contract performance can include such diversity as:

- Tri-Service organizations have needs that impact on the problem
- FCRCs and Associate Contractors are involved in the work
- Government laboratories have ongoing, related research programs

- NATO compatibility requirements must be met

Example 9.4.6 is an example of an understanding of the roles that the many organizations within the high energy laser community play in the research, development, and testing of a prototype operational system

9.2.7 UNDERSTANDING THE ENGINEERING CHALLENGES

Sometimes it is difficult to separate an understanding of the engineering challenges facing the customer from an understanding of the engineering work to be accomplished (which is described in the Technical Approach), but there is a difference. The engineering matters discussed or described in the Problem Understanding section of the proposal can include:

- The engineering codes and ordinances influencing engineering designs
- The availability and capability of existing hardware and software systems
- The reliability of candidate hardware and software to be procured
- The methods to reduce the logistics burden on operating forces
- The perils of using hardware from foreign sources

Note: if in doubt as to how to address this understanding, consider moving all discussions related to engineering challenges to the Technical Approach Section.

Example 9.4.7 is an example of Understanding the Engineering Challenges.

9.2.8 Understanding the Key Issues Associated with the Problem

The contracting agency is well aware of the many issues associated with their procurement, issues that require creative approaches to management, financial, and organizational problems. When you understand these issues, the customer develops a belief that you will work earnestly to assist with their resolution. The issues can include:

- The program requires the use of proprietary information or items
- The program is constrained by budgetary considerations
- A major test facility and test program will be required for the system
- Special security matters will influence personnel and facility requirements
- Interoperability issues will impose major restrictions

Example 9.4.8 is an example of special security matters that will influence facility requirements.

9.2.9 Understanding of a Type of Work

Normally, the Government will review the technical approach section of the proposal to determine if your proposal demonstrates a method for performing the work that will be successful. In such instances, your technical approach will be sufficient evidence that you understand the work to be performed. However, there will be instances in which the proposal team is faced with a RFP that does not require a specific technical approach, but instead, requires the bidder to demonstrate an understanding of certain types of work to be performed. In these instances, in your problem understanding section of the proposal, it is necessary to prove that you have the fundamental understandings needed to accomplish that type of work, usually during a multitude of assignments.

Example 9.4.9 is a response to a certain type of work, Transportation Security Analysis that was submitted in response to a Department of Transportation solicitation. In fact, we had to prepare similar responses to six other technical types of work, and we used the following as an example to these other responses.

9.2.10 UNDERSTANDING THE MANAGEMENT CHALLENGES

In some proposals, particularly when ghosting a competitor, it is suggested that an understanding of the management challenges associated with the contract be included in the Problem Understanding section. In this proposal response, you should describe your understanding of the management challenges associated with the work to be performed after award on contract. Some examples of key management understandings include:

- the special requirements of CSCS and CSSR reporting systems
- the special challenges associated with sophisticated planning networks
- the work situations that require rapid buildup and build-down
- the need to use special planning and estimating models and data bases

Example 9.4.10 is an example of an understanding of the more complex cost-schedule reporting systems required by the Government in major contracts and the special needs associated with those systems.

9.2.11 UNDERSTANDING OF SPECIAL PROGRAM REQUIREMENTS

In some proposals, the special, unique requirements of the customer is an item of major importance, and the problem understanding section must address stated and unstated matters as diverse as:

- special security requirements associated with the work

- use of the customer's facilities for performing the work
- need for government or special testing facilities
- desire for the winning contractor to hire the incumbent's personnel
- proven capability to finance a major GOCO facility operation
- need for major resources and facilities near the customer's site

Examples of these types of special contract requirements include such diversity as: requiring a war gaming support staff to work within a security vault, requiring a technical support staff to work at overseas sites, and requiring an approved SCI-approved security facility. Most of these types of proposal requirements are addressed in the "Other Information" section of the proposal.

9.3 WRITING GUIDELINES FOR PROBLEM UNDERSTANDING SECTIONS

9.3.1 GENERAL WRITING GUIDELINES

Write As If A Textbook Author - The most important guidance for the writers of the problem understanding section is to write in a very impersonal style; like a college textbook. Write in an aloof and detached style, avoid slang and acronyms, do not attempt to inject humor, do not use vague or undefined terms, and do not imply any undue familiarity with the customer. Cite references when essential, but do not burden the section with excessive citations.

Omit the Personal Pronouns in Writing - Avoid the use of personal and impersonal pronouns in writing about your understanding of the customer's problems. This exclusion includes the following personal pronouns: "we", "our", "they", "us", and "you". Remember, the problem understanding section should read like a textbook, and textbooks do not use personal pronouns.

Spell the Customers Name in Full to Show Respect - Show respect for the customer and other Government agencies by spelling out their complete name. Do not use an abbreviation such as USN instead of the Navy or the U. S. Navy. Of course it is permissible to use abbreviations when they are used as adjectives, such as "the FEMA facilities" or "the OMB publication".

Controlling the Grade Level - It is essential that the problem understanding section meet the editorial guidelines for the grade level of the text. It is recommended that the highly technical matters, such as an understanding of the key technologies, be written at a grade level of 11.0 or lower. It is recommended that other versions of the problem understanding be written at a grade level less than 9.0, preferably less than 8.0.

Adhering to the Proposal's Editorial Guidelines - The Proposal Manager issues editorial guidelines and editorial policies at the start of the proposal writing effort, and proposal writers must adhere to these directives. The purpose of the guidelines is to ensure uniformity, discipline, and consistency in the writing style, even though many different writers may be employed on the proposal.

Avoiding Too Many Complex Graphics - While the message in the problem understanding is in the words, graphics must be used for those matters that would require an excessive number of pages if described in words; like a wiring diagram or planning network. Just try to adhere to the standard of seven items (maximum) in each graphic.

Write Only What You Know Well - Do not attempt to write about topics or issues with which you are not familiar. Read all current publications related to the problem to ensure that your knowledge is current, particularly in matters such as programmatic issues or key technologies.

Show Respect for the Customer's Problems - If you think that the customer's problem is simple or trivial, then you do not understand the problem. The problem is real, and if you do not recognize this fact, then you should not be planning or writing about the problem.

9.3.2 SPECIFIC WRITING INSTRUCTIONS

The specific DO NOT rules to be observed during the writing of the problem understanding section of the proposal are quite simple:

- Do not write about your team's contract experience
- Do not write about your team's technical accomplishments
- Do not write in a casual or overly familiar style
- Do not forget to cite references completely and often
- Do not use abbreviations, acronyms, slang, or jargon
- Do not minimize the problems the customer faces

The specific DO rules to be observed during the writing of the problem understanding sections are described in the Appendix entitled Writers Handbook. This short handbook provides specific guidance such as:

- Limit the length of sentences and paragraphs
- Use the customer's words whenever possible
- Write so that people with diverse backgrounds will all understand
- Concentrate on the problem as the customer has defined it
- Control the grade level of the text

9.4 EXAMPLES OF THE PROBLEM UNDERSTANDING TEXT

This section includes a series of one-page and two-page units that were prepared as essential elements within the Problem Understanding section of the proposal. These units present typical contents of ten different types of understandings. It is suggested that proposal writers can learn best how to write problem understanding responses by using these examples for guidance.

Example 9.4.1
Understanding of a High-Level Requirement
Coal Mine Health and Safety Act

Background

In 1969, the Congress passed the Federal Coal Mine Health and Safety Act (PL 91-173) and the President signed the law without delay. This Federal Coal Mine Health and Safety Act was in response to a major disaster at the Farmington, WV, underground mine of the Consolidated Coal Corporation. This Act was one of a series of health and safety acts that have been enacted by the Federal Government; some of these acts include:

- Federal Metallic and Non-Metallic Mine Safety Act
- Railway Safety Act and Longshoreman Safety Act
- Walsh Healy Public Contracts Act
- Occupational Health and Safety Act

In each of these federal initiatives in the field of health and safety, the federal government supersedes the state laws and regulations.

The FCMHSA

The Congress enacted into law a series of new, specific standards and requirements that addressed the following:

- Established limits for the amount of respireable dust to which a miner is exposed

- Established limits for the maximum noise to which a miner is exposed
- Dictated the need for chest X-rays, audiometric testing, and safety training
- Specified requirements for improved mine maps, signage, and communications
- Dictated stronger methods for assessing the permissibility for underground equipment
- Required mine operators to maintain more comprehensive health and safety records
- Required periodic dust sampling and occupational noise surveys

The FCMHSA addressed may additional areas of concern to coal miners and coal mine operators, including:

- A trust fund, funded by mine operators, was established to provide financial support to coal miners disabled by coal workers pneumoconiosis (Black Lung)
- MSHA inspectors were authorized to issue citations that resulted in severe fines being imposed on the mine operators for virtually every violation, however minor.
- The need for a reclamation plan, approved by MSHA, that provided design documentation and funding estimates.

The FCMHSA established a new organization, the Mine Safety and Health Administration (MSHA) to enforce the act. The Bureau of Mines was relieved of its regulatory responsibilities and redirected to research areas. Most of the USBM employees in the field offices were transferred to the MSHA and were then trained in the provisions of the new law.

Probably the most punitive aspect of the FCMHSA has been the deliberate emphasis on an adversarial relationship between the federal mine inspectors and the coal mine operators. Prior to enactment of this law, federal mine inspectors had the authority to point out a minor infraction that the mine operator could correct in a very short time, without a citation or a fine. This relationship does not exist at the present time because any infraction, however minor, must be cited and a fine must be assessed. Zero flexibility is the rule now.

Example 9.4.2
Understanding of a Critical Issue
Minimizing the Impact of Construction on Customer Operations

1. Our Understanding of the Need for Continued Embassy Functioning

During the construction of an annex to the U. S. Embassy in Beijing, China, the construction work must proceed quickly without any major impact on the functioning of the Embassy itself. This means that we must tailor our design and construction efforts so that our on-site construction effort will not interfere with the day-to-day operations of our Embassy. This requirement means that we must tailor our project, both the design and construction phases, so that our construction schedule and construction plans will ensure that the Beijing Embassy will be fully functional.

This requirement means that we must ensure that our construction facilities and construction activities are integrated into a plan for minimum impact on Embassy functions. It also means that we must ensure that our security activities will not result in any compromise to the integrity of the Embassy and the Annex to be constructed. We must establish a project management structure that enables us to maintain close liaison with Government personnel. The key features of our understanding of the need for ensuring continued functioning of the Embassy offices, facilities, and personnel include:

- We have identified a requirement for the design phase that directs our engineering and architectural staff to develop designs that will result in a construction effort that has minimum impact on Embassy functioning.
- We have identified a requirement for the construction phase

that directs our construction planning staff to develop plans, schedules, and procedures that ensure that our construction effort has minimum impact on Embassy functioning.

- During the Initial Site Survey, our site survey team will identify specific means by which we will minimize the impact of our construction activities on Embassy functions. We will solicit inputs from Embassy and FBO representatives.

- We will evaluate alternative sites for locating our storage and material handling areas, equipment parking areas, and our temporary offices so that we can plan our construction to be efficient while having minimal impact on Embassy functions.

- We have identified a requirement to construct a new, temporary Post One on one corner of the existing embassy, using a modular unit that will be installed with minimum impact on the Embassy functions.

- We can accommodate the requirement for the beneficial occupancy of the Annex in which we must move Embassy offices, facilities, and personnel into the Annex before the Embassy modification and renovation begins.

- Upon completion of the construction work in the Embassy, there is a requirement for the offices, personnel, and equipment in the Annex will be relocated to the Embassy prior to closing the project site.

2. Interfaces between Our Managers and Government Managers

Our management approach to accommodating the Embassy requirement for continuous functioning during the construction phase is based on:

- daily, face-to-face discussions regarding construction priorities and problems by our senior managers and the Embassy and FBO managers.

- frequent monitoring of construction during walk-throughs by our managers and Government managers on a weekly basis

- submitting written reports on the corrective actions taken by our managers in response to the concerns expressed by Government managers

- monthly presentations by our senior managers that describe our initiatives to ensure minimal impact on Embassy operations.

In these initiatives, we will go to the offices of the Government personnel (Embassy and Foreign Building Operation) for the discussions, presentations, and work sessions. We will prepare a list of action items following each meeting and report to the Government managers when we have completed the action items.

Probably the most important aspect of our interfaces with the Government managers is the fact that our Project Manager and our Construction Manager can make decisions without recourse to higher level corporate managers. Our managers have the authority to commit our corporation to corrective actions, to change the construction schedule (while still meeting the ultimate completion date), to commit their management reserve, to reassign personnel, and to implement get-well plans.

3. Responsibilities and Authorities for Ensuring Continuous Embassy Functioning

We understand that the project personnel responsible for ensuring that our construction work has minimum impact on continuing Embassy operations must have the needed authorities. During normal construction projects, we delegate an extensive suite of resources and authorities to our key project personnel who will be working at the construction site daily. The highlights of the responsibilities and authorities that we consider essential to ensuring minimal impact on embassy operations include:

- Project Manager- Meets daily with Embassy and FBO personnel to review complaints, to anticipate complaints, and to discuss remedial actions. Directs changes to construction procedures and schedules. Maintains project surveillance of activities that could impact on Embassy functioning. Implements Get-Well Plans.

- Construction Manager- Meets daily with the construction foremen and superintendents to discuss matters impacting on the continuous operations of the embassy, directs changes in the activities, schedules and to equipment usage.
- Safety Director- Reviews all work activities and equipment usage daily to ensure that Embassy operations and Embassy personnel are not exposed to hazards or potential accidents created by construction.

Example 9.4.3
Understanding of
The Status of a Project or Program

The OSDOC Program

The military services have conducted a series of tests and exercises and have completed many studies in the field of offshore discharge of containers (OSDOC) during an amphibious operation. These tests have demonstrated that containers can be unloaded across the beach when specific systems and equipment are available; troops have been organized and trained for logistics-over-the-beach (LOTS) operations. The OSDOC program has benefited from the studies, equipment, designs, and models that have provided a wealth of information and insights into LOTS problems and provided guidance for planning LOTS-OSDOC operations.

The Military Organizations Involved in the OSDOC Program

The U. Army has been the lead service in the OSDOC tests to date, with the Navy and Marine Corps making significant contributions. The specific organizations include:

- Army Transportation Engineering Agency
- Army Engineer Research and Development Laboratories
- Army Advanced Materials Concepts Agency

- Army Transportation Center
- Army Material Command
- Army Mobility Equipment Research and Development Center
- Naval Ships Systems Command
- Naval Ship Research and Development Center
- Naval Civil Engineering Laboratory
- Hunters Point Naval Shipyard
- Naval Ship Engineering Center
- Naval Facilities Engineering Command
- Military Traffic Management and Terminal Service
- Marine Corps Development and Education Command
- Department of Defense

The OSDOC I and II Tests

The OSDOC I and OSDOC II tests conducted by the Army, Navy, and Marine Corps have provided most of the quantitative data on the discharge of containers from containerships over the beach. The 1972 test (OSDOC II) was an in-depth evaluation of the alternative methods for unloading/discharging containers in a LOTS operation. This test utilized a variety of ships, lighterage, material handling equipment, beach equipment, other equipment available for LOTS operations, and ship-to-shore movements. The lighterage included LCUs, barges, pontoons, and LCACs. It was a major advance over the OSDOC I tests conducted in 1970.

The OSDOC tests concentrated on examining the feasibility and effectiveness of the offshore discharge of containerships within an operational environment. The tests examined matters as diverse as: interfaces with other ships, operations, and environments; testing several concepts and tactics for the employment of containerships within a systematic approach. Specific needs for new concepts, doctrines, equipment, and organizations for containership unloading were also examined. It was observed that an operational test and evaluation program (OTE) might be necessary to determine their operational effectiveness.

The Findings of the OSDOC I and II Tests

The OSDOC tests and other work performed by the services and their contractors definitely proved that the discharge of containers in LOTS operations was practicable. The tests and subsequent studies indicated that there a number of problem areas that must be addressed before an efficient; bully operational system can be deployed. The findings included:

- A productivity model must be developed to determine the preferred mix of LCUs, barges, pontoons, air cushion vehicles, and to develop tactics for their usage.
- The interfaces between ships (merchant, MTMTS, Navy) and LOTS equipment during amphibious operations must be identified and defined.
- The on-shore/beach requirements for equipment and concepts (SCATT, ELCT, HOPPER, etc.) must be determined
- The optimum mix of assets to perform offshore containership discharge must include: dedicated assets, contingency acquisition, peacetime subsidy, Delong platforms and barges, and Navy ships versus merchant ships.

Some Observations Relative to the OSDOC Tests

The Navy's amphibious forces and the Marine Corps cooperated with the Army in the evaluation of containership unloading across the beach. However, the Navy and Marine Corps have not really addressed the problems of containership unloading when port facilities are not available. The Navy and Marine Corps have concentrated their attention and resources on the assault phase, with minor attention to general unloading and to unloading follow-on shipping. It appears that the only experience, data, models, and analyses related to offshore discharge of containerships are resident within the U. S. Army.

Example 9.4.4
Understanding of a Technology
Atmospheric Effects on Laser Radiation

Laser Propagation Losses in the Atmosphere

High energy lasers generate extremely high power levels that are concentrated into a small beam focused onto a target. While the laser devices generate power levels in the megawatts, the target receives only a very small fraction of that energy. The difference in power between the laser devices and the target is largely due to propagation losses incurred by the laser beam due to atmospheric conditions. Laser propagation losses are due to four major atmospheric phenomena that are unavoidable in a maritime environment, including:

- Scattering - in which laser radiation is scattered by aerosols (suspended particles)
- Absorption - in which laser radiation is absorbed by gases, clouds, rain, and mists
- Turbulence - in which varying wind conditions and wind shears deflect the laser beam
- Blooming - in which the heated atmosphere creates a lens effect that defocuses and spreads the laser beam

Since these phenomena exist in all maritime environments, laser propagation losses will always be a problem in maritime environments.

Absorption is the greatest source of laser propagation losses, to the point that over 80 percent of the energy leaving the beam director is lost before the beam reaches a target at a range of five kilometers. As a general rule, absorption losses increase as the wavelength of the laser radiation decreases, meaning that in the earth's atmosphere, lasers in the ultraviolet frequencies have significantly greater propagation losses than lasers operating at infrared frequencies. This general rule, losses versus wavelength, has exceptions in the form of windows, or small frequency bands, in which propagation losses are significantly less than at higher or lower frequencies. For example, a major window occurs in the mid-infrared band, at about 1.5 microns, permitting chemical lasers to operate more effectively than other lasers in the atmosphere.

Scattering is a minor source of laser propagation losses when compared to absorption losses; it causes propagation losses of only 10 percent over a distance of five kilometers. These scattering losses are almost uniform over all frequencies and are relatively easy to measure and predict. Since these particles (aerosols) are associated with such phenomena as cosmic dust, high-altitude particles, industrial emissions, and long-range dispersion of fine particles, all laser beams will be attenuated in all environments.

Turbulence reduces the effectiveness of lasers as weapons in the earth's atmosphere, because it defocus the laser beam and adds to the difficulty of maintaining a beam on a specific spot. Micrometeorological conditions, which are very unpredictable and are difficult to measure remotely, cause the laser beam to move, even when the beam director does not move. For example, under only moderate turbulence conditions, a concentrated (2-inch) spot on a target can become a less-concentrated spot with a diameter approaching five inches. Such a change reduces the effective power density on the target by a factor of approximately six.

Thermal Blooming causes severe defocusing of the laser beam when the air between the beam director and the target (the beam path) become heated. This heating of the air, largely due to absorption, creates what is best described as a convex lens using air to form the lens instead of glass. A 2-inch spot on the target can easily become a 4-inch spot (with a loss of power density of about four) when severe blooming occurs. Only a change in the beam path or a wind across the beam path can overcome the effects of thermal blooming.

A great deal of research has been conducted into laser propagation losses by the Naval Research Laboratory, the White Sands Missile Range, the Army's Atmospheric Science Laboratory, and the Air Force Weapons Laboratory. This research has resulted in an extensive data base on propagation losses for many atmospheric conditions, many power levels, and many frequencies. This data base, in turn, has been used to develop several computer modes (e. g., LASE, Phillips models) that compute the propagation losses likely to be encountered in many different situations.

Example 9.4.5
Understanding New Operational Requirements
Airport Capacity Demands

The Need for Increased Airport Capacity

For the foreseeable future, air traffic in the United States is projected to far outpace the growth in airport capacity. This increased demand, when coupled with systematic constraints (ATC, ground access, environment, cost) make the problem of airport planning very complex. It is almost a certainty that the need for increased airport capacity will significantly outpace the rate at which new airports are designed and constructed or existing airports are upgraded in major, expensive construction efforts.

Recent analyses have pointed out that, in light of the long lead-times required to site and build airports, capacity relief over the short to mid-term must be through measures that improve the efficiency or throughput of existing systems and facilities. Such measures can be grouped into two major categories:

(1) measures that increase the effective capacity of existing major airports by more efficient allocation and organization of their facilities.

(2) measures that increase the utilization of alternative (or reliever) airports by making them more attractive and accessible to travelers, shippers and airlines.

The existing major airports are already operating at a level that approaches their maximum capacity, and only minor improvements can be realized in this approach in improving their capacity. Most of these airports cannot increase their capacity to handle the growing needs of the air cargo and general aviation users without an significant, adverse impact on their capacity to handle passenger operations. Therefore, it appears that new and different airport facilities will be needed to handle the needs of airport users in the near future.

The Use of Alternative Airports

Alternative airports, ones that are not used extensively by major airlines and air cargo firms, fall into four general categories:

- Major new airports can be constructed and used principally for passenger operations, leaving air cargo and general aviation to use the existing airports.
- Smaller civil facilities (such as Long Beach, Oakland, Hobby, or Lakefront) that are underutilized can be used for certain aircraft, like general aviation..
- Existing military air bases that are being demilitarized and turned over to local authorities (such as Scott AFB and Homestead AFB) can be viable facilities
- Small facilities, new or existing, can accommodate VTOL or STOL operations (such as London Docklands, Toronto Island Airport, and Meigs)

The key to developing the potential that resides within these alternative airports lies in their being available to airlines, travelers, and shippers in a minimum amount of time. These users, have concerns with matters such as air traffic control, ground access problems, and availability of space at new facilities. For air carriers, these alternative airports must have adequate instrument departure, approach, and landing capabilities; ready availability of takeoff and landing slots, reasonable landing fees, user charges, favorable lease terms, and suitable terminal/maintenance facilities.

For shippers and travelers, the key issues associated with alternative airports are total travel time, which includes ground access time and flight frequency. In addition to roadways, rapid transit systems and other ground transportation systems must minimize total travel time. Issues such as sufficient parking, adequate passenger terminals, and freight warehouses are also important matters.

Key Issues Associated With Increasing Airport Capacity

Probably the most critical issue associated with the use of alternative airports is the timeline associated with the FAA system for upgrading its air traffic control systems; the FAA seems to move at glacial speed when planning, procuring, and installing more air traffic control capabilities. The next most critical issue is the very long time required to construct a new, major airport; construction times range from six to ten years, not including the delays associated with funding and community outreach. The process of converting an existing military base to commercial usage is inordinately long and complicated because of the process involved with utilization plans and community involvement. And then the issue of separating air passenger service from general aviation is always a political quagmire.

Example 9.4.6
Understanding of Associated Contractors and Other Organizations
Organizations Involved With the High Energy Laser Program

1. **The Naval Commands and Laboratories Involved With the HEL Program**

   High Energy Project Office (PMS 405) - The Navy Project Office within the Naval Sea Systems Command that is located in the Crystal City area of Arlington, VA. The program office has overall responsibility for all research, development, design, engineering, and testing activities by Naval elements and by the contractors involved in the development of a high power chemical laser. The Project Office began operations in 1972; its staff is organized into a Plans Section, Systems Analysis Section, System Engineering Section, a Technology Section, and an administrative staff.

   Naval Sea Systems Command (NAVSEA) - The Navy's high energy laser program was assigned to the Naval Sea System Command because the weapon system was to be installed on board Navy combatant ships. NAVSEA provides administrative, procurement, office, library, and other types of support to the High Energy Laser Project Office, in addition to serving as the Navy's office for management oversight..

Naval Research Laboratory - The Navy's lead laboratory for support of the high energy laser program, providing invaluable expertise in high power optics and laser propagation. NRL, which is located in Washington, DC, provides support to high level management review groups and to technology assessments.

Naval Weapons Laboratory - The Navy laboratory, located at Dalhgren, VA, that specializes in weapons effects; it provides support to the high energy laser program in the matter of threats, specifically, the effectiveness of warheads on Soviet anti-ship cruise missiles.

Naval Missile Center - The Naval facility that works closely with the Naval Weapons Laboratory in the testing and evaluation of large shaped charge warheads and their effects.

David Taylor Research Center - The Navy facility that provides detailed experimental data on the effectiveness of shaped charge warheads after detonation.

2. The Army and Air Force Organizations Involved with High Energy Lasers

Army Missile Command - The home of the Army High Energy Laser Special Project Office, located at the Army's Huntsville, AL, Arsenal. The AHELSPO was responsible for the development of a mobile electric discharge laser, a prototype of which was installed on a tracked vehicle for demonstration.

Air Force Weapons Center - The organization responsible for the development of an experimental weapon system in which a high power gaseous discharge laser was installed on a Boeing 747 aircraft for in-flight testing of a concept. This system has yet to prove feasible for use as a tactical weapon system.

White Sands Missile Range - The facility at which the High Energy

Laser System Test Facility was being constructed at WSMR will provide all of the administrative, security, logistical, and management support needed during the testing of the high energy lasers. The test facility will be located at the site of the old MAR facility.

Army Corps of Engineers - The Army organization responsible for the design and construction of the High Energy Laser System Test Facility; the Houston office of the COE is the lead organization for the construction of high technology facilities.

3. The Principal Contractors

TRW - The major defense contractor responsible for the design, fabrication, testing, and operation of the MIRCL high power laser device; TRW operates at the Capistrano Test Site where the Navy's high power laser, in a prototype version, is being tested and evaluated when engaging missiles fired from the nearby Marine Corps facility.

Hughes - The major defense contractor responsible for the design, fabrication, testing, and operation of the HEL Pointer-Tracker is also responsible for the installation of the pointer-tracker at the High Energy Laser Test Facility; provides expertise in high power optics, tracking systems, and major software applications.

Pratt and Whitney - The major defense contractor, a subsidiary of United Aircraft, responsible for the design, fabrication, testing, and operation of the Beam Transfer Subsystem for the High Energy Laser Weapon System; provides expertise in high power optics, beam ducting, and laser beam conditioning.

McDonnell Douglas- The major defense contractor working as a subcontractor to Brown and Root in the design of the High Energy Laser System Test Facility; also the developer of the important software system used for automatic aim point selection and maintenance. Provides support to Brown and Root in areas such as system safety, and system integration.

Brown and Root- One of the largest Architectural and Engineering Design and Construction contractors in the nation, responsible for the preliminary and final design of the High Energy Laser System

Test Facility. The firm selected to provide construction management services to the General Contractor selected by the Army Corps of Engineers.

Science Applications International Corporation- The principal contractor to the HEL Project Office, providing a wide range of technology, systems engineering, systems analysis, and planning support from a dedicated facility in Arlington, VA, plays a significant role in effectiveness analyses, design reviews, test design, and budgeting.

4. The FCRCs and Other Organizations

Facility Engineering, Inc. The engineering design firm working under contract with NAVSEA to support the formal design reviews associated with the Brown and Root designs for the High Energy Laser Test Facility.

MIT-MITRE - The Federal Contract Research Center under contract with the Navy to provide some unspecified technical support to the High Energy Laser Program. Principal activities seem to be as a spectator at some meetings.

New Mexico State University - The Physical Sciences Laboratory of NMSU is the prime contractor for the operation, maintenance, and support of the High Energy Laser Test Facility at White Sands Missile Range.

Example 9.4.7
Understanding of an Engineering Challenge
Pointer-Tracker Accuracy

On the Subject of Tracking Accuracy

The top-level specifications for the pointer-tracker to be used with the Navy High Energy Laser Weapon System dictates an accuracy of 1 micro-radian when acquiring, tracking, and engaging an incoming cruise missile. This accuracy requirement means that the jitter, or noise, experienced in measuring the range and angles between the pointer-tracker and the incoming cruise missiles must have a maximum standard deviation of 1 micro-radian. Note: one micro-radian is one-millionth of 57.3 degrees. It is noted that most tracking radars used at missile test ranges have a noise factor, or jitter, of about 1.5 mill-radians in angle track and that their range tracking noise is in the order of plus-minus 12 inches.

The Atlantic Missile Range and several USAF classified sites have been using a state-of-the-art radar system for tracking ballistic and cruise missiles for over ten years. This radar, the FPS-16, is the greatest radar system in the world, and it certainly has the lowest tracking noise, or jitter. Its angle tracking noise, which is probably in the range of 100 micro-radians, is probably due to several important technical matters, like:

- The FPS-16 radar uses optical sensors to assist in tracking at short ranges
- The radar is built onto an extremely stable base with a rigid structure
- The radar has extremely sophisticated software for processing data
- The radar uses data algorithms such as 11-point and 15 point smoothing
- The radar has the best technicians and engineers in the country for support

The effectiveness analyses associated with the High Energy Laser Weapon System indicates that a tracking accuracy of one micro-radian is necessary for the high energy laser to be competitive with other Close-In Weapons Systems used for defense against incoming cruise missiles. This accuracy is essential if the laser beam is to remain focused on a single spot for several seconds, a condition necessary for the laser energy to burn through the skin of incoming cruise missiles and to destroy critical components within those missiles.

In conclusion, it appears that laser pointer-trackers must have a tracking accuracy about 100 times better than the best of the current radar systems.

Operational Matters that Impact Tracking Accuracy

The problems that a pointer-tracker for a high energy laser weapons system will face in their usage within a combat environment include those associated with the atmospheric conditions, the characteristics of the missile, the personnel employing the weapon, and the shipboard constraints associated with the installation. These problems include:

- The effects of thermal blooming and atmospheric turbulence on the propagation of the laser beam from the pointer-tracker and the incoming cruise missile. Turbulence will introduce angle tracking errors greater than 1-2 micro-radians consistently.

- Cruise missile construction characteristics that cause the laser beam to wander while focused on the skin (with radar systems, this matter is called glint). Further, hardening of the missiles will require the beam to remain focused on a single spot longer.

- Shipboard operating conditions that can introduce major problems because the ship will twist due to the torque associated with the sea conditions. Also, exhaust gases from the stacks can alter the beam path and attenuate the beam itself.

- Ship crew members will include trained technicians and untrained officers to maintain, align, and calibrate the advanced technology weapons system. Calibration and alignment particularly will be very stressing while at sea in a combat environment.

The Engineering Challenges Facing Design and Development Personnel

The engineering challenges will prove to be most stressing, because the pointer-tracker must overcome the environmental conditions over which man has no control; elementary physics and introductory meteorology say that environmental conditions will always be unpredictable. Experience in military operations says that the enemy will develop countermeasures in a very short time after a new weapons system is developed. For example, the enemy can easily increase the thickness of the missile skin in vulnerable areas and can protect inner components (like guidance system, fusing system, and warhead) with minor insulation once the high energy laser weapons system become operational.

Probably the greatest challenge facing the designers of a radar or optical tracking system is the need for the angle tracking system to respond to rapid changes in direction and for the range tracking system to respond to dramatic changes in ranges to the target. Basically, any servomechanisms within the pointer-tracker have one major constraint:

In order to respond the rapid changes in ranges and angles, the servomechanism must have a very wide bandwidth with little or no smoothing. Wide bandwidths mean that more noise is accepted and generated within the angle and range tracking systems. It is an axiom that one cannot design a very responsive servomechanism without a major increase in the system noise. The angle tracking noise or "jitter", increases as the servomechanism is r equipped to respond quicker. This characteristic of servomechanisms cannot be overcome (God made it that way) and it is especially true in quick response servo systems. Jitter will always tend to defocus the laser beam.

Somehow, the pointer-tracker and the laser beam must overcome the adverse environmental conditions, resolve shipboard installation matters, and overcome enemy countermeasures. Additionally, the laser system must be designed to be simple enough for operation by 18-19 year old sailors and maintained by slightly more experienced navy technicians.

Example 9.4.8
Understanding a Design and Construction Requirement
Design of Security Barriers

Our Understanding of Design Requirements for Passive Barriers
Definition- Passive barriers are physical constructions that deny

passage by personnel or vehicles to a sensitive site. Passive barriers can include such diversity as: concrete structures, metal fences, stone walls, ditches/ponds/lakes, dense vegetation, and metal railings. Passive barriers are generally permanent installations that do not move, do not require maintenance, and do not need personnel to operate. They are a major physical security asset because of their ease of construction, low overall cost, and their long lifetime.

Role of the System - Passive barriers are the first line of defense for a facility or building needing protection. Passive barriers present a major obstacle to intrusion by the average person or typical vehicle and can provide major protection from blast and small arms. Frequently, passive barriers are used to direct intruders into routes or areas in which other security systems are very effective, and they are used extensively in conjunction with active barriers. Sometimes, passive barriers are used by guards and security personnel for protection when engaging intruders or potential intruders.

State of-the Art of the System - The state-of-the-art for passive barriers has not advanced significantly in many years, and it is not expected that technology advances will be realized for passive barriers in the foreseeable future. Concrete, earth berms, ditches, chain-link fences, and thorny fences have not changed in recent years. It is expected that existing designs, materials, and usage procedures are adequate for this system and that advances in the state-of-the-art or major changes in existing designs will not be necessary.

Problems/Limitations of the System - Passive barriers are difficult to reposition and, therefore, provide little flexibility in responding to new, different security situations, and the time required to modify or relocate passive barriers can be quite long and the expense quite high. Further, passive barriers can be penetrated by determined, highly-trained parties who can scout the barriers at their leisure. Passive barriers too close to the structure being protected cannot always provide improvements in blast protection and in physical security in general.

Sources for Procuring the System - Simple, movable concrete barriers can be purchased on the open market from local concrete mixing plants. Or, concrete can be purchased from local sources and then mixed at the site, using leased equipment. Materials and supplies for fencing and metal barriers can be purchased readily from local vendors. Or passive barriers can be constructed using local contractors and leased equipment. The approach to procuring the barrier materials and constructing the barrier will depend very much upon the design of the barrier itself.

Possible Countermeasures - Passive barriers of concrete are relatively unaffected by conventional countermeasures. Normally, massive amounts of chemical or mechanical energy are required for blasting concrete barriers; shaped-charge warheads, however, are extremely effective against concrete structures, even though they do not produce a major breach in the barrier. Fences are quite vulnerable to penetration by determined people using readily-available hand tools, except when fences are used in conjunction with detection systems. The enemy forces may just create larger car or truck bombs using even more powerful ANFO material.

Improvements in the System - While technological breakthroughs are not likely for passive barriers in the foreseeable future, innovative designs using current systems, materials, processes, and technologies can improve the effectiveness of passive barriers. This is particularly true in designs that incorporate kevlar coatings to contain spall, use two closely spaced barriers to minimize the effectiveness of shaped charges, and barriers that deflect blast waves away from the facility being defended.

System Cost Drivers - The construction of passive barriers and the removal of passive barriers require a not-insignificant amount of time and dollars. In fact, over 70 percent of the system lifetime costs are the initial construction/installation cost. Once the passive barriers are constructed, however, the costs for maintenance and repair over a 20-year lifetime are minimal, and personnel operating costs are almost non-existent.

Special Considerations - The design of passive barriers must be considered within the context of an overall security design. As an important element within the overall security system, the design engineers must ensure that the passive barriers are integrated with the active security systems.

Example 9.4.9
Understanding of a Type of Work
Transportation Security Analysis (TSA)

What TSA Is

Transportation Security Analysis is a structured approach to assessing the vulnerability of a transportation system to a wide range of likely or possible threats. It is the analytic process by which vulnerabilities and threats are identified and quantified, countermeasures are identified and evaluated, and preferred security measures and means can be identified. It provides security planners with the information needed to develop the most effective security program.

Specific TSA Activities

A wide range of threats are described in terms of their severity, likelihood, and impact. Vulnerabilities are identified in terms of their susceptibility to damage, destruction, or neutralization. Security, damage control, and mitigation approaches are described in detail and their effectiveness against a wide range of threats are quantified and ranked. Many times, the work will include threat analyses, vulnerability analyses, tradeoff studies, simulations, field tests, and exercises. When the various security measures are ranked, a detailed life cycle costing activity is frequently needed to estimate the relative costs of the measures.

Critical TSA Issues and Matters

Probably the most critical element is the TSA effort is the definition of a threat that is credible, quantifiable, and believable. In this matter, the results of damage or destruction to transportation facilities and systems during the period from WW II to the present are analyzed, and their likelihood and impact on our systems are estimated. In some matters, it will be necessary to conduct simulations, tests, and exercises to develop information where there is no usable, detailed information available.

Users of TSA

The users of the results from transportation security analyses include: design engineers, security forces, reaction teams, operations and maintenance personnel, and risk management specialists. The users, in effect, include all organizations associated with a project, facility, or system, from the design phase to the construction phase to the operational phase. Higher level managers use the analyses to prepare management plans, to develop funding estimates, and to allocate resources to security initiatives. Construction contractors and equipment manufacturers use the result of the TSA to build survivability into their work.

Special Resources Needed for TSA

The needed resources will include a diversity of documentation, analytic models, special resources, including: facility and system design documentation, operations and maintenance handbooks, technical intelligence related to threats, and samples of equipment and systems.

The resource requirements may include field exercise areas, special security equipment, highly skilled threat personnel, special training programs and equipment, and security specialists. Intelligence is needed to define the capabilities of threat systems, organizations, and personnel.

Results of the TSA

The results of the Transportation Security Analyses will include such diversity as: identifying the need for improved design and construction criteria, new security training initiatives, and additional security structures and systems. Other TSA results will identify and quantify the need for more threat-related information, the need of upgraded security forces, and a forecast of possible damage from threats. The analyses can provide the specific information needed to prepare security plans, to train security forces, and to select security systems and equipment. And when a costing effort is included, the TSA will provide documentation needed for budgeting.

Example 9.4.10
Understanding of Management Challenges
Understanding of Cost Schedule Reporting Systems

The Three Types of Cost-Schedule Reporting Systems

The federal government specifies three type of cost schedule reporting systems to be used by contractors in DOD Instructions. The cost reporting systems include:

- **Contract Funds Status Report** - which is submitted quarterly by the contractor.
- **Cost Schedule Status Report -** which is submitted monthly by the contractor
- **Cost Schedule Control System -** which is submitted monthly by the contractor.

The Contract Funds Status Report is usually restricted to small contracts for services, studies, and similar efforts. The Cost Schedule Status report is required for multi-year, medium-size contacts for hardware and software development, special studies, and research efforts. The Cost Schedule Control System reports are required for major programs with over $20 million in research and development services and over $100 million in production efforts.

The Contract Funds Status Report is the simplest form of cost reporting; the Cost Schedule Control System report is an extremely complex cost reporting system. The Cost Schedule Status Report is at an intermediate level of complexity, but it is not a simple system by any measure.

The Special Requirements of the CSSR and CSCS Systems

The CSSR and the CSCS requirements begin with three major project planning tools: a very detailed Work Breakdown Structure, a very detailed project schedule, a list of the many project milestones, and a planning network. Their requirements also include a very detailed description of: the project deliverables, the organization of the project staff, and the resources allocated to the project. Traditionally, both the CSSR and CSCS require a Project Management Plan that provides a top-level description of all the items described above.

Both the CSSR and the CSCS system require a Work Breakdown Structure (WBS), which includes a WBS Index and a WBS Dictionary. The WBS is a structured summary and a hierarchical breakdown of the specific tasks (into work packages) to be performed during the project. Typically, the work packages are limited to three months and to an estimated budget not greater than $50,000. This means that a two-year research study with an estimated value of $4 million will require 24 CSSR reports for a total of at least 80 work packages. Note: the actual number of WBS work packages will probably be in the order of 300-350. A major design, development, testing, and production project (requiring CSCS reports). Extending over a period greater than five years will probably require a WBS with over 5,000 work packages.

The Navy seems to prefer a WBS based on a Type-Of-Work structure, in which the work to be performed is the principal concern. Normally, the Navy WBS for a research and development or production program reaches down to the seventh or eighth level before it actually addresses the hardware and software to be developed. The Air Force, however, on a major weapons procurement program, organizes its WBS work with hardware and software as the principal concern. The Air Force WBS for major programs reaches down to the seventh or eighth level before it actually addresses the type of work to be performed.

The Resources Needed to Respond to CSSR and CSCS Requirements

Both the CSSR and CSCS reporting requirements dictate an appreciable manpower effort, a major software system, and many essential capabilities during the planning phase of the project. The planning effort for the CSCS reporting system requires about three times the manpower required by the CSSR. The preparation of the WBS Index and Dictionary for a project with only 300 work-package project will probably require at least 150 man-days (based on 2 pages per man per day). The preparation of a WBS Index and Dictionary for a major program requiring CSCS reporting, based on a minimum of 2,000 work packages, will be in order of 1000 man-days.

The major resources required for a CSSR reporting system begins with a computer system for accruing, allocating, and summarizing detailed technical and cost information associated with specific WBS work packages. Typically, the manpower required for CSSR reporting is at least two personnel working within the contractor's project office, supported by corporate cost accounting reports on a monthly basis. The resources required for a CSCS reporting system begin with the need for a validated (by a government team) system using computers and manual tools to prepare the reports to the Government. Note: the costs for developing a validated CSCS will probably be a minimum of $8 million. At least four members of the project management staff will be dedicated to the CSCS activities.

When variance analyses are required because of differences in cost budgets and actual costs for specific WBS work packages, several members of the engineering staff must be assigned for 5 to 10 days each month to the task of explaining the reasons for such differences and to write the variance analysis. The costing estimating effort needed during the planning of a program that requires CSSR and CSCS reporting is a major activity. Consider, when cost estimates must be prepared for 1,000 work packages and when cost budgets and cost forecasts must be prepared for those work packages, at least 100 man-days will be required, assuming no text or documentation must be written by the cost estimators.

The WBS must be supported by project/program planners who prepare the schedules, milestone charts, planning networks, lists of deliverables, and similar items. It is probable that, for 1000 work packages, the preparation of the master schedule, the planning networks, and milestone charts will require at least 20 man-days. Much of this time is associated with the preparation of inputs to the computer-based systems and in the integration of the lower-level schedules prepared by the technical groups, like the systems engineering staff, the testing staff, and the logistics staff.

CHAPTER 10

UNDERSTANDING THE WORK TO BE PERFORMED

10.1 UNDERSTANDING THE TOP-LEVEL RFP AND CONTRACT ISSUES

10.1.1 THE SOW, WHERE THE WORK IS DESCRIBED IN THE RFP

The Statement of Work, Section C of the RFP, describes the tasks and subtasks to be accomplished and the products and services that will be delivered to the Government. Ideally, when the tasks and subtasks described in the SOW have been accomplished by the contractor, all contractual requirements will be completed. So, a careful, thorough reading of the Statement of Work is the first step toward understanding the work to be accomplished after award of contract.

The Statement of Work in Section C, which is frequently augmented by attachments in Section J, is prepared in accordance with Mil Hnbk 245C, the government guide to its technical and contract personnel. The statement of work clearly states if the tasks and subtasks will result in a product or in services. Products include hardware, software, firmware, and other tangible items. Services also include a wide range of studies and technical efforts.

10.1.2 THE BIG DIFFERENCE BETWEEN SHALL AND SHOULD IN THE SOW

When reviewing the SOW, the reader must pay special attention to two verbs: shall and should. Shall; means that a task or subtask is mandatory in order to fulfill the requirements of the contract. If shall requirement is not accomplished by the contractor, the contract is in default. Should means that the contractor must consider the matter, and in the real world, the contractor is advised to accomplish all should items in the SOW also.

Mil Hndbk 245 presents a list of verbs approved for use in the SOW, followed by a separate list of verbs that are not approved for use in the SOW. Read this handbook completely, because it is the Bible for preparing Statements of Work. If you do not understand any words in the SOW, refer to the Government dictionaries, such as: JCS Publication 1, The Joint Dictionary, and The Army Dictionary. Note these Government and Military dictionaries should be on the bookshelf of every Proposal Manager and every proposal specialist.

10.1.3 THE STATED AND THE IMPLIED SOW WORK REQUIREMENTS

The SOW will state many work requirements, such as the tasks, subtasks, deliverables, reviews, and will refer to numerous references. These unambiguous statements are readily identified as topics to be addressed in the proposed work program. Further, all stated requirements in the SOW are almost certainly the basis for evaluation standards, so all SOW statements must be considered in the outlining of the proposal.

The SOW will not state all requirements in all matters, but the

Proposal Planner must be capable of deriving implied work requirements for the stated requirements. For example, if a SOW requirement refers to planning and reporting the work, there is an implied requirement for monitoring and controlling the work because these four items are the basics for managing a project, as described in an important DSMC publication on project management.

The Proposal Manager, Volume Leaders, and Proposal Planner must be aware of the implied work requirements in order to develop a complete list of proposal standards.

10.2 UNDERSTANDING THE CONTRACT DELIVERABLES

It is an absolute imperative that the Chief Engineer, Proposal Manager, Proposal Planner, and the Volume/Plan leaders have a full understanding of the deliverables and the schedule for the delivery of all items. This means that your corporation and the subcontractors must have the contract experience, the personnel skills, the problem understanding, the facilities, and the management tools/systems needed to develop hardware and software systems, to perform the studies and analyses, and to provide the technical services required by the customer.

10.2.1 The Hardware Deliverables

Virtually all RFPs for the development and delivery of hardware to the Government will include references, specifications that govern the performance, design requirements, and other characteristics of the hardware. These references and specifications will include:

- Performance Specifications
- Fabrication Specifications
- Military Standards
- Design Specifications
- Environmental Specifications
- Data Processing Standards

- Technical References
- Materials Standards
- TEMPEST Requirements
- SOW Requirements
- Testing Standards Specifications

The Chief Engineer and his/her staff must assemble a complete set of the specifications, standards, references, and other requirements governing the hardware to be developed and delivered. These documents, which are referenced or implied in the RFP, cite the many technical hardware requirements that must be included in the system design requirements data base. The technical specialists must be sure that your corporation can develop the hardware and that the hardware will satisfy the Government's expectations without exception or deviation.

Frequently, the development of hardware will require special testing facilities, special tooling, high-cost machines, CADD-CAM hardware and software, and new or different computer systems. Again, the Chief Engineer and his staff must determine which, if any, of these items are needed and the cost for acquiring the items.

10.2.2 THE SOFTWARE DELIVERABLES

All RFPs for the development and delivery of software systems to the Government will include references, standards, and specifications that govern the performance of the software systems. The requirement documents include:

- Performance Specifications
- Military Standards
- Technical References
- Testing Standards Specifications
- Special Security Requirements
- Design Specifications
- Data Processing Standards
- SOW Requirements
- Software Reuse Directives
- Data Rights

The Chief Engineer and his/her software specialists must assemble a complete set of the specifications, standards, references, and other requirements governing the software to be developed and delivered. These documents, which are referenced or implied in the RFP, cite the many performance and design requirements that must be included in the system design requirements data base. The technical specialists must be sure that your corporation can develop the software and that the software system will satisfy the Government's expectations without exception or deviation.

Frequently, the development of software, particularly major software systems will require special testing facilities, CASE tools and other special software, and new or different computer systems. Again, the Chief Engineer and his staff must determine which, if any, of these items are needed and the cost for acquiring the items.

10.2.3 STUDIES TO BE PERFORMED AND SERVICES TO BE PROVIDED

The Government contracts for a wide range of technical, management, and administrative support services and for an even wider range of studies to be performed by the contractor. Some examples of the studies and services that have been specified in hundreds of RFPs and their supporting documentation include:

Studies Statistical analyses, system lifetime costing, cost effectiveness analyses, systems evaluations, requirements analyses, technical forecasting, vulnerability analyses, survivability analyses, tradeoff studies, economic forecasting, reliability- maintainability analyses, logistics analyses, requirements analyses, scenario development, simulations, technology forecasting, model and simulation development.

Services Data collection, data analysis, operations support, maintenance support, test support, test planning, computer center management, repair services, construction management, vehicle maintenance, aircraft rework and repair, equipment and facility operation, data base maintenance, technical documentation preparation, and architectural engineering design.

The Proposal Manager, Proposal Planner, and Volume Leaders must have the technical skills and management expertise needed to fully understand the types of services to be provided and the studies to be completed.

10.2.4 THE DOCUMENTATION TO BE DELIVERED

The Proposal Manager, the Volume Leaders, and the Chief Engineer must have a broad and deep understanding of the documentation to be delivered during contract performance. This understanding must encompass deliverables as diverse as:

- Monthly Status Reports
- Cost Schedule Reports
- Plans and Specifications
- Invoices and Billings
- Spare Parts Listings
- Training Aids and Materials

- Review Agenda and Reports
- Technical Reports
- Interim and Final Reports
- Operating Manuals
- Maintenance Manuals
- Engineering Drawings

An in-depth understanding of the documentation to be delivered during contract performance is important for two reasons: (1), the labor required to prepare the deliverables must be accounted for in the Work Breakdown Structure, and, (2), the costing effort must include the expenses incurred in the preparation of the deliverables. Rest assured that the documentation requirements associated with a typical contract can be in the order of 10 to 15 percent of the total contract value. Every item listed in the CDRL and the SOW must be reflected in the WBS and in the costing.

10.3 UNDERSTANDING THE SPECIAL CONTRACT REQUIREMENTS

10.3.1 UNDERSTANDING THE CSSR-CSCS REQUIREMENTS

One of the most difficult tasks in a proposal for a major system development contract or for a major support program is to develop the complete structure needed to satisfy their financial reporting requirements. Whereas smaller work programs require only a Contract Funds Status Report, major programs require either a Cost Schedule Status Report (CSSR) or a Cost Schedule Control System (CSCS). The detailed requirements of the CSSR and the CSCS reporting systems are described in DOD Instructions and every proposal specialist must know the key features of the two systems. Some of the features include:

- Both the CSSR and CSCS require detailed Work Breakdown Structures
- Both the CSSR and CSCS require very detailed schedules, networks, and milestones
- Both the CSSR and CSCS require an extensive cost estimating effort
- The CSCS is very much more complex and demanding and is labor intensive.
- The CSCS will require at least one dedicated specialist on the management staff
- The CSCS is used to measure financial, cost, and schedule performance
- The CSCS will require major efforts to explain cost or schedule variances

The CSCS and CSSR requirements mean that project work and deliverables must be planned, costed, scheduled in great detail, and these matters must be updated every couple of days. A later section of this book will address the matter of preparing the project management information and cost-schedule data in more detail. Note: if you do not know the difference between these two reporting requirements and the level of work needed by the two requirements, then either develop that understanding very quickly or find someone who already understands cost-schedule reporting requirements to be your right-hand man.

During a proposal for a major multi-year contract, I prepared the WBS, schedules, milestones, work-around plans, cost estimates, project management plan, staffing plan, financial plan, and other planning documentation for CSSR reporting. I was highly motivated to do a superior job in this assignment, because I was being bid as the Deputy Project Manager, and I would be responsible, among other things, for the cost-schedule reporting system. I hated to lose that competition (we lost on technical matters), but I had a maniacal satisfaction when the Government used my planning work to monitor the contract performed by the winning competitor.

10.3.2 Understanding the Cost Realism Requirements

More competitive procurements are lost because the bidder did not understand the matter of Cost Realism. Basically when the RFP states that cost realism will be considered in its evaluation process and in the selection of the winning competitor, the matter becomes very serious. Typically, incumbent contractors lose their follow-on contract because they assert: "Our costs are realistic because we are currently doing the work, and we know what the costs should be." Trust me, that approach to cost realism in your proposal is a shortcut to unemployment. I know, because a Group Manager in my company said those very words after I offered to prepare a cost realism section for his cost proposal. He did not respond to this RFP requirement and, shortly thereafter, he had to fire over 350 employees when we lost. I later told the Group Manager that you cannot respond to the requirement for a cost realism section by an assertion.

The most important thing about a cost realism requirement in your cost proposal is that you must assign the task of preparing the response to the best member of your proposal team. Do not leave this critical item to a contracts person, to someone needing coverage, to someone who does not have a foggy idea what to do or you are almost certain to lose the competition, regardless of the work put into the technical volume, management volume, or plans. Regardless of whether your costs are the lowest, you must prove that your costs, and only your costs, are realistic.

10.3.3 ACCOMMODATING THE GOVERNMENT CONTRACT MONITORS

The review of the RFP documentation will usually provide a firm basis for estimating the amount of time required of the Project Manager and the project's technical staff for dealing with the Government contract monitors. Unfortunately, that documentation may not really provide the detail needed for staffing and costing, and the documentation may only provide clues as to the type and amount of contract monitoring that will be associated with the contract. Whatever the source of information about accommodating Government contract monitors, the Management Volume Leader must provide a detailed statement on this matter.

The Government contract monitoring activities during contracts for technical support, technical studies, and technical services are largely associated with the periodic project status reviews. These status reviews are frequently as often as once a month and are virtually always at least once a quarter. Technical monitors may meet with key members of the project staff on a very frequent basis. For example, when working on a SETA contract with the Navy High Energy Laser Project Office, my personal technical monitor was in my office in an adjacent building at least twice a day.

Many contractors do not realize that, during major system

procurements, the Air Force will establish a contract management team equipped with Sun Workstations to monitor contract
performance on a near real-time basis. These USAF teams usually work at the contractor's job site and use the documentation
developed by the contractor to monitor cost, schedule, and technical performance. The inputs to the Air Force workstations are
the contractor-developed plans, schedules, milestones, cost data,
Work Breakdown Structure, work-around plans, and other planning documentation. The USAF then monitors project status on a
near real-time basis, which means that, in many instances, they
have quicker insights into the project status than the contractor's
management staff. A horrible thought is getting a nasty gram from
the Government before you know you have a problem.

10.4 UNDERSTANDING THE RESOURCES NEEDED BY THE WORK

10.4.1 Special Facilities Needed by the Work

The Proposal Manager, Chief Engineer, Volume and Plan Leaders,
and the Proposal Planner must identify the special facilities that
will be required to accomplish the work specified in the RFP.
Sometimes, the Government will specify the type of facilities
needed during contract performance and during the proposal
evaluation phase. Some examples of the special facilities that
may be specified or may be merely implied include:

- TEMPEST-approved test sites, laboratories, computer centers,
and work areas
- Security safes, security vaults, and security work areas
- Need for 24-7 guard services and special intrusion detection
systems
- Testing laboratories with certified equipment and supplies
- Machine shops, welding shop, sheet metal shops, and car-
pentry shops

- Firing ranges, test ranges, and explosives storage areas
- Cover for special activities capable of being observed by space vehicles
- Airfields, anchorages, aircraft, ships or boats

The Proposal Manager, Chief Engineer, Senior Scientist, Senior Test Engineer, and Facilities Specialist must be able to identify these facility requirements from a reading of the RFP, the Standards and Specifications, and the other documentation. The Government may believe that if the bidder does not know what special facilities are needed by the contract work, that bidder is not competent to perform the work.

10.4.2 SPECIAL TOOLS, SYSTEMS, AND ITEMS NEEDED BY THE WORK

The same technical and management team used to determine the facility requirements will concurrently define the special tools, systems, and assets needed to perform the work as described in the procurement documentation. The special items can include:
- CASE tools tailored to the software systems being developed
- CSCS software systems for cost-schedule performance assessments
- Special equipment for testing hardware and software systems
- Word processing, spread sheet, and data base software compatible with customer systems
- Data input formats tailored to the PERT-Artemus system of the customer
- Spare parts and maintenance supplies for test items and test facilities
- Special support and supplies from manufacturers of major hardware items
- Training aids, handbooks, documentation, and equipment for operating personnel

- Four-wheel drive vehicles, vans and panel trucks, forklifts and cranes

As a universal rule, proposals for hardware and software development contracts have the greatest requirement for special tools, systems, and items. Technical services contracts can have appreciable requirements, but these efforts will always require less than the hardware and software development projects.

10.4.3 SPECIAL SKILLS OR EXPERTISE NEEDED BY THE WORK

The special skills or expertise needed to accomplish the work as described in Sections C and J of the RFP must be identified at the earliest possible time after receipt of the procurement documentation from the customer. The special management and technical skills required by the work will be used to develop position descriptions for key personnel, which are then used to select the key personnel whose qualifications will be described in the personnel and resumes sections of the proposal. The special technical expertise required by the work will be used to expand on the position descriptions for key engineering and scientific personnel, which are used to select the technical leadership for the project team.

Some of the special skills or expertise required by the work, based on an in-depth analysis of Sections C and J of the RFP, can include such diversity as:

- Computer modeling, data base development, simulations, and data processing
- Risk management, configuration management, and financial management
- Nuclear weapons effects, biological agents, and chemical warfare systems
- Systems engineering, systems integration, and systems evaluation

- Software design, software development, software testing, and software reuse
- Cost-schedule reporting systems, and performance measurement systems
- Schedule, milestone, network, and WBS development
- Technical documentation, technical plans, and management plans and systems
- Threat analysis, vulnerability and survivability, and scenario development

This analysis of the RFP requirements for skills and expertise needed to perform the work also provides the structure for the selection of the contracts to be cited in the experience section of the management volume. The experience of the key personnel, the corporate contract experience, and work requirements must be consistent, meaning that the key personnel being bid should be the people who performed similar work in the contracts cited in the experience section.

On a big, important proposal to the Defense Nuclear Agency, the Proposal Manager was selected on the basis of his academic achievements and his technical work for DNA. This high-level technologist did not really appreciate the need for consistency in the proposal and he removed me from the proposal team for protesting too much. When we lost the competition, the President of the corporation wanted to know why, since he had been waiting for this procurement for at least 15 years. I pointed out that the RFP had defined the skills, expertise, work experience, and educational requirements for the staff. I then pointed out that not one resume for any key person had a single line about their qualifications in any of the position requirements. And I pointed out that very few, if any, of the key personnel had worked directly on any of the contracts cited in our experience section in the Management Volume. Talk about falling on your own sword.

10.4.4 THE NEED FOR A SYSTEMS DEMONSTRATION CAPABILITY

During the procurement of major software systems, the Government for over ten years, has required bidders to demonstrate their software systems before contract award. This requirement means that each bidder must establish a full-up computer facility with the hardware, operating system, applications software as proposed, and must demonstrate that their software meets the benchmark requirements. This requirement is particularly demanding (and usually very expensive) since the bidder must have a fully operational hardware and software configuration for its demonstration of its software system. When the system must operate in an approved TEMPEST-proof facility, the costs become more than significant.

The need for a systems demonstration facility is a critical matter and a major procurement effort must be initiated without delay. Most bidders barely have enough time to assemble and check-out the hardware and software required for such a demonstration, so the need for such an activity must be recognized at the first reading of the procurement documentation. Then the costs and schedules for the facility must be approved by high-level corporate officers, since the facility will inevitably prove to be a major undertaking.

10.5 UNDERSTANDING THE RFP-REFERENCED DOCUMENTATION

Some key member of the proposal or design staff must be assigned responsibility for reviewing the latest version of each reference cited in the RFP and its associated documentation. This means that the Proposal Manager, Volume Leaders, Proposal Planner, Chief Engineer, and other key personnel must read the references in order to prepare a winning proposal. Missing an important proposal requirement by not reviewing the publications referenced in the RFP is one shortcut to losing the competition.

Every RFP has a reference list in the procurement documentation, in addition to those references cited in a listing of clauses in Section H of the RFP. For example, when the RFP mentions Mil Std 2167A, you know that software must be developed in accordance with the process and procedures cited in this very important standard. In fact, the entire design effort will be driven by Mil Std 2167A. The RFP referenced documentation can include:

- Military standards, specifications, instructions, policies, and handbooks
- Performance, design, test, and other specifications
- Federal and Department Acquisition Regulations
- Data Item Descriptions in the Contract Data Requirements List
- Code of Federal Regulations, U. S. Code, Executive Orders
- Cost Accounting Standards, Financial Reporting Requirements

It is wise to establish a proposal library with the latest versions of the references cited in the procurement documentation. The latest versions can be obtained from the Naval Publications Center or the Government Printing Office.

10.6 UNDERSTANDING THE MAJOR RISKS IN THE WORK

10.6.1 THE RISK MANAGEMENT APPROACH

Every major program, whether a study or system development effort, involves some degree of risk. All major programs involve some degree of technical, schedule, cost, and quality risks, with some risks being very serious and some risks being completely manageable. What is most important in this matter of risks is to convince the customer that your management approach has the tools, methods, and procedures to reduce or control risks.

The Defense Systems Management College has published several handbooks addressing the methods for managing risks. In these handbooks, the Government has identified the following risk related activities:

- Risk Identification
- Risk Mitigation/Control
- Risk Analysis
- Risk Reporting

It is highly recommended that elements of risk management be addressed in the management volume of the proposal, even if compacted into just one paragraph by severe page limitations.

During the competition for the development of an advanced technology fighter for the Navy, every major aircraft company stated in their proposal that there were no risks associated with their approaches, technologies, and designs. The Secretary of the Navy, John Lehman, then recommended that the design, development, and testing of the fighter be performed under a fixed price contract. After the high-level corporate officers of the bidders suffered a near heart attack and retracted their no-risk statements, the Navy issued a cost reimbursable contract. The lesson; if there are risks, never claim that you are proposing a no-risk work program.

10.6.2 THE MAJOR TECHNICAL RISKS

It is an axiom that there are always technical risks associated with any contract for the design and development of hardware and software. In proposals for such contracts, the major technical risks must be identified and analyzed by the proposal management and planning staff and by the senior members of the design team. The technical risks can include such diversity as:

- CASE tools cannot be extended or modified for the software
- Design analyses cannot be achieved in breadboards or brass boards
- Manufacturing technology will not be available for advanced materials

- Commercially available computers will not be as effective as forecast
- Flight testing or field testing may be restricted due to national emergencies
- Hazardous exposure limitations may be changed by OSHA, FEMA, EPA, CDC

It is noted that, as a general rule, proposals for studies and services have very few technical risks and that when risks do exist they are relatively minor in nature. In such proposals, the only appreciable technical risk is that the customer might decide to change the scope and complexity of the work after the contract has been awarded. But such technical changes (or re-directions) are not within the sphere of interest of the proposal team.

Every technical risk must, of necessity, become the subject of a work-around plan prepared by either the Proposal Manager and/ or the Chief Engineer. Each plan must address the need for a back-up approach or solution to every risk that has been identified and analyzed. These plans, be forewarned, involve a significant commitment of personal, facilities, resources, and management attention. Nevertheless, these risk mitigation plans are imperative.

10.6.3 THE MAJOR SCHEDULE RISKS

Schedule risks are a fact of life in all contracts, small, big, and gigantic. For example, during any contract for the design and development of hardware and software, there will always be major schedule risks that are associated with the technical risks. For example, during multi-year study or services contracts, the scope of work can be changed, the schedule for deliverables can be altered, and the staffing requirements can be modified.

Schedule risks can include such diversity as: the Government stretching funding to cover a longer period of performance; late delivery of critical GFI, GFE, GFF; occurrence of natural disasters; power shortages and brownouts, adverse environmental conditions, and changing the design or the technical approach. It is always wise to recognize these schedule risk during the planning phase and to have some slack built into the project schedule.

10.6.4 The Major Cost Risks

Look for the major cost risks associated with the work program as you envision it. First, consider the major cost risks that are beyond the control of the corporation or the Project Manager which includes the following categories:

- Changes in the costs associated with materials, equipment, and supplies purchased during the lifetime of the contract.
- Changes in the costs due to labor settlements that increase salaries and fringe benefits for employees.
- Changes in the costs associated with public services and public utilities, unforeseen weather conditions, and public transportation systems.
- Changes in the costs for local, regional, state and federal taxes, and changes in long-term climatic conditions.
- Government-mandated conditions, such as security and airline restrictions, that have a financial impact on the contract work.
- Major changes in the cost-of-living index and its impact on wages and supplies.

Then compile a data base of the major cost risks that can be (and should be) managed by the corporation or by the Project Manager, which can include the following risk categories:

- Unforeseen difficulties associated with the application of new technologies
- Growth in the salaries of exempt employees

- Excessive overtime pay for non-exempt employees
- Unrealistically high expectations for new software (CASE) tools under development
- Use of overly optimistic cost estimating algorithms for work-around plans
- Use of unsubstantiated assumptions and SWAGs for cost estimating

It can be categorically stated that if a project or program has any technical risks or schedule risks, then there will be cost risks without any exception. You can bet on this fact and never lose any money.

CHAPTER 11

KNOWING THE COMPETITION

11.1 IDENTIFYING THE COMPETITION AND THEIR STRATEGIES

It is imperative that you know the competitors that you will be facing in a major competition so that you can counter their strengths and expose their weaknesses. It is your duty as a loyal citizen to inform the Government about the shortcomings and infamies associated with your competitors.

11.1.1 IDENTIFYING THE COMPETITION

Several very effective methods, all legitimate and ethical, are available for identifying the competitors that you must beat in order to win the contract. Some of these methods include:

Checking the Offerors List - When attending a Pre-proposal Conference, check the names of the people and the companies that they represent on the attendance register, recording as much as you can without causing discomfort to the customer. Remember that most of the firms at the Pre-proposal Conference will be looking for an opportunity to team with a larger company as a subcontractor and that only a few of the firms attending the conference will bid as a prime contractor. You should be able to separate and identify these firms easily. Representatives of the firms wishing to be subcontractors but without a connection will give you their business cards and meet with you at a later time.

Checking the Commerce Business Daily - Conduct a search of all contract awards listed in the Commerce Business Daily for the customer and learn which firms have received contracts from that customer in the past five years. The CBD will cite the contract number, date of award, value of the contract, and other brief information. The earlier notices to potential offerors, published by the CBD for major procurements, will contain more complete descriptions of the work associated with the contract.

Reading the Competitor's Annual Reports - Buy one share of stock in any of the publicly traded companies that compete with you, and you will receive their annual reports. Several items in their annual reports should be of great interest to you:
- descriptions of their major contracts and business areas
- detailed information of their financial status
- descriptions of their legal problems and shortcomings
- descriptions of their facilities and key personnel

Hiring a Newspaper and Journal Clipping Service - Hire a clipping service to provide you with articles about your competitors from newspapers, from business journals and magazines, and from professional publications. These information items can prove of great interest because they may indicate the direction in which your competitors are heading. Clipping services are quite reasonable in costs and are very quick to respond. Check the Want Ads of the New York Times, the Washington Post, and the Los Angeles newspapers to learn which of the competitors are recruiting for the contract for which you are preparing a proposal.

Interviewing Applicants for Employment - In the present employment environment, many engineers and software specialists are almost in the category of transient workers, and many of them may be applying for a job at your corporation. Notify the Personnel Department that you want to interview any job applicants currently working or recently working for your competitors. Be put on the applicant's interview schedule, but meet with that person outside of your proposal center.

Discussing Technical Matters At Professional Meetings - Make it a point to talk to as many of the employees from your competitors at professional society meetings, because such meetings are viewed by many a neutral ground. You should keep the conversations as technical as possible and avoid giving too much information about your plans.

Talking with Manufacturer's Representative - Salesmen for high technology products are a great source of information about your competitor's hardware plans. Companies request quotes on major hardware items as part of their costing plans, and this information is not, as a rule, and designated as proprietary. Just ask, and you will learn. Note: watch what you say about your plans because the competition is probably asking about your plans also.

Meeting with Firms Having Contracts with the Customer - During every major and some minor competitions, there may be firms that have current contracts with the customer but are unable to submit a proposal. These firms can provide a great deal of information about the customer because they have great insights into the customer's internal workings, key personnel, and contracting preferences.

11.1.2 DIVINING THE COMPETITORS STRATEGY

Truly, preparing an estimate of the strategy associated with each competitor is closely akin to a black art. Few firm and fast rules are available in the matter of competitor strategy, but the following generalizations are true in virtually all procurements:

- **The Incumbent's Strategy -** Every good incumbent contractor will stress continuity, retention of trained personnel, in-depth knowledge of the problems, staffing certainty, and proven resources. Invariably, the incumbent contractors will cite the risks associated with the introduction of any new contractor, the delays and uncertainties likely to be associated with a change in contractors, and the time needed for a new contractor to make many errors in learning the job.

- **The New Technology Strategy -** Every good competitor trying to replace an incumbent contractor will cite the advantages of new technology infusion, fresh approaches to the problems, use of state-of-the-art hardware and software, and the use of newly improved engineering tools and data bases.

- **The Better Management Strategy -** Every competitor should expound on the management initiatives that it will bring to the program. They should emphasize the management areas in which the Government is weak or the incumbent contractor is severely lacking and expound on the ways in which their management is proven to be better.

- **The IRAD Reduces Risks Strategy -** Those competitors who have sponsored an Independent Research and Development Program at their expense in order to gain a competitive edge will certainly state that they have minimized risks already. This is a powerful strategy, but it must begin long in advance of the proposal effort.

- **The Name Recognition Strategy -** Some companies hire senior retired military officers, senior laboratory scientists, and senior politicians to be proposed as their Project Manager, Corporate Officer Responsible, or Senior Advisor Committee

Members. In these instances, the competitor emphasizes the fact that their management understands the customer's problem best. Read the local newspapers to determine which competitor is announcing the hiring of a senior person for work related to the procurement being bid.

- **The Fresh Blood For Old Problems Strategy** - When an incumbent has held a contract for a long time, it is very effective to cite the customer's need for a more enlightened management and technical personnel who have cutting edge technological skills. Emphasize fresh views, unbiased opinions, fresh approaches, new models, and new skills. Inevitably, every incumbent contractor will have had some problems with some member of the customer's staff, so this strategy will offer the customer new hope.

11.2 KNOWING THE CUSTOMER'S OPINION OF THE COMPETITORS

Knowledge about the Government agency's opinion of the competitors, and your own company, is a bit difficult to obtain. Nevertheless, it is still possible to obtain some information through legitimate, ethical means, such as:

1. If the Government agency continually renews on-going contracts with a competitor, then conclude that the competitor is meeting its contractual obligations.
2. If the Government agency has an award fee contract with a competitor, it may be possible to obtain the award fee reviews under the Freedom of Information Act.
3. If any Government agency has instituted legal proceedings, issued "show cause" notices, or canceled any contracts with your competitors, that information is in the public domain.
4. If a Government employee has joined your company lately, interview that person to obtain information about how the Government personnel feel about the competitors.
5. If an employee of a competitor has joined your company

lately, interview that person to assess how the Government personnel felt about their previous employer.

6. If you cannot discover some degree of dissatisfaction on the part of the Governments contract and technical personnel with a competitor, then you have a real dogfight on your hands. It is well that you realize such a situation early in the competition.

11.3 CHECKING THE CONTRACT PERFORMANCE OF THE COMPETITORS

Checking the performance of the competitors when working for the procuring agency is a very important activity during the early phases of the proposal planning. If a competitor is found to have performed poorly on a contract with the procuring agency or on a contract for similar work for another Government agency, this information can be used to develop win strategies, win themes, discriminators, and stakes to the heart. Now, how do you check the competitors?

- If you can get access to the Government's automated data base that contains information on the performance of contractors, such as the one maintained by the Army Material Command, this is an excellent source.

- If you can hire a clipping service, you can obtain information relative to the cancellation of major contracts and law suits following contract cancellations. The clipping service will provide, for a fee, all newspaper and journal articles

- Check the web sites of disgruntled employees from your competitors, and you may obtain insider information about your competitors. Talk to former employees of your competitors at professional meetings and during interviews at your company.

- Check the Commerce Business Daily for notices of contract funding increases that were not due to increased scope of work. Check the business sections of the local newspapers to learn about law suits relative to contract performance.

Remember that this research into the performance of your competitors should encompass technical performance, cost performance, and schedule performance. Cover all bases, so that your proposal can address these matters in a professional way. Remember, your competitors are verifying your contract performance in order to skewer your corporation in their proposal.

In recent editions of the Washington Post, in the Business Section, articles relative to a Government cancellation of a major software development contract and a legal suit for damages against American Management Systems have been quite detailed; AMS had a gigantic cost overrun for a software system that did not work. Also there was an article about TRW that described the cancellation of a major software development contract by HCFA cited an unusable system with a $65 million cost overrun.

11.4 IDENTIFYING THE WEAKNESSES OF THE COMPETITION

The Acquisition Manager (or Marketing Specialist) associated with the procurement should identify the weaknesses of each competitor as seen from the viewpoint of the customer. Every competitor has something that their managers do not want to become common knowledge within the community or with the customer. The Acquisition Manager must identify the weaknesses, major and minor, of each competitor, and these weaknesses become an integral part of the marketing intelligence used to formulate the win themes.

The weaknesses of the competitors can be of many types, but in all cases, the weaknesses must be from the viewpoint of the customer. For example, the Government agency may view instances in which one of the competitors raided other corporation's staffs in order to fulfill a contract in the past as a good practice unless you point out the problems created in other major, critical contracts with the Government and cite the inability of that contractor to retain a good staff. I recommend that you have a person posing as an adversary to test your statements about the weaknesses of the competitors.

The weaknesses of the competition can be in many activities, skills, and areas. It is wise to use and cite information that has been published in other sources or has been compiled in other data bases to document those weaknesses, whenever possible. Such sources include:

- Contractor performance data base maintained by the Army Material Command
- Reports from court cases maintained by commercial databases
- Public records related to contract performance reviews by the Government
- Information received under the Freedom of Information Act
- Articles published in professional and technical journals and newspapers
- Information gleaned from Help Wanted advertisements by competitors

Do not hesitate to use any legal or ethical means for gathering information from other sources. Frequently, while with my last employer, I tried to be part of the employment interview process when technical or management personnel from one of our deadliest competitors were seeking employment with my corporation. I frankly admitted to the applicant that I wanted to know more about their most recent employer because of a market research effort in which I was engaged. I stated at the onset that they should never reveal proprietary information, classified information, or information covered by the Privacy Act.

I believe that honesty and openness in all respects is the only policy in this matter. Remember that you may not want to hire someone who violates the restrictions of his recent or previous employer. The President of BDM, Earl Williams, frankly and firmly stated that the corporation would not hire an unethical or unscrupulous person and those interviewers would not ask for privileged information during an interview. Note: I suspect that 99 percent of the marketing specialists that I have known have never displayed any respect for my opinions or Earl's standards.

Words of Advice: NEVER identify a weakness in a competitor that your corporation also has. Get an independent third party to assess and report your weaknesses. Be very guarded in the matter of believing your line managers about your own weaknesses

11.5 SELECTING SILVER BULLETS FOR KILLING COMPETITORS

Once the Acquisition Manager (or Marketing Specialist) has identified the weaknesses of the competitors, the Proposal Manager takes charge. Hopefully, the Proposal Manager has a killer instinct in the matter of competitive proposals. But if the Proposal Manager does not have this attribute or does not feel that it is a gentlemanly endeavor, he/she should call upon a proposal person with the killer instinct.

Every corporation should have a proposal specialist who takes great pride in killing the competition and who excels in this activity. That person is best described as "one who drives a stake through the evil heart of the competition". This specialist will determine when and where in the proposal the win themes, discriminators, and other strong statements regarding the competitors will be inserted. Essentially, these "kill the competition" matters become proposal requirements.

The "Silver Bullets" can be of three general types. The more gentlemanly type of Silver Bullet is the use of positive win themes that extol your corporation in areas in which the competition is weak but where you do not mention a competitor by name. The slightly aggressive type of Silver Bullet is the citing of contractual problems associated with the competitors that are a matter of public record. The most aggressive type of Silver Bullet is when you produce evidence of bungling, mismanagement, defaults, and non-responsiveness on the part of the competitors.

When SAIC was a subcontractor with the Flour Corporation in the competition for a technical and management support contract with the Foreign Building Operation of the Department of State, I

concluded the Executive Summary with these Silver Bullets:

- __*__ *has been banned from federal contracts for non-performance.*
- __*__ *must pay a $1+ billion legal settlement with a dissatisfied customer.*
- __*__ *is an aerospace manufacturer that has never built a building overseas*
- __*__ *has a history of subcontracting to PLO-controlled subcontractors*

Always remember that the proposal is a major cost to the corporation, that the contracts resulting from the winning will help the corporation significantly, and that there is no glory whatsoever in being second. You owe it to your co-workers, your stockholders, and your pension to do everything that is legal, ethical, and moral to kill the competitors. Tell the truth about the evildoers and incompetents. The truth will set you free and win contracts.

Remember, a competitive proposal is not a race between equals in which the most gentlemanly company wins. It is a situation in which only the winner wins. Your proposal must provide the Contracting Officer or Source Selection Authority with good information about your corporation and deadly information about the competitors.

I was a Volume Leader for a system development proposal, a competition in which we had two local firms as our subcontractors, both of which had competed against us in earlier proposal efforts. When they read an Executive Summary from one of those earlier proposals, which I had written, they were stunned by the way that I had described their ineptness, lack of conscience, and basic malaise. Their managers asked me how I could write such things about them and still team with them. I merely replied "Then you were the enemy. Now you are an ally. Our allies are all good people".

11.6 WHERE YOU KILL THE COMPETITORS IN THE PROPOSAL

The **Executive Summary** is the first place in the proposal in which you begin your program to vilify and kill your competitors. The Source Selection Authority and the Contracting Officer can plainly see why your corporation is the "Best Buy" for the Government and why your competitors are a terrible buy. Since one of the major purposes of the Executive Summary is to provide the SSA or CO with the rationale for awarding the contract to your corporation, it is proper to point out the reasons for not selecting one of the other competitors. In fact, you have a moral obligation to inform the customer, the Government, of these matters.

Other sections of the proposal offer the skilled proposal planner/specialist the opportunity to kill the competitors. For example:

In the **technical approach** section, if we know the competitor's approach, cite the reasons we rejected that approach when we selected our approach.

In the **facilities** section, cite capabilities that definitely overshadow the facilities of the competitor, such as offices much nearer to the customer.

In the **contract experience** section, if we know of competitors cost overruns, cite our on-budget performance in similar contracts.

In the **personnel** section, highlight the on-time performance and commitment of our project personnel, when we know a competitor has delivered late.

In the **management** section, if the competitor has a record of management problems, expound on the proven ability of our manager.

Remember, you must attack and neutralize every competitor in your proposal. Do not overlook even the slightest competitor or the slightest opportunity.

I call this proposal activity "driving a stake through their hearts".

Part III

EARLY PLANNING
AND ORGANIZATION NEEDS

CHAPTER 12

THE EARLY PROPOSAL PLANNING ACTIVITIES

12.1 RESOLVING THE TOP-LEVEL PROPOSAL ISSUES

12.1.1 FORMULATING A VISION OF THE PROPOSAL

It is wise for the Proposal Manager to discuss the proposal with the Corporate Officer Responsible, Acquisition Manager, Marketing Specialist, Proposal Center Manager, and other corporate resources in developing a vision of the proposal. But these consultations do not relieve the Proposal Manager from formulating his own vision of the proposal its organization, its strong messages, and its style. Be assured that the Proposal Manager's vision of the proposal is the only one that truly counts, because he/she will be the only one facing the corporate firing squad.

When I was managing a proposal (or a volume) with a 100-page limit, I posted 100 pieces of blank paper on the wall. I allocated these 100 pages out to the various volumes and sections, based on the proposal outline. Next, I allocated the pages down to the modules and units within the sections, again relying on the proposal outline. Then I reviewed the entire range of proposal requirements from all sources (RFP, DAR, etc.) and prepared a sketch of what I thought each page should look like. I identified the graphics and the topics of paragraphs as this thought process continued. In the end, I knew what the proposal was going to look like and what it would contain.

Remember, someone on the proposal team must have a vision of the proposal, the volumes, and the plans from the onset. While it is possible to change this vision as the proposal is being written, changes should be few and far between if you have a good vision. This effort to describe the proposal or volume down to the page, graphic, paragraph, and is not as difficult as it may seem, so do not hesitate to try it.

12.1.2 DEFINING THE PROPOSAL PROCESS TO BE USED

The Major Factors that Determine the Proposal Process - The proposal process used in the preparation of a winning proposal is dependent on the resources, facilities, and skilled personnel that are available; the effort needed to prepare the proposal; and the funds available for the proposal effort. The possibilities associated with a wide range of proposals can cover a universe bounded as follows:

Quick-Response Proposals for Delivery Orders - These proposals are usually 20 pages or less in length and usually must be submitted within ten days. Prepared by a team of two or three skilled technical persons, and supported by local word processing and graphics specialists, all working in their normal facilities.

Proposals for Multi -Year Technical Services - These proposals are frequently limited to 100 pages per volume (Technical, Management). Usually prepared by a proposal team working in a corporate proposal center. With full service word processing and graphics support or working at a site dedicated to the proposal effort. They must be submitted within 60 days.

Major Proposal Accompanied By A Major System Design - These proposals are associated with a high-value contract that requires two distinct teams (design, proposal) working in concert during a 120-150 day period. The final proposal and system design documentation are major efforts that require extensive facilities, a large staff of skilled personnel, and support and resources from corporate publications and proposal centers.

The Range of Proposal Processes From Which to Choose - The Corporate Officer Responsible and Proposal Manager should consider the full range of options available for the planning, writing, and production of a proposal. The decision will have a major impact on the cost of the proposal and the quality of the proposal, for sure. These options cover the following range:

1. Prepare the entire proposal within the division and its resources, using the local technical and administrative staff in existing division facilities for planning, writing, managing, reviewing, editing, word processing, graphics, and production.
2. Prepare the proposal using the local technical and administrative staff for . planning, writing, managing, and reviewing and contracting with a corporate service center for editorial, word processing, graphics, and production support
3. Prepare the proposal using a corporate proposal and publications center for support in the key areas of office space, office services, office equipment, editing, proofreading, word processing, art-graphics, and printing. Use division personnel for managing, writing, and reviewing.

The advantages of contracting with corporate service centers are many, including: the preparation of high quality proposal volumes, the availability of a wide range of skilled personnel, the ready availability of facilities and resources essential to producing a quality proposal, the availability of facilities and resources tailored to the proposal process, and the use of a structured approach to proposal development. The disadvantages associated with the use of corporate service centers are: the high costs for travel and daily expenses when people are working at distant sites, the absence of skilled personnel from the Division offices, and the inability of the Division Manager to hide the costs of the proposal in an obscure cost account.

The advantages of developing a proposal using the resources within the line organization are many, including: meeting special security requirements with existing resources and facilities, producing the proposal at less cost since travel expenses are negligible, the ability to phase technical people into the proposal with least indoctrination, and the availability of proposal writers to handle emergency needs within the line organization. The disadvantages associated with this concept include: lack of quick access to corporate proposal resources, lack of access to proposal specialists within the corporation, tendency of managers to divert technical writers to daily crises, and lack of experienced planners and writers from corporate resources.

12.1.3 Identifying and Acquiring Special Facilities and Resources

The matter of facilities and resources can become a critical matter, particularly during a proposal for the design of a major system or during any proposal with special security requirements. So, an early effort to ensure that the proposal and design efforts are not hampered by lack of facilities and resources is important. It is highly recommended that, immediately after receipt of the first procurement document, the Proposal Manager and the Chief Engineer acquire the following or have guaranteed access to the following:

For Special Classified Proposals - Safes, vaults, TEMPEST-tested work areas, removable hard drives, limited access controls, approved computers and software, approved destruction system, personnel clearances, approved work spaces, visitor control system, secure local area network with approved server, guard services, and Special Security Officer support.

For System Design Proposals - Engineering work spaces, engineering data bases, engineering handbooks and references, computers with similar hardware and software, local area network, conference rooms, manufacturers catalogs, engineering handbooks, military handbooks, specifications and documentation, library room/annex, rooms for meeting vendors, drafting tables and equipment, system demonstration facility, support from a major computer center.

Remember that these special facilities and resources are in addition to those needed by the proposal team. Planners for major system development proposal must begin planning for their extensive, sophisticated requirements as early as possible. When security is an issue, the facilities and resources must be collocated, which creates a major demand for a single work area. During the system design and the preparation of the design specification, colocation of the design team is essential.

The proposal and design teams for a major classified combat intelligence system for the Navy required Martin Marietta to lease another separate work area in the Denver area and to have an extensive security sweep of that area prior to the arrival of the design team. A full array of capabilities and equipment was needed and special guard and courier services were necessary. The destruction of all preliminary drafts and suggested designs by an approved security organization was necessary. Members of the design team and proposal team were instructed not to discuss the design or proposal effort outside of the specially cleared facility.

12.1.4 ACCOMMODATING THE SECURITY REQUIREMENTS

When the procurement documents are classified, the proposal and the supporting documents, in virtually every instance, will be classified. If the procurement involves the development of a classified system, the design and the design documentation, in virtually every instance, will be classified also. In those proposal and/or design efforts that involve special security requirements associated with Code Word, Black, or SCI classifications, many stringent security requirements must be satisfied.

So, during classified procurements the proposal and design efforts must meet security requirements that can include such diversity as:

- Obtaining special access clearances for personnel, equipment, and facilities
- Restricting the reproduction of any proposal or design material
- Special destruction of material by cleared personnel
- Working in vaults or specially-cleared facilities with TEMPEST-tested equipment
- Special handling of hard drives which are removable from the computers
- Restricting access to the proposal facilities and equipment
- Controlling the use of internet and corporate networks that are not secure
- Using the STU-III equipment to encrypt and decrypt telephone transmissions

The Proposal Manager must prepare a Proposal Security Plan for each classified proposal and all members of the proposal team and design team must acknowledge in writing that they have read the plan and understand it. This plan should be prepared in cooperation with the Security Officer or the Special Security Officer, who will decide the level of classification to accord to the plan itself.

These security measures are in addition to those normally associated with: using safes approved for the storage of classified material, controlling access to proposal spaces by personnel whose security clearance and need to know have not been verified, using a code name for the proposal instead of a descriptive title, and requiring all proposal and design personnel to display their security badges at all times.

12.2 SELECTING THE KEY PROPOSAL MANAGEMENT STAFF

Line managers and the Corporate Officer Responsible are responsible for selecting the key personnel to manage the proposal staff during the preparation of the proposal.

- Proposal Manager
- Management Volume Leader
- Proposal Planner
- Past Performance Volume Leader
- Technical Volume Leader
- Cost Volume Leader
- Review Team Leaders
- Plans Volume Leaders

For major system development proposals, additional key personnel are essential for the preparation of the system design, the system specifications, and the technical documentation. These additional key management personnel include:

- Chief Engineer
- Costing Specialist
- Subcontractor Specialist
- Plans Leaders

Ideally, the selection of the proposal management staff should be somewhat in the following sequence:

1. A senior line manager and the Corporate Officer Responsible select the Proposal Manager, the Chief Engineer, and the Technical Volume Leader from their staff.
2. A senior line manager or the Corporate Officer Responsible selects the Management Volume Leader from their staff or hire a senior member of a proposal center in that role.
3. The Proposal Manager and the Technical Volume Leader

select the writers for the technical volume from a pool of engineering, scientific, and technical personnel within the line organizations and from a pool of approved consultants.

4. The Proposal Manager and the Management Volume Leader select the writers for the management volume from a pool of personnel within the line organizations, from the consultant list, and/or from the proposal center and its on-call staff.

5. The Technical Volume Leader and the Management Volume Leader select the personnel (Leaders and Writers) for the preparation of the supporting plans and Past Performance Volume.

6. Normally, a high-level corporate manager assigns a Contract Specialist to work as the Cost Volume Leader. If a Senior Costing Specialist is assigned to a systems design proposal, he/she should become the Cost Volume Leader.

7. The Chief Engineer selects the engineers, designers, and specialists for the design team from a pool of qualified technical personnel within the corporation, the subcontractors, and a pool of approved consultants. Notes: (1) the Production Coordinator, a key proposal person, is usually designated by the manager of the corporate proposal center;(2) the roles, authorities, and responsibilities of the key proposal management personnel are described in a later section related to proposal organization.

The criteria for the selection and assignment of the key management personnel to the proposal and design teams, in order of importance, include:

Proposal Manager - Technical skills and proposal development skills are of equal importance in the selection of this manager. Given a choice, proposal skills should receive more weight than technical skills and experience in the selection of this key person. The ability to assess the productivity of the writers, to measure the progress of the volumes, and the skills needed to deal with management and subcontractors are imperative.

Chief Engineer - Technical skills and related experience in system design are of greatest importance in the selection of this manager. The ability of this technical leader to write well during intense periods with harsh schedules is of near-equal but secondary importance. Experience in systems designs efforts completed during short time periods is also a necessity.

Technical Volume Leader - Technical skills, related experience in the technologies, and an in-depth understanding of the problem are of greatest importance of this manager. The ability to plan, assign, monitor, and control work by technical writers is of near- equal but secondary importance. Experience in proposal leadership roles is very important.

Management Volume Leader - Technical background, proven management skills, and extensive experience in the preparation of management volumes, past performance volumes, and management plans are of greatest importance. The ability to plan, assign, monitor, and control work by writers is of near-equal but secondary importance.

Above all other matters, people should never be assigned to a proposal solely on the basis of their being available at that time. In certain circles, such people are called "Noodlers", in that they go through the motions of working but produce little or nothing.

12.3 PREPARING THE PROPOSAL SCHEDULE

12.3.1 A Top Level View of Proposal Schedule Issues

For most Government and industrial procurements, all volumes of the proposal (technical, management, cost, past performance, plans) must be submitted on the same day. Since these procurements represent over 95 percent of all competitive procurements, I will address them in detail in this section. It must be recognized that the approach to proposal scheduling presented in this section is based on the proposal process described in an early part of this book, a process that is largely driven by the milestones associated with the formal reviews and the major types of actives.

It must be recognized that proposals that require a major system design effort create a need for a schedule that is quite different from the normal proposal schedule. The development of a system design, because of its scope and complexity, takes about three times as long as the preparation of the proposal itself. Also the costing of a major fabrication or production effort requires much more time for the cost volume than the technical and management volumes of the proposal. Consider the following time factors:

- The US Air Force prefers to issue a design specification about three months prior to the issuance of the RFP itself. This allows the contractor to begin the system design early, so that the system design and the proposal itself can be submitted at the same time. Sometimes the USAF directs the contractor to submit the cost proposal one or two months after the proposal and system design.
- The Navy seems to prefer to issue the design specification and the RFP at the same time, with the contractor submitting the proposal at an earlier date than the design and cost documentation. Procurement for a ship to be constructed in accordance with a Navy-provided design, the cost proposal was required to be delivered 60 days after the technical and management proposal.

12.3.2 A Systematic Approach to Preparing the Proposal Schedule

When tasked to prepare the proposal schedule, the two most critical inputs facing the Proposal Planner or Proposal Manager are the time at which the Bid-No Bid decision is made (the starting time) and the time at which the proposal must be delivered to the designated customer representative, normally the Contract Officer. From these two dates, a detailed, realistic proposal schedule can be developed with reasonable confidence. Of course, the Contract Officer may issue a RFP amendment that specifies an extension in the due date, at which time the schedule must be revised.

The approach that I prefer to the preparation of the proposal schedule is largely based on the proposal process that has been defined at an earlier date. In this approach, I prepare a milestone chart that depicts major start-stop dates of the overall proposal and for major activities and events; concurrently, I prepare a Gantt Chart that indicates the duration of the various activities. This concurrent use of a time-line schedule and a milestone chart is very effective.

Step One - Begin the milestone chart with two milestones, the start date and the delivery date. These milestones bound the proposal process time-wise.

Step Two - Start working backwards from the delivery date, allowing one day for delivery, three days for final production, and if necessary, one day for final security reviews. Prepare the time-lines on the Gantt chart and the milestones associated with these activities. Typical milestones include:
>   Delivery of final smooth draft to production staff
>   Completion of production and security activities
>   Delivery of the proposal to the customer

Step Three - Define when the Gold Review will be conducted and allocate all time prior to that date to the preparations for the review. Typically, the Gold Review will not be sooner than three days after the Bid decision and not later than seven days after the Bid decision. The time required to prepare for the Gold Review is largely driven by the demands for dealing with subcontractors, the compilation of the proposal requirements, and the development of the proposal outline. When the Gold Review is completed, the major proposal writing effort begins.

Step Four - Define when the Red Review will be conducted and allocate one day (normally) or two days (maximum) for the review itself. As part of theRed Review, I schedule a minimum of one day for the production staff and the Proposal Manager to prepare for the Red Review, with two days being more likely. The Red Review must be completed in sufficient time for the Proposal Manager to make the mandated revisions to the proposal; I usually reserve at least two days, preferably four days, for the proposal staff to make the necessary changes prior to the final production, security, and delivery activities.

Step Five - At this point, you know when the proposal writing will begin and when the proposal writing must stop. Now, define when the first complete draft will be ready for the Blue Review by the Proposal Management staff. The Blue Review is a one day event, with very little preparation, other than the time needed to Xerox the existing text and graphics, to put the text, and graphics in a notebook. Personally, at the Blue Review, I almost always have a complete, near-final copy of my volume, and expect few changes or additions during the post Blue writing period.

Step Six - Allocate the time between the Gold Review and the Red Review to the Proposal Writers, minus the time required for the production of the Red Review version of the proposal. Some Proposal Managers prefer a schedule in which the time between the Gold Review and the Blue Review and between the Blue Review and the Red Review is divided equally.

That is a matter of choice and I have no major preferences in this matter, but it must be observed that there really is not much time to be divided

Step Seven - Begin the preparation of cost-related data to be provided to the Volume Leader of the cost proposal and to the leaders of certain supporting plans not later than the time of the Blue Review. Do not wait until the last moment for this activity because the assumptions about purchases and labor hours, two critical matters, must be coordinated with the overall cost proposal effort, the cost estimating assumptions, the staffing plan, and the procurement plan

12.4 PREPARING THE PROPOSAL DIRECTIVES, POLICIES, SYSTEMS

The Proposal Manager must prepare a series of proposal documents that provide basic information to all members of the proposal team. The purpose of these documents is to ensure that:

- the higher level managers fully understand what is being undertaken,
- the proposal staff is working from an unambiguous set of instructions,
- the proposal system and schedule are understood by all
- the system design team is integrated with the proposal writing staff
- the proposal, plans, and specifications meet very high editorial standards

12.4.1 THE TOP-LEVEL PROPOSAL DIRECTIVE

The **Proposal Directive** is prepared by the Proposal Manager, supported by the Acquisition Manager and the Corporate Officer Responsible. The directive addresses the top-level concerns of the proposal team, design team, support personnel, and higher-level management for information that is critical to decisions to be made during the preparation of the proposal.

Part I of the Proposal Directive includes a summary of procurement-related information, which describes the customer, the reasons for the procurement, the procurement process being used by the customer, the type of contract, and the major procurement milestones. Key customer personnel and their roles in the acquisition process are presented.

Part II of the Proposal Directive describes the key issues associated with the procurement documentation, the major technical requirements in the SOW and specifications, the more serious risks associated with the work, the investment required to complete the contract, and the technical workaround plans envisioned. Other matters such as the roles of associated contractors and FCRCs, the special facilities and resources required by the contract are also discussed.

Part III of the Proposal Directive describes the corporate approach to winning the competition, including the strategies, win themes, discriminators, and other procurement matters. This part identifies the key proposal, design, and cost personnel and their responsibilities; and it also includes a description of the proposal process, the proposal and design facilities to be used, and the corporate resources committed to the proposal. Key subcontractors and their key personnel are identified and their roles are discussed. Other matters such as cost reduction initiatives and risk management activities are addressed also.

Part IV of the Proposal Directive presents the results of the early proposal and design planning efforts, such as schedules and milestones, proposal requirements and outline, and design issues and special studies. The material presented in the Gold Team Review is included, as are the special proposal related policies and procedures. The roles of corporate support personnel and resources during the proposal and design efforts are presented.

Part V of the Proposal Directive addresses a large number of somewhat lesser, but important, issues such as special security requirements, control of proposal drafts, dealings between the various organizations involved in the proposal, subcontractor roles and their design and proposal responsibilities, and interfaces between the proposal and production teams.

12.4.2 The Proposal Policies, Plans, and Instructions

Every proposal effort should have proposal policies, plans, and instructions issued to by the Proposal Manager to the Proposal Team. This set of documentation is essential to the efficient management of the proposal staff, proposal facilities, proposal operations, and proposal documentation. The policies and instructions ensure that every member of the proposal team understands:

- how the proposal will be planned, written, reviewed, and published
- what the security requirements are and how they will be enforced
- how the volumes will have a common structure and writing style
- where the proposal and design resources are located and how to acquire them
- which forms will be used during the costing effort
- who is empowered to deal with subcontractors on contractual matters
- how proposal records, documents, and material will be destroyed
- who is empowered to access corporate files, records, and data bases

Probably the most important elements of this set of proposal policies and plans are:

(1) The Editorial Policy, a one-page statement that governs the writing style and production of the proposal and the design documents.

(2) The Proposal Security Plan, a five or six page statement of the policy and procedures governing classified and proprietary information.

(3) A statement of the roles, authorities, and responsibilities for personnel assigned to the proposal, review, design, production, and costing teams.

12.5 PREPARING MATERIAL FOR THE GOLD REVIEW

The first formal review in the proposal process is the Gold Review, in which higher-level management (the Gold Team) has the opportunity to review the work done during the planning for the overall proposal effort. In this review, managers receive a series of presentations that inform them about the key factors that will determine the chances of winning a contract. Formal presentations by key personnel are accompanied by viewgraphs, handouts, outlines, other written material, and all are collected into a three-ring binder. In these presentations, the key acquisition and proposal personnel prepare material in their areas of responsibility, such as:

- a discussion by the Acquisition Manager of the customer, the overall procurement, and the competition. The presentation should include a competitive assessment, a discussion of special issues, the identification of key customer personnel are identified, and a summary of the unstated requirements. Hopefully, the probable winning cost will be included.

- a presentation by the Proposal Manager regarding the approach to winning, scope of the proposal effort, major proposal issues, and corporate commitments necessary to win. The proposal process and proposal facilities should be described, the key members of the proposal staff should be identified, and costs for a winning proposal should be presented.

- a presentation by the Proposal Planner of the proposal outline, customer requirements, win themes and discriminators, and special requirements in the procurement documentation. proposal schedule and milestones are presented. The proposal schedule and milestones should be presented.

- a discussion by the Cost Planner of the major cost factors, scope and complexity of the cost proposal, effort needed for cost documentation, special costing requirements, and cost proposal milestones. The level of effort needed to prepare the cost inputs and the cost realism portion of the cost proposal should be presented.

- a presentation by the Chief Engineer on the technical requirements of the system, technical risks and workaround plans, special facilities needed for the design effort, facilities needed after contract award, level of effort needed to prepare a winning design, special matters such as a system demonstration site, and security requirements.

The key proposal, design, and acquisition managers should not have any doubts about the massive effort needed to prepare for the Gold Review. Time, resources, personnel, and support services must be allocated to this planning activity.

CHAPTER **13**

IDENTIFYING THE PROPOSAL REQUIREMENTS

13.1 UNDERSTANDING THE PROPOSAL REQUIREMENTS

Many of the organizations responding to the Request for Proposal think that all evaluation matters are contained in Section L of the RFP. This is a major misconception because the Federal Acquisition Regulations specifically state that **proposals shall be evaluated against the evaluation standards**. Yet these same regulations specifically prohibit the Government agencies from publishing the evaluation standards. It seems an insoluble situation in which the proposal team must prepare responses that are being evaluated by a set of unknown standards.

The Government recognizes this matter and ensures that the evaluation standards are embedded within the procurement documentation, without them being overtly labeled as evaluation standards. This means that the Proposal Manager, Proposal Planner, Volume Leaders, and other proposal specialists must detect and identify the evaluation standards within the Request for Proposal, the supporting documentation, the referenced publications, the covering letter, APBI material, and the Federal Acquisition Regulations.

While the evaluation criteria and proposal instructions, as presented in Sections M and L, respectively, of the RFP, will always be the primary sources from which the evaluation standards are derived, the other sources of proposal standards must not be overlooked. Remember, if the proposal does not have a response to an evaluation standard, then the Government evaluator will assign a zero value in his/her scoring. Fail to respond to enough evaluation standards, and your proposal cannot win the competition.

Small proposals may have only fifty evaluation standards, but many large proposals for technical services and studies may have between one hundred and two hundred evaluation standards. Remember that proposal evaluation standards are used by the Source Selection Evaluation Board to determine the degree of compliance and the relative ranking of the competitors. So, you must respond to the evaluation standards or you will lose the competition.

13.2 IDENTIFYING THE RFP-DRIVEN REQUIREMENTS

The purpose of identifying those proposal requirements included in the Request for Proposal and its supporting documentation is two-fold:

First, you must review the RFP to ensure that your corporation meets all of the mandatory requirements of the procurement. Unless you prove that you satisfy the mandatory requirements in every respect, your corporation is not a competent bidder. Next, you must review the RFP and its supporting documentation to ensure that you have the complete package and that you have all references cited in the procurement documentation.

Second, you must review the RFP and its attachments in order to develop a list of the proposal requirements. These requirements, in turn, are the basis from which you must develop a list of proposal evaluation standard. This two-facet activity is necessary so that the proposal will have a response to every evaluation standards. Having a response to every evaluation standard is the only method for ensuring that the proposal is complete and compliant and that the proposal will receive the highest evaluation score.

The principal sources of the proposal requirements are the Request for Proposal and its attachments. The major sources for the proposal requirements and, eventually, the evaluation standards, are contained in the following seven parts of the procurement package.

Section M Evaluation Factors - Defines the factors and sub factors considered in the evaluation of the proposal, indicates the relative importance of the evaluation factors and sub factors, and provides guidance on subjects of importance not included in Section L.

Section L Proposal Instructions - Provides preparation instructions to bidders, specifies page limitations, defines critical editorial matters, specifies topics to be included in the proposal, lists and names the required volumes, and specifies the number of copies to be submitted.

Section C Statement of Work - Describes the services, products, or materials that the Government is procuring. Specifies the major tasks and activities to be performed and the general process or schedule for performing the work. Describes the objectives of the procurement, the general requirements governing contract performance, and the role that the Government will assume in its control of contractor work.

Section A - Includes the Standard Form 33 for RFPs and Standard Form 18 for RFQs. Includes the Solicitation number, the name and address of the Contract Officer, place for submittal of the proposal. Describes the type of procurement, the date for submission of proposals; contains brief description of the procurement.

Attachment: Technical Specifications - Define the technical aspects of the hardware, software, or firmware to be developed by the contractor; describe the performance, design, and technical requirements, provide specific information on materials and supplies to be used by the contractor, specify the testing, IV&V, and documentation requirements.

Attachment: Contract Data Requirements List - Specifies

the number and type of deliverables from the contractor to the Government, cites the references governing the contents of the deliverables, specifies the schedule for the submission of deliverables, and provides special instructions for certain deliverables.

Attachment: Form DD-254 Security Requirements - Defines the classification of the proposal and the work program, provides instructions on handling of classified hardware and software, the need for personnel and facility clearances, the need for special security measures, and the level of access granted for additional information.

It is important for the Proposal Manager, Volume Leaders, and Proposal Planner to review other sections of the procurement documentation for clues to evaluation standards in other important areas. These sections should include:

Covering Letter - Describes in general terms some information about the procurement and the work resulting from the contract

Section B - Includes the listing of supplies or services and the price/costs for these items and for major contract activities, deliverables, and items supplied to the Government.

Section H - Contains the special contract requirements, including s clear statement of any special requirements that are not included elsewhere in the clauses and sections.

Section I - Contains the contract clauses required by law or by the CFR, includes clauses expected to be included in the final contract.

Section J - Includes a listing of all attachments including the title, date, and number of pages, plus the attachments themselves.

Section K - Contains the representations, certifications and other statements of offerors or quoters. Includes those solicitation provisions that require certifications, representations or submission of other information.

It is recommended that the Code of Federal Regulations, part 15.406, become an essential item for every proposal specialist to remember.

13.3 IDENTIFYING THE FAR-DRIVEN REQUIREMENTS

The Federal Acquisition Regulations and the Defense Acquisition Regulations are a source of some critical evaluation factors and standards. For example, the FARs, states the quality that shall be evaluated in all procurements. The DARs state the requirements for cost schedule reporting systems during major procurements. These items and the other possible evaluation-related requirements from the FARs and DARs must be included in the listing of proposal requirements.

When the FARs or DARs state a requirement for the proposal, the statement is quite abbreviated, usually in the form of a few words. This brevity means that the Proposal Planner must refer to other Government documentation for a better understanding of the proposal requirements. For example:

The FAR statement regarding the evaluation of quality must be examined in light Government handbooks, instructions, and documentation related to quality. For example, most quality-related references address the issues of organization, personnel skills, records and reports, authority and responsibilities, and training for quality programs.

The DAR statements regarding cost reporting systems must be examined in light of the DOD Instructions regarding Contract Funds Status Reports, Cost Schedule Status Reports, Cost Schedule Control Systems, and Work Breakdown Structures.

When the Government handbooks, instructions, and manuals are examined, the Proposal Planner can make a very good estimate of the evaluation standards associated with the brief mentions in the FARs and DARs.

13.4 IDENTIFYING THE OTHER REQUIREMENTS

The Proposal Requirements Dictated by Related or Referenced Documents - The Government will reference many documents in the Request for Proposal and the attached documentation, and the Proposal Manager and the Proposal Planner are obligated to review these procurement publications to identify the other Proposal Requirements. The other proposal requirements are contained in publications such as the Federal Acquisition Regulations, Defense Acquisition Regulations (and other Department acquisition regulations), handbooks and instructions, and Code of Federal Regulations. These requirements must be identified and included in the proposal requirements data base.

The Proposal Manager, the Proposal Planner, and the Volume Leaders must review all referenced and relevant documents to identify the other proposal requirements. This means that when the RFP lists the references without including the text for those references the proposal management team must read and understand all of the referenced items. Many proposals have lost because the references were not checked and understood; a prime example being not knowing the difference between a Drug-Free Workplace Program and a Drug-Free Workplace Plan.

The Design Requirements Dictated by General and Technical Specifications - The Government will prepare a specification for a hardware or software system that defines the performance and design criteria that must be satisfied by the system being developed, (Such as the maximum weight for an aircraft). The Government will also reference many technical specifications when procuring a system that is applicable to a wide range of systems, (Such as the range of environmental conditions under which the system must operate).

The technical specifications can include Performance, Design, Fabrication, EMI-EMC, TEMPEST, and Test Specifications. The general specifications can include those associated with Quality Control, Materials Testing, Technical Documentation, Data Base Structure, Construction Standards, Reviews and Audits, and Configuration Management. When preparing the design requirements data base, these specific and general system requirements must be included, and these design requirements must be satisfied by the design team.

The Proposal and Design Requirements Not Stated or Identified in the Procurement Documentation

Every customer has a list of items, capabilities, and resources that it wants during and from its procurements. These requirements, which are not stated in writing, are important to the customer, and the customer expects the winning contractor to satisfy these requirements. Such requirements can include such diversity as:

- providing offices, office equipment, office services, and office support for their staff when they are monitoring work in progress at your facilities.
- using software systems that are compatible with those used by the Government to ensure ease of transmission of project data and drawings.
- ensuring that emerging technologies can be integrated into the system at some indefinite date in the future with minimum disruption of service.
- Maintaining a full operational capability in a command center when a new hardware- software system is being installed to replace an existing system.
- Hiring those incumbent contractor personnel judged by the Government to be particularly skilled and productive.
- Replacing those personnel designated by the customer as having skills no longer needed when you are the incumbent contractor.

As a general rule, the Acquisition Manager obtains this information from the customer in personal contacts well in advance of the time at which the procurement documents are issued. In most normal procurements, the Government technical and management personnel are free to talk about these preferences prior to the formal procurement activities begin. After the procurement process begins, they are not free to discuss such matters. Of course, the staffs of commercial and industrial clients are free to talk of such matters at any time, unlike Government personnel.

Earl Williams, President of the BDM Corporation, taught me several important lessons, the most important being that Government employees are eager to answer your questions so that you will prepare a better proposal and be a better contractor. However, Government employees cannot volunteer information, but they can sure answer questions. So you must ask questions before they will provide insights and information to you. This lesson has been very important during my 25+ years of preparing proposals to the Government.

13.5 IDENTIFYING THE PROPOSAL MANAGER'S REQUIREMENTS

13.5.1 THE WIN THEME-ASSOCIATED REQUIREMENTS

The Proposal Manager complies a listing of **win themes** that cite the many benefits that the customer will accrue if your corporation wins the contract. Win themes are positive statements that can be said about your corporation and your subcontractors. It is recognized that all of your win themes are not unique to your corporation and your team, but you must still present those win themes anyway. Even though some, if not all, of the competitors can present some of the same win themes (what I call the "Ho-Hums"), you must still include them

in your proposal. If you don't include those Ho-Hum themes, then the competitors' themes become unique to their proposals. Examples of some win themes include:

- Our corporation has contract experience in every technology essential to the development of the ballistic missile defense program of the Army.
- We have seven major computer centers, twenty development and test laboratories, and five major engineering centers that support our technology projects.

- We have been supporting the Defense Science Board, Army Science Board, Air Force Science Board, and Navy Research Advisory Board for over twenty years.
- Our scientists and engineers have successfully completed over 400 Independent Research and Development Projects in the past 20 years.
- Our Architecture and Engineering services subsidiaries have been working continuously in environmental remediation for over 15 years.
- Our pool of skilled personnel includes over 17,000 engineers, scientists, analysts, managers, technicians, and administrators from which we can staff this program.

The Proposal Manager, Proposal Planner, and the Volume Leaders determine where the win themes are to be inserted into the proposal and assigns those items to specific writers. The writers must integrate the win themes into their text or graphics.

13.5.2 THE DISCRIMINATOR-ASSOCIATED REQUIREMENTS

The Proposal Manager identifies the **discriminators,** which are actually win themes that are unique to you, your team, and your proposal. None of the competitors can make the same claim as you, so your offer will include advantages or benefits that only you will provide to the customer. Discriminators win competitions, without a doubt. Some of the discriminators that I used in my employer's proposals include:

- We are the only company that has built explosive detectors used by the FAA in airports.
- We can support the customer from over 175 offices located nationwide.
- We supported (24-7) three RSNF command centers continuously during Desert Storm.
- We have never had a contract terminated for cause in over

6,000 projects over 23 years.

- Our corporation is owned by its employees and their pensions depend on good work.
- We developed the carbon-fiber materials used to protect space capsules during reentry.
- Our hospital information software system was judged the best by DOD.
- We are the only contractor supporting high energy laser programs of all three services.
- Our team developed all of the systems being integrated into the Air Force CCCI segment.
- Our correlator-tracker developed by IRAD funds is the most advanced system in the world.

Usually, the Proposal Manager and the Volume Leaders determine when, where, and how the discriminators are to be integrated into the proposal and, as a general rule, attend to this matter themselves. The discriminators are too critical a matter to be left to an unskilled writer.

13.5.3 THE STAKE-THROUGH-THE-HEART REQUIREMENTS

The stake through the heart matter addresses two issues: the weakness of the competition and your own weaknesses. You must assume that the competitors know about your problems and shortcomings and will bring such matters to the attention of the customer in their proposal. The only means that you have to counter their actions is to admit that you had problems or shortcomings during certain contracts. After which, you describe the lessons learned and the remedial actions that you successfully implemented. Always assume that the competition has someone as deadly as me directing their stake-driving effort.

I consider it to be my sacred duty to inform the Government, or any customer, of the shortcomings, defaults, and disasters associated with our competitors. Government or customer personnel may not fully appreciate how incompetent, mismanaged, and unmotivated the competitors are. Your customer may not be aware of legal actions taken against those competitors or the failures of systems that they developed. It is a higher calling to expose them.

Since most people working on proposals, whether planning or writing, are hesitant to take on this necessary activity, I usually reserve this activity for myself.

During a major competition in which my corporation was the prime contractor, managers from two of our subcontractors came to me in regard to my stake-in-the-heart efforts during an earlier competition when these two firms were our competitors. They were very concerned. I explained to them that, previously, they were incompetent, unethical bunglers, but now that they were teamed with us, they were, once again, competent and ethical.

CHAPTER 14

PREPARING THE PROPOSAL OUTLINE

14.1 THE IMPORTANCE OF THE PROPOSAL OUTLINE

The preparation of the proposal outline is one of the most critical activities during the proposal process because the outline is used for so many purposes by so many different members of the proposal team. The major uses of the proposal outline into which the proposal requirements have been allocated include:

The **Proposal Manager** uses the outline to assign work to the proposal staff, monitor work by the proposal staff, assess the status of the proposal, manage the proposal resources, prepare a cost budget for volumes and plans, estimate the production demands, and identify special resource requirements,

The **Proposal Planner** uses the outline to allocate the proposal requirements, establish the page budgets for sections or chapters of the proposal, prepare the proposal schedule, identify potential problems, identify the writing requirements, develop the compliance matrix, prepare a WBS for proposal activities, and estimate the resources required for the proposal.

The **Volume and Plan Leaders** use the outline to define a structure for managing the writing of the volumes and plans, use as a structure for the detailed planning of their volumes and plans, make writing assignments to the writers, assess the status of their volumes and plans, report progress to the Proposal Manager, identify critical issues and demands at an early date, and manage their budgets.

The **Review Teams** use the proposal outline to make their review assignments, check on compliance with the proposal instructions, verify the compliance matrix, evaluate the logical organization of the proposal, and define the organization of their review comments.

The **Production Coordinator** uses the outline to plan the production process, assess the productivity of the volume and plan writers, determine the amount of work on hand and pending, and assemble the volumes and plans.

Basically, the proposal outline is used by every person involved with the planning, preparation, writing, and production of the proposal. It is the first major element in the preparation of a compliant, complete, winning proposal.

14.2 KEY PROPOSAL PERSONNEL WORKING IN THE OUTLINING

The principal people working in the development of the proposal outline are the Proposal Manager and the Volume Leaders. These members of the Proposal Management Staff have the following roles and responsibilities:

Proposal Manager ensures that all proposal requirements are entered into the proposal requirements data base, provides guidance to the Proposal Planner on his/her vision of the proposal, integrates the proposal outlining activities with the outlining required for design volumes and plans, prepares and publishes the Editorial Policy that specifies the style and format for titles used in outlining.

Proposal Planner compiles the proposal requirements data base, defines the number of volumes to be prepared, determines the titles and contents of the sections, prepares the initial proposal outline with the proper titles, allocates proposal requirements to the proposal volumes, allocates the volume requirements to the sections within the volumes, prepares an interim outline with the proposal requirements included beneath the titles, and then audits that outline to ensure that all proposal requirements are addressed.

Volume Leader reviews the volume outline prepared by the Proposal Planner, breaks the macro requirements into a series of detailed requirements, develops the volume outline down to the module or unit level, inserts the lower level titles into the expanded volume outline, allocates the volume requirements down to units, pages, and paragraphs. This detailed volume outline is provided to the Proposal Planner and Proposal Manager for a complete detailed proposal outline.

It is noted that many proposals do not have a Proposal Planner. When the Proposal Team does not include a planner, then the duties of the Proposal Planner must be performed by the Proposal Manager and the Volume/Plan Leaders, in addition to their other responsibilities. If the proposal team does not include experienced Volume Leaders either, outlining will probably become a "Mission Impossible" assignment for the Proposal Manager.

14.3 THE SPECIFIC ACTIVITIES ASSOCIATED WITH OUTLINING

14.3.1 PREPARING THE PROPOSAL REQUIREMENTS DATA BASE

The Proposal Planner, or the Proposal Manager on smaller proposals, will compile a proposal requirements data base that lists all proposal requirements. These requirements, as described previously, include:

The RFP-Stated Requirements The RFP Implied Requirements
The FAR/DAR Requirements   The Proposal Win Themes
The Proposal Discriminators The Other Customer Requirements
The Second-Tier Requirements

Typically, this proposal requirements data base will be prepared using the EXCEL tabular format with columns allocated to the following matters:

Column 1 Requirements Identification Number - that is unique to each requirement, so that every requirement can be tracked

Column 2 Source of Requirement - that relates the requirement to its source, such as the RFP, DAR-FAR, Win Themes, Specification, etc.

Column 3 Source Paragraph Number - that refers to the location of the requirement in its source document

Column 4 Volume to Which Assigned - that specifies the proposal volume or plan where the requirement will be addressed

Column 5 Section-Paragraph to Which Assigned - that specifies the location of the response to the specific requirement

Column 6 Statement of the Requirement - that has a textual statement of the requirement as close to the exact wording as possible

It is important to recognize that a design requirements data base must also be prepared for the system design team. The design requirements included in that data base are derived from the Request for Proposal, the Design Requirements, the System Requirements, and the referenced documentation or publications. The major difference in the format for the System Requirements Data Base and the Proposal Requirements Data Base in that most of the system design requirements are allocated to a subsystem, equipment group, or configuration item within the overall system architecture.

14.3.2 Determining the Number of Volumes and Plans to be Prepared

The proposal instructions in Section L of the Request for Proposal will state the number of volumes to be submitted, the titles of the volumes, and the page limitations associated with the volumes (if any are limited) of the proposal. The Section L instructions should also include the number and type of plans, the design documentation, and other supporting information to be submitted with the proposal. These instructions, which are critical items in the proposal requirements data base, will state the number, types of volumes, and plans to be submitted. Typically, Section L instructions state requirements for:

- the stand-alone volumes required in virtually all proposals, which will include the Technical Volume, Management Volume, Cost Volume, and Past Performance Volume
- the stand-alone supporting volumes required in many proposals, which can include the Project Management Plan, Quality Assurance Plan, Total Quality Management Plan, Staffing/Recruiting Plan, Facilities Plan, Transition Plan, Procurement Plan, and Security Plan

The RFP documentation related to the design of a major system will certainly specify the stand-alone volumes associated with the design volumes that must be submitted with the proposal. These volumes can include: System Performance Specification, Design Specification, Software Capability Plan, Facilities Plan, Installation and Checkout Plan, System Transition Plan, Test Plan, Quality Control Plan, Software Development Plan, Training Plan, Logistics Plan.

It is noted that the Contract Data Requirements List cites the plans to be submitted after contract award; as an almost universal rule, the CDRL requirements are based on the Data Item Descriptions in the AMDSL. When a preliminary plan is to be submitted with the proposal and a complete plan to be submitted after contract award, the CDRL will describe the volumes needed.

The Proposal Manager and the Chief Engineer should be very involved in the process of determining the number and types of volumes to be prepared and submitted with the proposal. Only the Proposal Manager and Chief Engineer have the high-level vision needed to recognize the requirements and their implications.

14.3.3 Determining the Sections in the Volumes

The Volume Leaders, or maybe the Proposal Planner, will determine the number of and titles for sections (or chapters) within each of the volumes. The principal references for the sections within the volumes are within Section L and Section M of the Request for Proposal. The preferred method of identifying the number of and title for the sections is:

When outlining the volumes with the evaluation criteria being given priority over the proposal instructions:

- Refer to the evaluation factors in Section M. The evaluation factors for the volumebecome the titles for the sections within the volume. For example, when the evaluation factors are entitled "Key Personnel, Contract Experience, Management Approach, Facilities," four of the sections within the management volume will use these titles for their responses. When the evaluation factors are entitled "Technical Approach, Problem Understanding", two of the sections within the technical volume will use these titles for their responses. You now have the beginning of an outline for the volume.
- Next, refer to the proposal instructions in Section L. The instructions may be listed by volume or they may be presented in a single list for the entire proposal. Usually, the proposal instructions do not have a hierarchy so that you know which are the most important items, so it will be necessary for you

to group them functionally. For example, several items in the proposal instructions may be related to contract experience; in this instance, group these items under what appears to be the highest-order or highest-ranking item with the most impressive wording.

- Next, integrate the sections based on the evaluation criteria and the proposal instructions so that material from both of these sources are reconciled and redundancies are eliminated, It is recommended that the sections based on the evaluation criteria be given higher visibility whenever possible and that the proposal instructions be subordinated to them. You now have most of the outline for the volume.

- Finally, integrate the Section L and Section M proposal requirements for the volumes with the proposal requirements that are based on other sources (such as quality, per the FARs), on the win themes, and on the Proposal Manager's instructions. These subjects and their titles could be something like "Our Independent Research and Development Program", "Our Leadership in Technology Application", and "Our Overseas Offices For Support of this Project". You have now identified the major sections in your volumes, based on the totality of the proposal requirements.

When outlining the volumes with the proposal instructions being given priority over the evaluation criteria:

- First, refer to the proposal instructions in Section L. The instructions may be listed by volume or they may be presented in a single list for the entire proposal. Usually, the proposal instructions do not have a hierarchy so that you know which the most important items are. So it will be necessary for you to group them functionally. For example, several items in the proposal instructions may be related to contract experience; in this instance, you should group similar items under what appears to be the highest-order or highest-ranking item with the most impressive wording.

- Next, refer to the evaluation factors in Section M. The evaluation factors for the volume become the titles for sections within the volume. For example, when the evaluation factors are entitled "Key Personnel, Contract Experience, Management Approach, Facilities," four of the sections within the management volume will use these titles for their responses. When the evaluation factors are entitled "Technical Approach, Problem Understanding", two of the sections within the technical volume will use these titles for their responses.

- Next, integrate the sections based on the evaluation criteria and the proposal instructions so that material from both of these sources are reconciled and redundancies are eliminated. It is recommended that the sections based on the evaluation criteria be given a lesser visibility whenever possible and that the proposal instructions be dominant. You now have most of the outline for the volume

- Finally, integrate the Section L and Section M proposal requirements for the volumes with the proposal requirements that are based on other sources (such as quality, per the FARs), on the win themes, and on the Proposal Manager's instructions. These subjects and their titles could be something like "Our Independent Research and Development Program", "Our Leadership in Technology Application", "Our Overseas Offices For Support of this Project". You have now identified the major sections in your volumes, based on the totality of the proposal requirements.It can be readily observed that the two approaches above entail the same activities and that only the precedence in the sources of the requirements for sections has changed. In the final outline, the major difference in the two approaches will be a slight difference in the ordering of the section titles.

In ninety percent of its procurements, the Government states an unambiguous requirement for these sections in the Management Volume:

1. Project Management, or Management
2. Project Organization
3. Key Personnel
4. Facilities or Resources
5. ontract Experience

In virtually all of its procurements, the Government states a very focused requirement for these sections in the Technical Volume:

1. Problems Understanding
2. Technical Approach
3. Response to the Statement of Work

To these requirements, the Proposal Manager must add, at a minimum, the following items to be included in the Technical and Management Volumes:

- **Technical Volume sections** - Highlights of Our Technical Volume, and Our Independent Research and Development Program
- **Management Volume sections** - Highlights of Our Management Volume, Our Quality Initiatives, and Other Essential Information

When the sections have been identified and named, the proposal outline will look something like that shown in Figure 14.3.3-1 below:

When outlining the supporting plans, attachments, and special volumes, the procurement documentation will specify the format for most of the supporting plans and attachments by referring to references such as the Data Item Descriptions in the AMSDL. In many, if not most instances, the Government will modify the referenced DIDs to fit the specific needs of their organization. So be alert.

```
        Volume I       Technical Volume
            Section 1      Highlights of Our Technical Volume
            Section 2      Our Understanding of the Problem
            Section 3      Our Technical Approach
            Section 4      Our IRAD Program
        Volume II      Management Volume
            Section 1      Highlights of Our Management Volume
            Section 2      Project Management
            Section 3      Project Organization
            Section 4      Personnel and Staffing
            Section 5      Contract Experience
            Section 6      Facilities and Other Resources
            Section 7      Other Essential Information
```

Figure 14.3.3-1 Typical Sections within the Proposal Volumes

I have found that the DID instructions are not complete and are frequently ambiguous. In such procurements, I have always added to the DID-based outline so that our proposal would be enhanced by the supporting plans and documentation. As for the Past Performance Volume, the Government should specify the information to be included in its RFP or the RFP attachments. When the RFP instructions on this volume appear to be lacking, refer to the Army Material Command publication on this subject.

I suggest that you add several sections to these proposal-related documents that are not always addressed in the DID and AMC instructions to cover items such as References, Safety, Special Items, and Security.

14.3.4 DETERMINING THE MODULES/UNITS WITHIN THE VOLUMES AND PLANS

Once the sections within the volumes have been identified, a tougher task emerges, determining the next indenture in the outline, which is the module or unit level. For this activity, the person preparing the outline begins with the section requirements which are then allocated to the module level. As a general rule, the subjects and titles of the modules and some units are based on the key words within the evaluation sub factors and the lower level proposal instructions.

If the Evaluation Factors or Proposal Instructions dictate a title of Project Management for the section, the key words at the sub factor level could include: Management Tools, Risk Management, Management Approach, Management Responsibilities and Authorities, With these key words, plus the requirements of the Proposal Manager, the section outline can be developed to the next level, which might include:

Section 2 Project Management
2.1 Highlights of Our Project Management Approach
2.2 Our Management Tools, Systems, and Data Bases
2.3 Responsibilities and Authorities of our Project Manager
2.4 Our Approach to Risk Management
2.5. Our System for Managing Our Subcontractors

This process is repeated for every section within the proposal volume, again based on the key words within the procurement documentation and the Proposal Manager requirements.

14.3.5 PLANNING AT THE PAGE AND PARAGRAPH LEVEL

Just when you thought that outlining has been tough, the next step in the outlining process demonstrates the real meaning of the word tough. At this lowest level of the proposal outline, you must envision what will be allocated to the pages and what the pages will look like. You will have to move from the actual proposal requirements stated in the procurement documentation to those requirements that are inferred in the documentation. Only the brave, experienced, and dedicated succeed in the next step in the outlining process.

Remember that the title "Unit" means a maximum of two pages, with one page being the usual number of pages required for a unit response and that somewhere between three and five paragraphs will be associated with each page. Finally, remember that a graphics or visual impact item must be included within each unit. It can be seen that, at this level of the outlining, you are determining the topics of paragraphs and type of graphics to support the paragraphs. This means that when you complete the outlining down to this level, you can (must) envision what almost every page is going to look like.

The Volume Leader and the writers must identify the key phrases or key words that will be the subject of the paragraphs and identify what type of graphics will accompany the text. First, remember that you cannot have one graphic per paragraph because that would result in too much of the proposal being devoted to graphics. Remember, proposal evaluators on the SSEB read words and do not admire or enjoy the graphics; a strong statement of opinion, by the gentleman who was the Head of the SSEBs for all major procurements at NAVAIR once upon a time.

At this phase of the outlining, I recommend that the writer prepare a sketch of each page, with a layout that may have four paragraphs with some visual impact item (like titles, bullet listing, bold print, underlining, etc.) or a layout with two or three paragraphs with one graphics item on a page. This approach has a way of focusing the writer's attention quickly, because the writer is deciding what the page will look like, what the paragraphs will address and what graphics or visual impact items will be included.

The best advice that I can provide to the writer who is outlining at the page, paragraph, and individual graphic item level is:
- Ensure that every sub factor in the evaluation criteria has a title in the outline

- Allocate one paragraph to each key word in the proposal requirements
- Ensure that one graphic, however small, is presented once every two pages
- On pages without graphics, ensure that there is a visual relief textual item*
- Avoid lists in a paragraph, using bullet or numbered listing whenever possible
- Prepare a sketch of each page as the outline is being defined

* This can include titles, bullet listings, bold print, changes in margins, and underlining

When working on the Chemical Demilitarization proposal to the Army, a five year, $300 million plus competition in which my employer was the incumbent contractor, I was responsible for the Contract Experience section and the Past Performance Volume. At the first review of the storyboards, I posted 32 pages on the wall, with a sketch of every graphic and the topics of every paragraph denoted. When the proposal was completed about eight weeks later, my final smooth section of the proposal looked exactly like the sketches on my storyboards. I had a vision of my work down to the individual paragraph subjects and the supporting graphics. And I produced that vision. Incidentally, we won the competition on the basis of our contract experience.

14.3.6 ALLOCATING THE PROPOSAL REQUIREMENTS TO THE OUTLINE

The Volume Leaders who prepared the detailed outline for their volume know best when and where the response to each proposal requirement is addressed. No other person has a better vision of the proposal volumes, so the Volume Leader performs the allocation during the preparation of the detailed outline and the page layouts for his/her volume. Basically, the Volume Leader allocation process is one of "cut and paste" on their computer, cutting from the proposal requirements data base and pasting in their volume where the response to the requirement will be written.

The allocation of proposal requirements can be done in an iterative step, in which all volume requirements are pasted under the title of the Section. Then these section-level requirements are cut and pasted into the modules within the section, immediately following the titles of the modules. Then, the module-level requirements are cut and pasted into the units within the module, immediately following the titles of the units.

Once the proposal requirements are pasted into the outline down to the unit level, these requirements become the basis for the page layouts and the graphics. By parsing the unit level requirements into key words or short phrases, the topics of individual paragraphs and supporting graphics is known. This allocation process will not be difficult because the titles used in the outline were developed directly from the proposal requirements themselves.

It must be noted that when the proposal requirements are pasted into the proposal outline down to the unit and page level, that the requirements will not be printed in the final version of the proposal. The proposal requirements are pasted into the outline at the page level are to ensure that the proposal writers are focused on the topic assigned to them and to make the Red Team Review a more effective effort.

14.3.7 Preparing the Compliance Matrix after Outlining

The most efficient time for preparing the compliance matrix is when the detailed outline has been completed, because all of the proposal requirements, especially the inferred or derived ones, are not know until the last. At that time, the preparation of the compliance matrix becomes an auditing technique to ensure that all responses to the proposal requirements have been identified and have been included in the outline. It is usually more effective and efficient for the Volume Leader to prepare the compliance matrix for his/her volume to ensure that the matrix is organized in a structure most suited for use by the Government proposal evaluation teams.

Always remember that the structure and organization of the compliance matrix should not be driven by the organizational structure of the proposal. The purpose of the compliance matrix is to guide the Government evaluation team to your response.

14.4 SPECIAL PROBLEMS ASSOCIATED WITH OUTLINING

The work associated with preparing the proposal outline and allocating the proposal requirements to the outline is more complicated than the section above indicated. The major problems inherent in almost every proposal outline include.

14.4.1 DIFFERENCES IN THE SECTIONS L AND M REQUIREMENTS

To many proposal specialists, the proposal instructions are the most important source of requirements related to the outlining of the proposal volumes. But to many, other proposal specialists, the evaluation criteria are the most important source of requirements related to proposal outlining. These specialists are vehement in their statements regarding the primacy of their requirements and fierce arguments are frequent and loud.

My preference is to outline according to the Section M Evaluation Criteria, because I want to get the highest score in the evaluation of the proposals. However, some guidelines relative to the relative importance of the proposal instructions and the evaluation criteria in proposal outlining are as follows:

1. If you organize according to the **proposal instructions**, subordinating the evaluation criteria, then you may present a problem to the members of the SSEB who must evaluate the proposal, using the evaluation standards. But organizing according to the proposal instructions will aid in determining if you are a compliant bidder.

2. If you organize according to the **evaluation criteria,** subordinating the proposal instructions, then you present a problem to the Head SSEB in determining if the proposal is compliant. But organizing according the evaluation criteria will ensure that you obtain a better evaluation rating by the members of the SSEB.

3. If the proposal instructions state unambiguously that "_the proposal volumes shall be organized into the following chapters or sections_", then you must prepare the outline in accordance with the proposal instructions. Remember, "shall" is the most important single word in any procurement document.

4. If the proposal instruction state that _"the proposal volumes shall include the following information",_ then you are free to prepare an outline based on the evaluation criteria. In this situation, the word "shall" has a different connotation. Prepare your proposal outline in accordance with the evaluation criteria without hesitation.

14.4.2 DECIDING WHICH PROPOSAL RESPONSES ARE MORE IMPORTANT TO THE CUSTOMER

Sometimes, the process of preparing the proposal outline is complicated by the fact that the person preparing the outline must make a wide range of critical decisions about the relative importance of your responses within the proposal. These decisions are driven by the importance of the responses in light of your vision of the proposal and the strategy for winning the competition.

Consider the following:

When the solicitation documents mention a key word or key phrase three of more times in its evaluation criteria, proposal instructions, statement of work, or background information, it is almost a certainty that the customer regards that matter as key to the success of the contract.

When the customer has placed very high weights in the evaluation criteria on a certain topic to be addressed in the proposal, it is a certainty that the customer regards that matter as critical to the success of the contract.

When responses to requirements of the customer fall in either of these categories (key to winning or critical to winning), you must ensure that your outline covers these requirements thoroughly in the outline so that the proposal responses will have very high visibility to the customer. Remember two axioms in the field of proposal preparation: First, the more important a subject is to the customer, the higher the visibility of the proposal response, and Second, the most important matters in the proposal are those matters of greatest importance to the customer.

14.4.3 DECIDING WHAT RESPONSES ARE MORE IMPORTANT TO YOU

As I stated above, you must subordinate your outline and your responses to the customer's desires and values. This does not mean that you must not let those customer concerns preclude you from presenting your win themes and discriminators or from describing key technologies or resources that you possess. You must prove that your concerns, your resources, your skills, and your technologies are of critical importance to the customer. The only negative aspect of allocating pages to your approach to winning the contract is that you devote fewer pages and less emphasis on the customer's wants.

If undecided in the relative importance of the responses related to the customer's desires and to your requirements, give the customer-related matters a bit more emphasis, with your matters a close second. But do not be a mere echo with your proposal. Innovation, technology, performance, skills, management, and facilities are essential to winning. You must convince the customer that what is important to your corporation is also very important to the customer. Never forget that your proposal is a sales document that will whet the appetite of the customer.

The Strategic Defense Initiative Office initiated a procurement directed to the development of system architecture for a space-based ballistic missile defense system. The SDIO wanted ten contractors to work for a year on the conceptual design of such a system. My corporate officers knew that we were not recognized as a major competitor in the design of space systems, but Fred Giggey a bold manager, decided that we would submit a proposal in which we demonstrated that our corporation had the technology base essential to such a system. We proved that we had the personnel, facilities, resources, and experience in all the technologies essential to a space based defense system.

We prepared a proposal with the theme that we would provide the SDIO with its technology base, the only bidder that did not respond directly to the solicitation. We convinced the SDIO that it needed our corporation in order to integrate technology into future systems. We won one of the ten contracts and we kept that contract for over ten years, during which our income totaled over $50 million. Not bad for a non-responsive proposal.

14.4.4 ALLOCATING PAGES DURING NORMAL OUTLINING

Section L, Proposal Instructions of the RFP, will specify the page limitations, if any. Ninety percent of the time, the limitations will be stated at the volume level; in very rare instances, the page limitations will be stated at the section level of the volumes. It is best to plan that the page limitations will be by volume only.

The process that I have found most effective for allocating pages, or partial pages, to the topics to be covered in the proposal begins with the pages that are needed structurally; If the page limitation is 50 pages for a management volume, allocate pages as follows:

- First, allocate one page for an introduction to each volume for high-lighting its contents and presenting the win themes and discriminators associated with that volume.
- Second, allocate one page in the management volume for "Other Essential Information" to present responses to all of the mandatory requirements.
- Third, allocate one page in each volume to the title page, which will also include the proprietary notice and the security classification information.
- Fourth, if the RFP requires a compliance matrix and if that page counts against the volume limitations, allocate one page per volume.

Note: I have noticed instances in which a creative Proposal Manager used the cover of the proposal volumes to present the information normally included on the title page and then did not include a title page within the volume itself. Essentially, the cover became the title page.

The most effective method for allocating the pages to the sections, modules, and units within the volume is almost certainly as follows:

Allocate the pages in the volume using a weighting system based on the evaluation factors and sub factors, using the following system:

Assume the management volume has a page limitation of 100 pages, that the volume is worth 40 percent of the total evaluation points, and that the evaluation factors for the volume are in order of declining importance. Also assume that the evaluation factors were contract experience, personnel, project management, organization, and facilities/resources. Then, using the volume outline suggested earlier, the sections should have the following number of pages:

Volume II	Management Volume	100 pages
Section 1	Highlights of Our Management Volume	2 pages
Section 2	Project Management	20 pages
Section 3	Project Organization	16 pages
Section 4	Personnel and Staffing	22 pages
Section 5	Contract Experience	26 pages
Section 6	Facilities and Other Resources	12 pages
Section 7	Other Essential Information	2 pages

The next level of the volume outline is based on the evaluation sub factors that are reflected in the next indenture of the volume outline can be weighted equally or be weighted in order of declining importance. Assume that the next level of the volume outline is based on the evaluation sub factors and that the section is limited to 20 pages. The probable number of pages allocated to the modules (2.1 to 2.6) is probably something like the following:

Section 2 Project Management	(20 pages)
2.1 Highlights of Our Project Management Approach	1 page
2.2 Our Management Tools, Systems, and Data Bases	4 pages
2.3 Responsibilities and Authorities of our Managers	3 pages
2.4 Our Approach to Risk Management	4 pages
2.5 Our System for Managing Our Subcontractors	4 pages
2.6 Our Quality Management System	4 pages

At this point, the Volume Leader and the Proposal Writers are ready to allocate pages and fractions of pages to the evaluation standards. As an example, for section 2.6 above, the following allocation of the four pages should be close to the following:

2.6 Our Quality Management System	(4 pages)
2.6.1 Highlights of Our Quality Initiatives	¼ page
2.6.1 Qualifications of Our QA Personnel	1 page
2.6.2 Organization for Quality Assurance	1 page
2.6.3 Responsibilities and Authorities of QA Personnel	¾ page
2.6.4 Quality Auditing, Monitoring and Reporting	¾ page
2.6.5 Quality Training for the Project Staff	¼ page

When page limitations are very severe, it can be noted that the results of allocating pages based on equal weighting and on declining weighting will result in almost the same number of pages or fractions of pages being allocated to the evaluation standards.

14.4.5 IMPACT OF SEVERE PAGE LIMITATIONS ON OUTLINING

In a perfect world, severe page limitations would not be a consideration. But we must live, work, and compete in an imperfect world. So it is in proposal outlining. I have seen RFPs that wanted the bidder to describe its understanding of twenty or more technologies in four or fewer pages. I have seen RFPs that wanted the bidder to describe its technical approach to a complex, long-term project in three or fewer pages. Sounds like a Mission Impossible assignment, doesn't it?

At the onset of the planning and outlining effort, the Proposal Manager, Proposal Planner, and the Volume Leader must decide how they will respond to the RFP requirements within the severe page limitations. I wish that there was some rule that would guide the planners and writers, but the decisions in such instances, in which there will be no response to certain evaluation sub factors or evaluation standards, should be made at the Proposal Manager level. These decisions relative to what is to be included and what is not to be included will determine if your proposal wins or loses.

To the Volume Leader or the Proposal Writer preparing a proposal or a volume with very severe page limitations, I recommend the following:

- Allocate your paragraphs to responses at the evaluation sub factor level
- Structure your sentences in the paragraph to respond to key words in the sub factors
- Weigh carefully the requirements to include win themes over key words in the RFP
- Obtain concurrence from the Proposal Manager on all decisions to omit responses

At the Red Team Review of a proposal that was limited to 20 pages of double-spaced text, the senior managers stated most strongly that the proposal did not show our strengths well enough, had left out essential material, did not demonstrate our understanding of the problem, and did not present a convincing technical approach. They decided that the proposal team was too inept and that they, the high-level corporate officers, would show the team how to prepare a winning response. The first draft of their proposal, assembled four days later, was over 100 pages of single spaced text, and they were still writing. Finally, when the cutting-to-fit effort was completed, the corporate officers decided that our version was the best that could be done. Such is the pressure of severe page limitations.

14.4.6 Cross-Referencing Problems during Outlining

When a proposal has severe page limitations, it may be impossible in many instances, to repeat information or to expound upon a critical matter. The problem is exacerbated by the fact that the proposal evaluation teams are focused on very specific sections or modules or very specific matters when evaluating responses against a set of evaluation standards directed to a specific subject. The SSEB evaluation teams may not have access to other parts of the proposal or may not be inclined to look in other parts of the proposal for responses. In such instances, the proposal man receives a low rating by an evaluation team when the proposal has a good response in another part of the proposal.

The only methods for overcoming the problem of inadequate space in the proposal to repeat information that is the same for two or more requirements are:

- Insert cross reference into the text that direct the evaluation team to other sections.
- Prepare a very detailed compliance matrix that directs the evaluation teams to all responses.

Do not assume that evaluation teams will search your proposal for a response to their evaluation standards when the response is not in their specific section of the proposal. You and your proposal will die if you do. Prepare the matrix and insert the cross-references.

14.4.7 Developing the Compliance Matrix While Outlining

During the preparation of the outline, the Proposal Manager, Proposal Planner, and Volume Leaders should be keenly aware of the proposal requirements and the place within the outline that they are addressed. This is probably the best time for the preparation of the detailed compliance matrix, a graphic in which every proposal requirement is tabulated and the place within the outline where the response to the requirement is satisfied. This is the best time because the proposal management staff has made all the decisions relative to the matter and is fully aware of the logic behind such decisions.

14.5 DECISION ON TYPES OF TITLES AND USE OF THEME SENTENCES

Prior to or during the outlining effort, two major decisions must me made: (1), what type of titles will be used and, (2), whether theme sentences following the titles will be used. Three types of titles can be used:

Examples

Short Titles	Technical Approach
	Management
	Facilities
Long Titles	Our Innovative Technical Approach
	Our Management Tools and Systems
	Our Extensive Facilities and Resources
Action Titles	Our Technical Approach Is Innovative and Low Risk
	Our Management Approach Ensures On-Schedule Performance
	We Already Have All Facilities Needed to Support High Technology Projects

The use of theme sentences is an effective method for stating the most important message in the text following the short title. Be warned that the use of theme sentences is usually reserved for editorial styles based on the use of short titles, since the Long Title and the action title as shown above already have themes or messages to the readers.

PROJECT MANAGEMENT

Our approach to project management is based on planning, monitoring, controlling, and reporting the work with discipline and structure.

The following advice relative to the selection of titles and the use of theme sentences that the Proposal Planner or Proposal Manager should be considered before making any decisions relative to these two outlining matters:

1. The short title tells the evaluator very little about the text that follows.
2. The short title without a theme sentence is really dull.
3. The theme sentence in a single column format is very effective.
4. The theme sentence is most effective when using the short title.
5. The theme sentence is too long for use in dual column page formats.
6. The theme sentence should not ever be longer than two lines.
7. The action title presents a strong message to the evaluator early.
8. The action title may be too long for effective use in a dual column page format.
9. The long title can be used well in single or dual column page formats.
10. The long title and action title do not need theme sentences following.
11. The long title and action title are best when using personal pronouns.

CHAPTER 15

ORGANIZING THE PROPOSAL TEAM AND ITS RESOURCES

15.1 THE ORGANIZATION STRUCTURE OF THE PROPOSAL TEAM

Virtually all proposal teams have similar organizational structures, in that all teams are led by a Proposal Manager who directs and coordinates the efforts of the Volume Leaders, Plan Leaders, and Production Coordinator. The typical proposal organizational structure, as shown below, has four Volume or Plan Leaders, a Production Coordinator, and a Proposal Planner reporting to the Proposal Manager.

Proposal Manager
Proposal Planner

| Technical Leader | Management Volume Leader | Cost Volume Leader | Plan Leaders | Production Coordinator |

This straight-forward proposal team structure seldom varies, except for: (1) those small, intense, short-term proposal efforts that cannot afford the structure, and (2) those major proposals requiring a substantive costing effort.

In the small, quick-response types of proposals, the organizational structure is much simpler, in that there are not any technical, management, or plans leaders, and all writers assigned to a very small proposal team report directly to the Proposal Manager.

On the very large system development types of proposal, the organizational structure becomes more complex, with a costing team working under a Senior Cost Analyst, a System Demonstration Team, and several teams for plans and specifications.

It is noted that the Proposal Planner seldom is a full-time, long-term member of the proposal team and that the Proposal Manager usually is responsible for the preparation of the Executive Summary, which could be considered a small volume.

15.2 THE ORGANIZATIONAL STRUCTURE OF THE DESIGN TEAM

Like all good organizational structures, the design team is tailored to the exact requirements of the system being proposed, which means that the single most important factor driving the organization of the design team is the product to be delivered to the Government. For example:

O   When the deliverable is a computer-based hardware system, the organization of the design team will reflect the demands for software and hardware specialists, supported by logistics specialists.

Example: On a major proposal to the FAA to procure, integrate, test, and install major computer systems at four FAA sites, we were told that existing FAA software compatible with IBM mainframes would be used with the hardware. Accordingly, we organized our design team to reflect the system architecture and the logistics support for that system, which meant that we had many computer hardware specialists on the design team.

○ When the deliverable is a computer software system, the organization of the design team will reflect the software architecture to be designed, tested, integrated, and installed.

Example: On a major proposal to the HCFA to develop a major software system for use in processing Medicare claims, we were told that the existing IBM computers owned by the government would be used with the software. Accordingly, we organized our design team to reflect the software system and its subsystems and configuration items, with only a few computer hardware and logistics specialists assigned to the design team.

○ When the deliverable is a fully integrated computer-based hardware and software system, the organization of the design team will reflect the demands for software and hardware specialists, supported by logistics specialists.

Example: On a major proposal to the Navy by Martin Marietta, in which my company was a major subcontractor, the deliverable was a computer-based system for processing tactical and strategic intelligence. The design team included five major contingents: computer hardware engineers, computer software specialists, system engineering specialists, logistics specialists, and test specialists.

Of course, on small proposals for systems with a value of $2 million or less, the design team may be comprised of a computer hardware engineer, a computer software specialist, a general-purpose hardware engineer, a test specialist, and a logistics specialist. Such a five-person design team for a small system is a luxury. On a proposal to develop a atmospheric sampling system installed on a pallet and carried aloft by a balloon, we had exactly five people on the design team and we also wrote the technical volume of the proposal.

15.3 RESPONSIBILITIES AND AUTHORITIES OF KEY PERSONNEL

The Proposal Manager is the most important person associated with the proposal and the Chief Engineer is the most important person associated with the system design. They are responsible for winning the competition and preparing the best design. These managers cannot be successful without the authorities necessary to meet these responsibilities. All Proposal Managers or Chief Engineers who does not demand the necessary authorities in order to meet their responsibilities are doomed to failure.

The Volume Leaders, the Cost Planner, the Proposal Planner, and the Plan Leaders are the other key personnel on the proposal team. The Plan Leaders, Lead Designers, and Senior Engineering Specialists are the other key personnel on the design team. The Production Coordinator is a very important person in the proposal process and is key to the preparation of a superior proposal.

15.3.1 AUTHORITY AND RESPONSIBILITY OF THE PROPOSAL MANAGER

Responsibilities - Preparing a winning proposal, selecting the proposal management team, recruiting the proposal writing staff, acquiring the needed proposal resources, dealing with subcontractors, approving all planning documentation, identifying the win themes and discriminators, keeping high-level corporate officers informed, conducting proposal team meetings, defining and controlling the proposal budget, participating in teaming and consulting agreements, preparing or approving the proposal planning documentation and policies, heading the Blue Team Review, and making the toughest proposal decisions.

Authorities - Approval of all proposal staffing assignments, control of proposal facilities and resources, approval of all charges against the proposal budget, controlling expenditures for all equipment and services, approval of all time charges against the proposal, approving the volumes and plans, approval of planning documentation at all levels, dealing directly with subcontractor management, removal of unproductive personnel from the proposal team, controlling all meetings and internal reviews, and selecting members for the Blue Team Review.

15.3.2 Authority and Responsibility of the Volume Leaders

Responsibilities - Preparing a winning volume, recruiting the volume writing team, assigning writing efforts to volume writers. reviewing work by writers, ensuring that all volume requirements have a response, meeting with the volume team at least once a day, extending the proposal outline down to the page and paragraph level, assigning work to writers from subcontractors, participating in the Blue Team Review, meeting the budget for the volume, meeting daily with the Proposal Manager, preparing WBS packages related to their area of responsibility, identifying the risks associated with their volume, and preparing the detailed cost data forms.

Authorities - Approving all material included in the volume, approving all text and graphics prepared by the writers, approving all costs incurred in the volume, directing the get-well plans for the volume, committing additional resources to the writing effort, assisting in the preparation of Subcontractor Data Packages, approval of all cost estimating forms and data related to their volume, and controlling the work performed by the writers.

15.3.3 Authority and Responsibility of the Proposal Planner

Responsibilities - Preparing the list of proposal requirements, preparing the top-level proposal outline, preparing the overall proposal schedule, estimating the manpower required to produce the proposal, identifying the key issues in the procurement documents, preparing much of the material for the Gold Review, assisting in preparing the high-level proposal directives and policies, assisting in the Blue Review, preparing status reports for the Proposal Manager to be submitted to higher management, and participating in the daily internal proposal reviews.

Authorities - Controlling the proposal requirements data base, approval of the final volume outlines, and controlling the page budgets.

15.3.4 Authority and Responsibility of the Production Coordinator

Responsibilities - Preparing the production-related directives and documentation, dealing with the proposal writers on editorial and production matters, assigning work to the production staff (editors, artists, graphics specialists, word processor operators, printers), maintaining the master copy of the proposal text and graphics, serving as the interface between the proposal team and the production team, preparing the volumes for the formal reviews, preparing the proposal for delivery to the customer, and ensuring that security requirements are met by the production staff,

Authorities - Enforcing the production and editorial policies, approval or disapproval of text or graphics received from the production staff, enforcing a standoff distance between writers and production personnel, control of the master copy of the proposal in its latest version, withholding of text and graphics from production that do not meet the editorial policy, and defining the last time (day and hour) for submission of material by the writers to the production staff.

15.3.5 Authority and Responsibility of the Senior Cost Estimator

Responsibilities - Deciding on the cost strategy, defining the costing policies and procedures, selecting the cost estimating models and systems, defining the detailed cost data requirements, identifying the cost proposal requirements, preparing the cost volume outline, allocating the cost proposal requirements to the outline, estimating the level of effort needed for the costing activities, preparing the detailed forms for collecting cost data, preparing the Cost Breakdown Structure, compiling the detailed cost data into the Cost Breakdown Structure, identifying and quantifying the cost risks, securing corporate approval of major contract expenditures, establishing the schedule for all cost related activities, and dealing directly with the Contract Specialist who prepares the complete Cost Volume.

Authorities - Enforcing the policies and procedures for preparing cost estimating data, controlling the level of detail in the cost estimating forms, approval of all costing assumptions, approving all costing inputs and estimates, approving costs from vendors and suppliers, control of subcontractor cost input data, and enforcing costing guidelines and policies at all levels,

15.3.6 Authority and Responsibility of the Chief Engineer

Responsibilities - Preparing a winning system design, selecting the design team members, defining the organization of the design team, developing the system requirements data base, defining the top-level architecture for the system being designed, allocating the system requirements to the architecture, assigning design work to the design team members, conducting daily design reviews, identifying the major risks associated with the system, ensuring the facilities and equipment are ready for the design team, preparing the schedule for the system design, assigning key personnel to prepare the technical plans and technical specifications, and participating in all formal proposal reviews,

Authorities - Approving all personnel assigned to the design team, approving all designs and associated design work, controlling the baseline configuration of the system, controlling the system requirements data base, approving all expenditures associated with the design team, controlling the work performed by subcontractor personnel working on the design team, and dismissal or replacement of design personnel as requirements change.

15.3.7 AUTHORITY AND RESPONSIBILITY OF THE PLAN LEADERS

Responsibilities - Preparing a compliant and complete plan that satisfies the customer requirements, preparing a plan requirements data base, preparing both the top-level and detailed outlines for the plan, preparing the schedule and milestones associated with the preparation of the plan, ensuring that the plan supports the system design or the work program presented in the technical volume, writing the text and preparing the graphics for the plan, ensuring that the plan meets the Editorial Policy, securing higher-level approval for all commitments and purchases in the plans, assigning work to plan writers, dealing directly with the other volume leaders and design team members, and planning get-well efforts for critical matters,

Authorities - Approving all text and graphics prepared by the plan writers, controlling all costs associated with the plan, replacing plan writers as the work load changes, controlling all data inputs to the plan requirements data base, committing resources to get-well efforts, and dealing directly with the other key proposal and design leaders,

15.3.8 ROLE OF THE CORPORATE OFFICER RESPONSIBLE

The role of the Corporate Officer Responsible is to serve as: the corporate representative for the competitive effort, the person responsible for acquiring corporate financing and resources, the corporate representative to the subcontractor management, and the leader of the effort to acquire the best possible design team and proposal team. His/her principal role is to represent the proposal and design teams to corporate management and to represent high-level corporate management to the proposal and design teams. Also, this key person will be very committed to the Gold and Red Team Review, serving as a team member in many instances. The Corporate Officer Responsible does not need to have extensive proposal skills or detailed design expertise, but does need to have the management skills needed to monitor a high-intensity effort.

15.3.9 Role of the Acquisition Manager

The role of the Acquisition Manager is the collection of information relative to the customer, the procurement, the competitors, the associated contractors, and FCRCs. Mostly, this information will be collected prior to the issuance of the procurement documents, with the balance of the information collected after the documents have been issued by the customer. The Acquisition Manager does not have an active role in the planning, managing, writing, and production of the proposal or the design.

The major role of the Acquisition Manager during the preparation of the proposal is that of an information resource. During the design effort, the role of the Acquisition Manager is much less significant because of the technical nature of the work. During the Gold Review and the Red Review, the Acquisition Manager provides valuable insights into the procurement and the customer. Hopefully, this manager can provide extremely valuable inputs for the development of win themes, discriminators, and other top-level matters.

15.4 DEFINING THE LINES OF COMMUNICATION AND INTERFACES

15.4.1 The Chain of Command

Within the Proposal Team - The chain of command within the proposal team is quite simple. The Volume Leaders, Plan Leaders, Proposal Planner, and Senior Cost Estimator report directly to the Proposal Manager. The Proposal Writers and the Plan Writers report to the Volume/Plan Leaders. Subcontractor personnel assigned to work as Proposal Writers report to the Volume or Plan Leader to whom they are assigned.

At the first meeting of the proposal team, the Proposal Manager must explain the chain of command from high level corporate managers to the proposal team and the chain of command within the proposal team. At periodic meetings of the proposal management staff, the Proposal Manager must restate the organizational structure to ensure that problems do not arise. It helps to post a large graphic that depicts the proposal team's organizational structure and identifies the key personnel within the proposal management team.

Within the Corporation - The chain of command within the higher levels of management should be quite simple. The Proposal Manager reports to the Corporate Officer Responsible. The Corporate Officer Responsible reports to the Group Manager. There should be no doubt about who reports to whom and when they report. The communications in this higher-level of management will include both written and verbal reports, with verbal reports being the most frequent method. As an almost universal rule, communications between the higher-level corporate managers and the proposal staff is limited to the reviews.

I was considered for employment as Proposal Manager for an Arsenal

Ship proposal in which four major companies had teamed with General Dynamics. During my interview with a group of high-level people, they described their concept for the management of the proposal. Basically, they had designated a five-person proposal management team that, as a group and as individuals, would issue orders to the Proposal Manager. Since I will not work for five managers simultaneously, I declined the offer to work on that proposal. I stated my policy of working for a single manager and not for committees, groups, or panels. I still believe that when there is no simple chain of command, a proposal or a project is destined for major problems.

15.4.2 THE MAJOR INTERFACES

Interfaces Within the Corporation - By definition, interfaces are those communications outside of the chain of command. Interfaces are the means by which work is coordinated and problems are resolved with minimum problems. The interfaces associated with the proposal ensure that the proposal stays on schedule, that all information needed for the proposal is available, and that personal conflicts are minimized. The major proposal interfaces include:

Volume Leader Interfaces - Leaders for the technical volume, management volume, and cost volume must have frequent and open contact with each other. These leaders meet regularly to ensure that the interfaces between their volumes are consistent and do not have any contradictions. The Volume Leaders normally meet once or twice a day in proposal management staff meetings, at which time interface issues are identified and resolved.

Production Coordinator Interfaces - The Production Coordinator, who works in direct support of the Proposal Manager, deals directly with the Volume and Plan Leaders, and works closely with the production staff. The Coordinator is the interface between the proposal team and the production staff.

<u>Cost Estimator Interfaces -</u> The Cost Estimator, who works directly for the Proposal Manager, is the interface between the proposal team and the contracts staff. The Estimator deals directly with any and all members of the design team throughout the design effort, with the Proposal Planner in the preparation of the Work Breakdown Structure, and with the proposal staff in those matters related to project management costs and systems.

<u>Design Team-Proposal Team Interfaces -</u> It is inevitable that the design team will join the proposal team when the system design is completed. This migration from the design team to the proposal team is sometimes difficult, but when the interfaces between the two teams are managed by the Chief Engineer and the Proposal Manager, problems should be minimal. Nevertheless, ensuring that this interface is controlled by senior managers is imperative.

Interfaces with Outside Organizations - It is inevitable that members of the proposal team, the design team, and the cost estimating team will deal with outside organizations like the subcontractors, vendors and suppliers, consultants, and potential employees. These interfaces are necessary and normal on all major proposal and design efforts, and with diligence, the interfaces can be very effective. It is the duty of the Proposal Manager and Chief Engineer to define these interfaces and issue guidelines governing these interfaces. Some examples of these interfaces include the following:

<u>Subcontractor Interfaces -</u> Subcontractor personnel who are working on the design team or the proposal team must fully comply with the team activities, while maintaining contact and providing consultation with their corporate managers. The interfaces between subcontractor personnel and other members of the design or proposal team should be seamless and informal.

<u>Vendor and Supplier Interfaces -</u> As a general rule, these interfaces are limited to members of the design team, the cost estimating team, and the cost proposal team. These interfaces are necessary to obtain detailed information on matters such as hardware characteristics and capabilities, software capabilities, hardware and software support services, special facility costs, construction costs, availability, delivery schedules, terms and conditions, and special restrictions.

<u>Consultant Interfaces -</u> When a consultant is not working exclusively in support of your proposal or design effort, then the interfaces must be very formal and understood by both parties. However, when the consultant is a member of either the proposal team or design team, then he/she is subject only to the normal restrictions of the design or proposal teams.

<u>Potential Employees -</u> When technical and management personnel are being recruited for a program to become active upon the proposal and design winning the competition, a formal wall must be erected as an interface. In effect, non-employees have no interface with the proposal effort in any way. Accept the possibility that the potential employees are, in fact, Trojan Horses.

15.5 PROBLEMS INHERENT TO PROPOSAL ORGANIZATIONS

Failing to Isolate Writers from the Production Staff - Without a doubt, the single biggest problem associated with the preparation of a winning proposal is to allow designers or writers to deal directly with the production staff. This problem area, which has resulted in more strife during the preparation of a proposal, has always been the result of writers and designers bypassing the Production Coordinator. It is my belief that the only times that the writer and the production staff worked well without a Production Coordinator were during five or six day efforts when there was only one person writing the proposal.

Failing to Integrate Subcontractor Personnel into the Proposal Team - Nobody ever said that it would be easy to convince subcontractors that they were trusted member of our team while restricting their access to certain activities, data bases, cost data, and proposal processes. But controlling the subcontractor personnel on a current proposal is a necessity, because they will be competing against you in the future. If the subcontractor personnel are not assigned specific tasks with firm schedules, they will begin to wander, talk, and read in unrelated efforts. They are members of your organization and they must be integrated with your staff.

Failing to Enforce the Chain of Command - When the proposal staff is organized into a formal structure, every member of the team knows his or her role and knows for whom they work. The members of the proposal team attend proposal-related meetings and deliver their text and graphics to a member of the proposal management staff. The members of the design team attend design reviews and deliver their analyses and designs to the design management staff. When proposal writers, detailed designers, and plan writers do not observe the chain of command, chaos reigns. The Proposal Manager must enforce the chain of command because it is the line of authority and the channel for reporting.

Failing to Define Specific Responsibilities and Authorities - The Proposal Manager and the Chief Engineer must define the responsibilities and authorities of the proposal team and the design team. It is not enough to assign a title to some senior individual. It is wrong to assign responsibilities to the members of the proposal staff and the design staff without assigning the authorities needed to meet these responsibilities. While this observation may sound like Introduction to Management 101, too many proposals suffer from the lack of such an unambiguous statement.

Failing to Control the Daily Meetings - As part of the organizational structure of the proposal team and the design team, the Proposal Manager and the Design Manager must determine who will attend the various meetings. For example, proposal writers do not attend the daily proposal status meetings which are limited to the Proposal Manager, Proposal Planner, Volume Leaders, and Production Coordinator, but the writers will attend the volume status meetings each day. The proposal writers do not attend the design reviews and design team status meetings and the design team members do attend the proposal status meetings. Failure to establish these organizational restrictions can cause major problems and major loss of productive man-hours.

The most mismanaged proposal in my career was the Medicare Transaction System proposal to HCFA. Initially, the proposal was struggling under the direction of a salesman who was appointed Proposal Manager without him ever having worked on a proposal team in any role whatsoever. His successor as Proposal Manager loved meetings and assembled the design team, the costing team, and the proposal team in two meetings each day. Every attendee was directed to describe their progress since the last meeting. Since each of the 30+ attendees took a minimum of two minutes to describe the little bit of work done since the last meeting, our two meetings each day required at least three hours total for every attendee. We could have prepared 20 pages of the proposal each day that we were not required to attend these meetings. But the Proposal Manager wanted good karma. WGAS

CHAPTER **16**

PLANNING THE SUBCONTRACTOR ROLES

16.1 DEFINING THE ROLE OF SUBCONTRACTOR PERSONNEL

Subcontractor personnel can be highly qualified to work on the proposal team or on the design team. Their technical personnel will work on the technical volume of the proposal and their proposal specialists will work on the management volume of the proposal. During the preparation of a proposal that includes a major system design, subcontractor engineers and specialists will work on the design team, while other subcontractor personnel will work on the proposal team.

As a general rule, subcontractor personnel will be employed primarily as writers for the technical volumes, management volumes, and supporting plans. In such assignments, the proposal writers provided by the subcontractors will work in areas such as:

In the **management volume**, subcontractor writers with proposal experience will prepare project descriptions for contracts awarded to their employer, resumes for key personnel from their corporation, and descriptions of their facilities and resources.

In the **technical volume**, subcontractor writers with strong engineering or scientific backgrounds will assist in the preparation of the problem understanding and technical approach in those areas in which their corporation will work after contract award.

16.2 COORDINATING THE SUBCONTRACTOR PROPOSAL SUPPORT

It is important that the Proposal Manager and the Volume/Plan Leaders prove their management skills through the ways in which subcontractor personnel are used during their assignment to the proposal team. The assignment of work to subcontractor personnel usually follows a discussion of the proposal needs and their skills. Then, when the Volume Leader identifies the areas or subjects in which the subcontractor proposal personnel are qualified, the Volume Leader assigns very specific writing assignments to those personnel.

The Volume Leader will be the principal member of the proposal management staff for dealing with the subcontractor personnel assigned to his/her volume. As a good management practice, the Volume Leader will assign a very specific part of the proposal to the writer, accompanied by a Writer's Folder, which will include examples of good proposal writing related to the assignment.

Since the proposal writers provided by the subcontractor will not know your process, your resources, or the skills of your proposal management staff, the Volume Leaders must spend considerable time to ensure that those writers are productive. This means daily contact and mentoring with the subcontractor writers, particularly during the early phases of the proposal. Every effort must be made to ensure that subcontractor writers, as well as writers from your own corporation, fully understand the critical role of their work and the way that their work is coordinated with other material.

16.3 INTEGRATING SUBCONTRACTOR SUPPORT FOR THE DESIGN TEAM

Generally, the Chief Engineer assigns subcontractor technical personnel to one of the major technical areas (Systems Architecture, Systems Design, System Test, Systems Logistics, Hardware Design, Software Design). The skilled technical personnel will be integrated into the design team, working on specific tasks assigned by the Chief

Engineer, Senior Design Engineer, Senior Systems Engineer, Senior Installation and Checkout Specialist, and Senior Logistics Specialist.

Probably the most effective technique for integrating subcontractor personnel into the design team is the daily design review meeting. In these meetings, a lead design engineer may describe the results of his team's design analysis and a discussion of the hardware items selected for a specific application. Or these meetings may describe the results of the training requirements analysis, followed by a discussion of the documentation to be developed. When subcontractor engineers and technical personnel attend such meeting every day, they develop a vision of the role that their support for the overall design and for the technical volume to be prepared upon completion of the design effort.

The Chief Engineer and his lead technical managers are responsible for ensuring that technical skills and experience of the subcontractor personnel are used to the maximum. It has been noted in every design effort at my employer that when technical expertise is used effectively that the subcontractor personnel are more effective in their contributions.

16.4 PROPRIETARY INFORMATION AND THE SUBCONTRACTORS

Security within the Proposal Team - Every time that a competitor becomes a subcontractor and works as a member of your proposal team, it is a certainty that the subcontractor personnel will learn much about your corporation and your proposal capabilities. Every subcontractor employee working on your proposal team should be viewed with a degree of suspicion, especially if the subcontractor sent a proposal specialist with its worker force. I know, because I supported many proposals in which my employer was a subcontractor to a major corporation that was destined to be a major competitor the future.

A very fine line exists between providing a subcontractor employee with specific information needed for the instant proposal and providing general information about your proposal process, your proposal resources, and your proposal centers. Smart and observant subcontractor personnel will learn of your corporate disasters, your contract failures, and your cost overruns during conversations with your staff. The competitors will use this information to "ghost" your corporation, your approach, and your experience in future proposals in which they are competing with your employer.

The Proposal Manager and the Volume Leaders should brief its proposal team members in this matter and impress them with the need to limit the type and amount of information made available to subcontractor personnel, particularly those with extensive proposal experience. Employees should be coached on the means by which information needed by subcontractor writers will be limited to need-to-know items without the subcontractors being aware of an active effort to control their access to your information and resources.

Transmission of Information to/from Subcontractors - It will be impossible to control the information that subcontractor personnel carry away from your facility in their minds. It could be nearly impossible to control the flow of your corporate information to their own corporation within their briefcases. And it could be very frustrating to control the transfer of proprietary data or other corporate information by Internet E-mail. When working as a subcontractor to an Arizona corporation on a space-related proposal, the guards at the entrances and exits searched briefcases for floppy disks. But they were ineffective in preventing other methods of removing proprietary information.

Probably the best methods to block or limit the transmission of data and proprietary information are:

- After each formal review, find all copies of the proposal and have an employee to destroy the unneeded copies immediately after the reviews.
- During the writing effort, allow the computers used by the writers to be used on an proposal network without access to outside sources.
- During the periodic volume meetings, have the Volume

Leader to discuss the matter of controlling proposal related information.

- Block all subcontractor personnel (and your own corporate employees) not on the proposal team from access to the proposal center network.
- Limit access by subcontractor personnel to your corporate data bases and to the. information provided by other subcontractors.

Once, while working on a proposal in which my company was a subcontractor to TRW, I had the opportunity to read the TRW proposal newsletter. The newsletter had a form by which employees could be placed on the distribution list for this very helpful proposal-related publication. I submitted the form, using my home address, without ever stating that I was not a TRW employee. For the next two or three years, I received the TRW proposal newsletter, which was a very informative item. I gained much insight into their process and their experiences. Obviously, their proposal security was rather lax.

16.5 TYPES OF DOCUMENTATION PROVIDED TO SUBCONTRACTORS

Two major types of documentation is provided to the subcontractors: (1), that documentation needed by the subcontractor to prepare their proposal to your corporation, (2), the material provided to the subcontractor personnel working on-site as a member of the proposal or design teams. Proposal-related documentation includes all information needed for the subcontractor to prepare its proposal to your corporation; this documentation is included in the subcontractor data package. Documentation provided to working members of the proposal team is included in the Writers Folder. NOTE: these two sets of documentation for subcontractors and their staff are described in detail in other sections of this book.

16.6 RECOGNIZING SUPERIOR WORK BY SUBCONTRACTOR PERSONNEL

When subcontractor personnel become very productive members of the proposal team or the design team, the Proposal Manager or the Chief Engineer is obliged to send a formal letter of appreciation to high-level managers at the subcontractors. This policy could be a mirror image of the letters of appreciation and recognition sent to the managers of your own employees. These letters of appreciation to subcontractor managers could almost be a form letter, but the letter should include specific references to the roles and contributions of those personnel. Make the letter appear sincere in every respect. But do not send a letter of appreciation for non-performers.

16.7 WORKING AS A SUBCONTRACTOR FOR A PRIME CONTRACTOR

When working as a member of a design team or a proposal team in which your employer is a subcontractor to a major corporation, you are obligated to deal with the prime contractor's staff in the most professional manner possible. This means that you accept your work assignments, that you deliver on schedule, that your work is consistently high quality, and that your efforts are integrated seamlessly into the overall proposal effort. These high-level matters are true, whether you are a member of the proposal team or the design team.

While working as a subcontractor on a proposal effort, every effort must be made to ensure that the work assigned to your corporation in the teaming agreement is not reduced summarily or arbitrarily. Further, you must ensure that your employer will receive work commensurate with its contribution to the proposal if you prepare 25 percent of the proposal, your employer should be eligible for 25 percent of the dollars after contract award. Since you know what is happening during the proposal effort, you are best qualified to monitor these matters.

Probably the most important advice to technical and management volume writers assigned to support the prime contractor's proposal is: to call upon your corporate resources, meet the highest editorial standards, deliver text and graphics on schedule, work hours as long as the prime contractor's staff, and ensure that your corporation is not exploited by any member of the team. Never accept any "Mission Impossible" assignments from any member of the proposal management staff.

CHAPTER 17

PREPARING FOR THE COST PROPOSAL

17.1 DEFINING THE WINNING COST OF THE BID

Many managers believe that determining the winning cost for a bid is little more than a combination of the black arts. Others believe that insider information is the only means for determining what the customer will pay for products or services. Most believe that it is truly impossible to approach the task of defining the winning cost with any degree of rigor and with any ethical process. But, I assure you, it is possible to develop a rational cost that should be the winning cost. While this costing process may have some flaws, it is better than a dart board or a vote by the uninformed.

Proposal Managers, Chief Engineers, Cost Estimators, and other people responsible for a winning cost proposal should consider the following approaches to defining the probable winning cost for a competitive bid:

For Technical Services Contracts - Collect cost information, under the Freedom of Information Act, if necessary, on similar contracts in which other firms have won competitions in which costs were a very important consideration. Assume that those firms that won services contracts in the past will bid similar low-cost personnel costs. Then plan how you will match these low costs in your proposal, or how you will justify higher personnel rates.

For Technical Studies Contracts - Collect cost information, under the Freedom of Information Act, if necessary, on research or technical contracts of similar scope and complexity in which research firms have won competitions in the past. Assume that the firms that specialize in the same type of contracts will compete against you. Then plan how you will convince the customer in your proposal that your costs are appropriate for the study.

For Major Military Contracts - Determine how much funding is available for the program, relying on the Five Year Forecast. This official DOD document identifies all major procurements approved for the military services and presents the year-by-year forecast for the costs associated with each major system. Since these costs include the money needed by the Government agencies to manage the program, it is prudent to deduct 15 percent from the annual forecasts to determine the amount of money available for the contractor.

For Software Development Contracts - Collect information relative to the estimating system that is used for man-hours required to design, develop, test, install, and operate a software system. Some customers prefer to use the COCOMO model, and some prefer to use the RCA Price model. These models require inputs such as: existing lines of code that can be used without modification, existing lines of code that can be modified, and new lines of code to be developed. The outputs from the models are the time required to complete the technical work, the man-hours required for various phases of the work, and total man-hours required for the entire effort.

For Hardware Development Contracts - Collect information relative to the costs of comparable systems developed for the customer in the recent past. Use cost estimating methods and algorithms to determine how much it will cost to design, develop, fabricate, test, install, and demonstrate the hardware systems. These two methods, comparable systems and cost estimating tools, are reliable enough to develop hardware costs. When special conditions, such as the use of innovative technologies, exist, the cost estimates will probably rely on engineering estimates and extrapolations from existing systems.

It is imperative that the estimate of the final set of cost data for a competitive proposal not be prepared when the technical and management volumes and the engineering designs have been completed. The costs to be proposed to the customer should be decided before the design effort really begins and the writing of the proposal starts. When the costs are known, the proposal and the design can be tailored to those costs. Waiting until the end of the design and the final draft of the proposal is not the time to begin cost cutting and cost compromising.

Stated simply, every proposal effort should begin with an estimate of the final costs to be proposed to the customer and the Proposal Manager (and the Chief Engineer) must prepare a proposal that meets this estimate.

17.2 REDUCING THE GOVERNMENT'S CONTRACT MONITORING COSTS

Very few contractors consider the costs incurred by the Government (or client) when performing its contract monitoring activities. Yet the costs to the customer can be significant for activities such as: monitoring contract performance, coordinating on-site visits, conducting audits and inspections, observing tests or demonstrations, and conducting formal reviews. Because these costs are important to the customer, they should be important somewhat to the Proposal Manager and the Cost Estimator. The following matters should be considered in developing the cost strategy:

Lower The Travel Costs for the Government Personnel - Avoid project reviews in places like New York City and Boston because of the high cost of lodgings. Avoided project reviews in places like Boise and Key West because of airline fares. Whenever possible, make an effort to control Government expenses by conducting formal design reviews at a location close to an airport and to a motel/hotel in order to reduce local travel expenses for Government personnel.

Lower the Costs for Computer-Based Financial Accounting - Ensure that your financial reporting system produces data in the detail and format needed for direct input to the customer's computer system (hardware and software specific). Do not require the customer to perform any data formatting and conversion; do it yourself.

Remember that the Government's contract monitoring team does not have unlimited funds and that your cost reduction efforts will be appreciated. In some instances, the difference in the cost for contract monitoring might be a decisive factor in the selection of the winning contractor. So, develop a strategy for assisting the Government in this matter.

17.3 DEVELOPING YOUR COSTING STRATEGY

The Design to Cost Strategy - In this strategy, for a technical services proposal, the Proposal Manager or Volume Leader develops a staffing plan in which the average labor-hour cost needed to win the contract has been determined and they meet this cost. For a technical study proposal, the Proposal Manager and Volume leaders define an organizational structure and a staffing plan to meet the maximum total costs being proposed and are selected to meet the not-to-exceed costs. For a major software development proposal, a strategic decision is made as to which of the two principal means for reducing design costs will be used; i. e., whether to change to lines of code estimates or to reduce personnel costs.

During a major procurement for SETA support to a high level Government agency, I had been told by the COTR, long before the RFP was issued, and that the Government estimated the fully-burdened labor rate for analysts, engineers, and scientist would be an average of $ 8,500 per month. The average labor rate for the 30-person staff that we bid was about $8,480 per month.

But I have been on many proposals for technical services during which managers prepared the staffing plan based on the sole criteria of full employment for his/her existing Division staff. In most of these efforts, it was not until three days before the delivery of the proposal that someone, usually the Acquisition Manager or Marketing Specialist, realized that the proposed labor costs were much too high to win. Agonizing re-staffing efforts combined with major cost cutting initiatives were very necessary because the staffing plan and initial costing were not focused.

The Low Cost Risk Strategy - In this strategy, a major effort is made to convince the customer that your approach presents minimal cost risks to the Government agency. This strategy means, of course, that your design team and proposal team must conduct risk analyses on all possible cost risks; positive, believable, logical actions must be specified in sufficient detail to convince the customer that your approach or design is certainly low risk. Be advised, that in order to have no cost risks, there must be no technical risks, which means that your design and your proposal must also reduce the technical risks to negligible or near zero.

I suggest that outside consultants who know the customer and technical leaders in your corporation be organized into a risk management team that identifies all technical and cost risks in an independent assessment. Having an outside view is important because the proposal team members and the design team participants will begin to believe what they have written in a very short time and they lose their objectivity. Use objective outsiders.

The Saluting the Flag Strategy - When all other cost reduction strategies fail, some Proposal Managers fall back on what I call the "full employment for retired military or civil service personnel" strategy. In this strategy, the proposal themes emphasize an extensive understanding of the problem, the many years of personnel experience in related programs, and the commitment of the retirees to working for the customer. Be advised, that this strategy is usable only when competing for high-image, high-level programs in which personnel costs play a relatively minor role in the selection of a winning contractor.

The Board of Directors of my employer had members, such as

Melvin Laird, who were invaluable in gaining an audience with the Source Selection Authority prior to the issuance of an RFP for high level procurements. Mr. Laird, because he has always been an honorable person with great prestige, was very effective in projecting an image of our company as a technology leader. Melvin always did what was best for the country, which really made him a great advocate.

A major design and construction firm had a policy of hiring many retired professional engineers from the Army Corps of Engineers, the Bureau of Reclamation, and similar Government agencies. These former Government engineers were great advocates for the firm, largely because they were always concerned about the services provided to their Government agencies.

The Sharpening the Pencil Strategy - Many techniques have been used by contractors to reduce the costs proposed for a specific procurement. These techniques include:

- using personnel with minimum required skills to lower direct labor costs
- establishing special cost center with lower direct overhead rates
- using subcontractors with lower direct labor rates
- performing certain management activities within another cost center
- using comparable and compatible foreign-made equipment
- traveling at Government rates for commercial carriers
- providing the minimum required to meet the contract requirements
- moving desirable but not required items to options
- using Government-provided facilities, equipment, and systems

The You Get What You Pay for Strategy - In this strategy, it is very important that a very skilled proposal writer be assigned responsibility for the Executive Summary and for parts of the various volumes. In this strategy, the writer presents a series of subliminal messages to the Government agency to the effect that; "Low cost means low quality. Our costs are driven by quality initiatives. We hire only the best technical personnel. We have committed extensive resources to this program. Our approach is truly the most cost-effective method. We are committed to the best approach, regardless of its cost impact." This strategy is best used when you cannot bid the lowest cost, no matter how aggressive your cost cutting efforts may have been.

Note: Be warned that each of these techniques can present problems, and that certain Government agencies can tolerate very few risks while other agencies are very accustomed to all types of risks.

17.4 IDENTIFYING THE RESOURCES NEEDED FOR THE COST PROPOSAL

17.4.1 THE RESOURCES NEEDED FOR A COST REALISM RESPONSE

The preparation of a cost realism response is characterized by a bi-polar condition, in that only one contractor has the truly realistic costs and that all other contractors do not have realistic costs. Your costs are realistic or they are not realistic, and you cannot win if your costs are unrealistic. So your cost proposal must have the best cost realism response, or the Government will add much larger costs to your costs to reflect their risks, eliminating your proposal on a cost basis. Be advised that your most talented writer-costing specialist must be assigned to the cost realism response.

When working as a consultant for a local technical services company, I was tasked to prepare a cost realism response. Since I had been working on the proposal team for about a week, I had an in-depth understanding of the procurement, the proposal, and the customer. I had also established a good working relationship with the corporate financial and contracts staff, so I had ready access to the needed information. Yet it required over 7 long days for me to prepare the cost realism response. The company won the

35-person, five-year technical support contract because it had the most realistic costs.

So, the resources needed for a cost realism response are: 7 to 10 man-days of labor, free access to the corporate financial structure, wage-hour surveys, fringe benefit surveys, and about twenty special publications.

17.4.2 THE RESOURCES NEEDED FOR SHOULD-COST ANALYSIS

The Should-Cost Analysis is an activity performed by the contractor in an effort to replicate the process by which the Government developed its estimate of the probable costs for an upcoming procurement. Essentially, the contractor's Should-Cost Analysis is an attempt to determine what money has been allocated to the procurement for which the contractor is bidding. This Should-Cost Analysis is useful when the Government's budget documents provide no data relative to the funding for the upcoming procurement and when your Marketing and Acquisition Specialists have no idea what level of funding is available for the procurement.

The Should-Cost Analysis can be based on a variety of analytic tools, some of which have been discussed earlier. The tools can include such variety as using data from:

- current contracts for technical studies of comparable scope and complexity
- software estimating systems used by the Government such as COCOMO
- cost estimating relationships developed by the corporation for hardware systems
- area wage surveys and fringe benefit surveys for SETA support contracts
- RFP-based estimates of the man-hours needed to perform the work

- use of existing or easily-developed cost estimating relationships
- subcontractor-provided cost data from other teaming agreements

My employer decided to submit a proposal for the development of a complex of inter-connected communications centers for use in times of national emergency. Our corporation submitted a proposal with a cost that was over $570 million. The Government had estimated the system costs to be less than $280 million. The winning contractor bid about $275 million. Our managers did not examine the agency's budget, a public document, and did not prepare a should-cost analysis. Apparently, our competition did their homework in should-cost.

17.4.3 THE RESOURCES NEEDED TO PREPARE THE COST INPUT DATA

Somehow, the Chief Engineer and the Proposal Manager must assemble the resources needed to prepare the basic cost input data that will be used to prepare the Cost Volume. The resources include forms, procedures, documentation, and instructions, such as:

- a general concept for how and where the contract work will be performed
- a complete detailed work breakdowns structure (Index and Dictionary)
- a project organization chart with position descriptions and staffing profiles
- a listing of all contract deliverables and their schedule
- a list of all formal reviews, audits, and demonstrations and their schedule
- the forms used by the technical staff to estimate labor hours
- the forms used to secure bids from vendors and suppliers
- the forms and procedures needed to obtain delivery schedules and costs
- the forms for requesting quotes from organizations providing technical support

- the budgeted amount of money by major WBS activities (Level 2 or 3)
- instructions regarding preparation of cost input data
- special assumptions approved for use in costing
- the Cost Breakdown Structure specified by the Government for cost reporting
- an understanding of the method for translating WBS costs to CBS costs

17.5 ADDRESSING THE MATTER OF COST RISKS EARLY

The Government will make an assessment of the risks associated with your approach or your design as part of the proposal evaluation process. If the Government foresees major potential risks in your proposed work program, the Government managers will add a sum to the costs that you have proposed to meet the anticipated risks. So, this means that your costs will be increased by the Government, and that the cost evaluation process will use the adjusted costs (yours plus theirs) to select the winning contractor. What does this mean to the proposal or design team? It means that cost risks must be considered and addressed as part of the proposal preparation process.

It is important to address cost risks in the risk management element of the proposal. And that means that a discussion of your process for identifying, evaluating, and minimizing risks is not enough of a response. Instead, a specific effort to identify at least one, preferably two, of the major cost risks identified by the design and proposal teams. Then the proposal must demonstrate that your approach, your design, your skills will handle the risks. Leave no doubt that you can handle every cost risk that arises during the contract.

17.6 PLANNING THE COSTING EFFORTS

The methods found to be most effective in developing competitive costs and in avoiding costing disasters during the preparation of a winning cost proposal include critical activities by management, by the design team, and by the cost estimator:

The Top-Level Cost Planning Activities

- agree to a cost strategy not later than the Gold Review
- prepare a cost reduction plan to implement the cost strategy
- designate the major areas in which costs reductions are most possible
- assign the best cost estimator in the corporation to direct the costing effort
- intensify the marketing effort for information related to the customer's funding profile
- agree on the final costs to be presented in the cost proposal
- select the cost estimating system and cost data base to be used
- modify the cost estimating models/relationships to fit the job being bid
- begin work on the cost realism section of the cost proposal
- evaluate information related to the competitors probable costs and collect more intelligence

The More Detailed Cost Planning Activities

- identify the major cost drivers at as early of a stage as possible
- collect cost related information from all available sources for a cost data base
- establish a cost log as a central repository for all cost-related information
- establish the financial structure needed to meet the cost bullets
- identify the efforts needed to reduce costs and cost risks
- identify and quantify the cost risks and prepare cost risk mitigation plans
- implement what is written in the cost realism response
- ensure that the management reserve is controlled by an iron hand

- ensure hardware and software designs are consistent with the cost being bid
- ensure the technical approach and deliverables are consistent with the costs being bid
- prepare personnel requirements based on technical and management skills and average salary

From the lists above, you can rightly conclude it is imperative in a major system development proposal to agree at an early date on the total costs for the work being bid. Then, if you concluded that one tailors the design, the staffing, and the approach to the dollars being bid in the cost proposal, you are correct. Remember that late surprises in proposal costing are very traumatic and that Herculean efforts are necessary to revise the technical proposal or designs at the last moment. Your market intelligence should provide the information needed to identify the winning costs and to avoid late crises if not, someone should be fired.

In proposals for procurements in areas as diverse as technical services, study and analyses, architectural and engineering design, and small system development, the above lists can be shortened a bit. It is recommended, that the cost planner think seriously before deciding to delete any of these activities. In all procurements, for example, you still need a cost strategy and all that it implies, information about the funding available and probable costs of the competitors, and a cost estimating system and cost data base.

During a major proposal to the FBI for a software development contract, my employer submitted its proposal to the Government with a detailed system design. As part of this submission, we included the detailed information used by our staff and by the Government personnel as inputs to the COCOMO estimating model. Like: lines of existing code to be used without modification, lines of existing code to be used after modification, and new lines of code to be developed. As part of the Best and Final Offer, some corporate managers wanted to reduce the costs proposed in our original submission to the Government. But we could not do that because we had documented the lines of code in detail, by configuration item and by source of the code. We could not reduce design, development, and testing costs after that original submission.

17.7 BEGINNING WORK ON LONG LEAD-TIME COST MATTERS

17.7.1 PREPARING THE WORK BREAKDOWN STRUCTURE

It is imperative that the proposal teams prepare the Work Breakdown Structure for the proposed project as early in the proposal process as possible, because the WBS is probably the most essential document in the cost estimating effort. The preparation of the WBS, however, is not a simple task, because it requires both a tabular index and a supporting dictionary. The preparation of a WBS index and dictionary provides the cost estimating staff with a complete summary of the work to be performed and the relationships between the various work efforts. The importance of the WBS to the cost proposal cannot be understated.

The level of effort required to develop a types-of-work WBS Index is relatively minor, even when the Index extends down to the fourth or fifth level. However, when that Index must be extended down to the eighth or ninth level of the WBS, the level of effort required for the index is not a minor concern. The time required preparing a WBS for a technical services or study contract should not require more than two man-days in most instances. For system design procurement, the time required for the preparation of a WBS may be two to four days, depending on the availability of an existing WBS Index and the skills of the preparer.

The preparation of a WBS Dictionary is a major activity and

the level of effort required for this activity is significantly greater and very much more difficult than the WBS Index. The WBS
Dictionary must describe the work to be performed, the major
activities to be accomplished, the inputs to and outputs from the
work, the schedule for performing the work, the personnel and
resources required for the work, and the special issues associated
with the work. As a first estimate of the level of effort associated
with a WBS Dictionary, use these planning factors as a guide for
estimating man-power requirements:

- Each WBS work package will require one typewritten page
  of text.
- Each typewritten page for a WBS work package will require
  one man-day to prepare.
- The prime contractor on a system development proposal will
  be required to prepare a WBS Dictionary for 600 to 800 work
  packages.
- Each subcontractor on a system development proposal will
  be assigned 50 to 70 WBS work packages.
- The prime contractor for a technical services, study or analysis, or A&E design proposal will be required to prepare a WBS
  Dictionary for 150-250 WBS work packages.

The level of effort required to develop a WBS Dictionary, based
on a types-of-work WBS, can range from three man-weeks for a
minor technical support contract of three years duration to over
six man-months for a major system development proposal.

17.7.2 Preparing the Cost Breakdown Structure

The Government requires contractors to report their costs in a
format and level of detail that is driven by their Cost Breakdown
Structure. Their Cost Breakdown Structure, which is an essential
part of the RFP, is based on the manner in which funding is allocated, monitored, and controlled by the Government. Basically,

the CBS is tailored to the Government's requirements and not to the contractor's requirements. In very few, if any, instances does the Government's cost structure correlate to the cost accounting and reporting system used by contractor. For example, the Cost Breakdown Structure is not consistent with the requirements for a validated Cost Schedule Status Reporting system or a Cost Schedule Control System. These two reporting systems dictate a structure based on the WBS, which most contractors use to plan and manage their work.

I have found that, in virtually every instance, contractors cannot plan, organize, manage, control, and report their work using the Government's Cost Breakdown Structure. Why? The CBS was not designed to support the work to be performed. This means that the contractor must develop a means for accruing its cost and reporting based on the WBS and then reporting its costs based on the Government's CBS. Such a reallocation of costs is necessary in spite of it requiring something between a magical process and a formal algorithm.

In summary, do not attempt to use the Government's Cost Breakdown Structure to plan, manage, and control the contract work. Instead, concentrate on planning the system or process by which WBS-based cost data can be translated into CBS-based cost data.

17.7.3 ASSISTING IN THE DEVELOPMENT OF A SYSTEM ARCHITECTURE

The cost estimator and cost proposal planners must participate in the development of a system architecture that will be used during the preparation of the cost proposal. This is particularly critical during the preparation of a proposal to the Air Force for a major system development contract. The system architecture is critical for a contract in which the Work Breakdown Structure is based on the hardware and software architecture. This is because the Air Force cost data bases and cost estimating systems are based on the hardware and software to be developed, not on the types of work to be performed.

When required to prepare a Work Breakdown Structure based on the hardware or software architecture, work packages describing the work to be performed do not appear before the ninth or tenth level of the WBS. This means that the top level architecture for hardware and software system must be defined very early in the design effort so that planning the cost estimating efforts can begin. A cost estimating specialist should assist the design team in the development of the system architecture so that the costing effort will have all necessary inputs.

Note: One of my major nightmares is being assigned to a system development proposal as the Senior Cost Estimator when the existing cost data base is based on types of work and the cost estimating relationships are based on the hardware architecture.

17.7.4 ASSISTING IN THE DEVELOPMENT OF A CONCEPT OF OPERATIONS

It is a major fact of life that 99 percent of the people working on a proposal have very little experience in the development of a concept of operations that provides all the information needed by the costing team. It is likely that an experienced Management Volume Leader is the best qualified person to prepare a concept of operations, because that person will be the most knowledgeable about essential cost-related matters such as:

- where the contract work will be performed (one site or multiple sites)
- what skills levels will be required for the project personnel
- what special facilities and resources will be required
- when major activities will begin and be completed

- how the project staff will be organized and deployed
- what are the contract deliverables and when are they delivered
- which subcontractors will perform work and what work will they do
- what resources will be provided by the Government (GFI, GFE, GFF)

It is likely that even an experienced Management Volume Leader will not know the type, amount, and depth of the information required by the cost estimating team. But when a cost estimating person works with and provides support to that Volume Leader, it is extremely likely that the resulting concept of operations will provide the information needed by the cost estimating team. Usually, this cooperative effort requires one long day of hard work by two people.

17.7.5 Preparing the Cost Data Log and Collecting Cost Data

If you wait until the RFP has been received to begin collecting cost data, it is too late, and your corporation is entering the competition blindfolded. Cost data must be collected and recorded into a logbook as a routine practice. The record should identify the source of the information, the date the information was obtained, the confidence that one can have in the information, and the follow-up information collection effort.

Cost data can be collected by many means and from many sources, all legal and open to the searcher. Of course, some people believe that cost data comes from illegal leaks by unethical people. But in the real world, the cost data is collected from the following sources:

- The Commerce Business Daily - the Government daily newsletter announcing the award of contracts and the dollar value of a contract with which you are familiar.

- Newspaper Announcement - the business section of the local newspaper that cites the contract awards made to local companies on procurement with which you are familiar.
- Wage Benefit Surveys - the national surveys conducted by the Department of Labor and the local area surveys conducted by a consortium of companies.
- Freedom of Information Act - the law that allows interested parties to obtain costing information about contracts not otherwise available without a FOIA request.
- Professional Journals - the publications of the professional organizations that include articles about the work being performed by competitors and their dollar value.
- Interviews with Competitor's Personnel - the interviews with personnel seeking employment with your company can reveal much information on benefits.
- Subcontractor Proposals to Your Corporation - their cost proposals will provide much information about their fully-burdened rates that will be valuable in the future.

Usually the Marketing Specialist and the Acquisition Manager will collect the cost data and will enter that data into a cost log. Note: marketing personnel seem to be talkers and not writers, and they communicate mostly by talking not writing. So beware.

17.7.6 PREPARING THE COST PROPOSAL OUTLINE

Cost Proposals for Major System Procurements - When planning a proposal for a major system development procurement, the preparation of the outline for the cost volume becomes a major activity. The Cost Volume outline is the means by which the Cost Volume Leader ensures that the volume includes; responds to all RFP requirements, all required representations and certifications, the cost realism and cost risk sections, and special matters such as costs for CLINs and CDRLs. Most such proposals also require a listing of every major hardware and software item to be procured, plus a summary listing of every major purchase of materials and supplies to be made during the contract. Every Cost Volume must include a detailed outline and should have a compliance matrix, both of which denote where every response to the volume requirements can be found. Additionally, the cost volumes submitted by major subcontractors to your corporation will likely be required with your cost proposal. The outline for such a cost volume should include the following major matters:

- Form 33 signed by a responsible corporate official
- Representations and Certifications signed by a responsible corporate official
- CDRL list and the costs for deliverables (if required)
- CLIN list and the costs for each CLIN item
- Table of Contents; Lists of Abbreviations, Acronyms, References, Compliance Matrix
- Listing of Major Procurements and Purchases and their schedule
- Cost Breakdown Structure and Work Breakdown Structure
- Brief summary of assumptions associated with cost estimating

When preparing a proposal for technical services, technical studies, A & E design work, analytic studies, and similar procurements, the cost proposal will include much of the same material as the system procurements, but the number of items and pages will be significantly less.

17.7.7 IDENTIFYING REQUIREMENTS FOR THE CSCS AND CSSR

The Request for Proposal will specify the type of financial reporting system to be employed by the contractor for tracking and reporting its performance. Three levels of financial reporting are described in the FARs, DARs, and DOD Instructions:

Contract Funds Status Report - used in small contracts and requires very little structure. Also requires quarterly reports.

Cost and Schedule Status Report - used in medium-size contracts and requires a WBS and a cost accounting system. Can be used for financial and schedule performance assessments. Also requires monthly reports.

Cost Schedule Control System - used in major contracts and requires a WBS and a major cost accounting system. Used for financial and schedule performance assessments. Also requires monthly reports, variance analyses, and plans.

When the RFP requires the contractor to implement a CSSR reporting system, the contractor faces an appreciable amount of work to prepare the inputs and to generate the outputs. It is highly recommended that every project requiring the CSSR system to be used have at least one financial person, plus a project planner, on the project management staff assigned to this responsibility. During the contract, there will be changes to the project schedule, activities, milestones, budgeting, and reporting, so both of these key individuals will be needed to revise the WBS, prepare cost estimates for the new or revised WBS work packages, and to prepare the cost inputs to the automated system used for CSSR records and reporting.

When the RFP requires the contractor to use a CSCS reporting system, the contractor faces an incredible amount of work to prepare its inputs and outputs, plus preparing the monthly reports and the variance analyses. It is highly recommended that a full-time staff of three to five financial and planning specialists be assigned to the task of implementing the CSCS. During the contract, there will be changes to the project schedule, activities, milestones, budgeting, and reporting, so these key individuals will be needed to revise the WBS and prepare cost estimates for the new or revised

WBS work packages. Preparing, reviewing, and approving the financial inputs, outputs, and reports, in addition to performing the variance analyses, will be a major effort that must be reflected in the cost estimates for WBS work packages related to project management.

Every contractor must be aware that the expense associated with the development and validation of a Cost Schedule Control System will probably be in excess of $6 million dollars minimum. In addition, the time required to develop and validate a new CSCS will be in the order of two years minimum. A requirement for the contractor to have a CSCS that has been validated by government specialists is probably the most severe mandatory requirement in the RFP. If you don't have one, you will probably be judged to be an incompetent bidder.

17.7.8 IDENTIFYING THE MAJOR COST DRIVERS

One of the first activities of the Senior Cost Estimator is to identify those parts of the proposed work program that are the high cost items. These items are referred to as the "cost drivers" because they largely drive the overall costing effort and represent the greatest amount of the costs being proposed. Examples of the major cost drivers include:

- For technical studies, technical support contracts, A & E design contracts, labor-related costs will certainly account for an overwhelming portion of the proposed costs. Subcontractor costs in such procurements are almost entirely labor-related costs.
- For software and hardware development programs, labor-related costs will account for a major portion of the proposed costs, followed by the costs associated with computer hardware and software resources and by special facility costs.
- For O & M, administrative support, and technical services

contracts, labor-related costs will account for virtually all of the proposed costs, followed by minor facility and equipment costs.

- For construction contracts, labor-related costs will account for over two-thirds of the total construction costs, with one-third of the costs related to materials, supplies, and equipment rental.
- For all contracts, the major cost driver is the fully-burdened hourly rate of the employees; the burden on those direct labor rates covers costs such as taxes and fringe benefits, direct and indirect overhead, general and administrative costs, and profit.
- On technical services contracts, the burden placed on the hourly rates paid to subcontractors can be a major cost driver. Such burdens can range from 45% to over 250%.
- On mega-procurements, such as operating a national laboratory, the cost of money, or the interest paid on money to fund the contract, is a major cost driver.
- On contracts in which extensive work is performed by subcontractors, the major cost driver is the double burden associated with the overhead, G & A, and profit of the prime contractor being added to the overhead, G & A, and profit of the subcontractor.

If the overall costs being bid on a major procurement are to be reduced, attention must be focused on the major cost drivers. Only reductions in the cost drivers can make the bid costs become more reasonable. Focus on them first.

17.7.9 Collecting Preliminary Quotes for High-Value Items

The Procurement Specialist can obtain preliminary, non-binding quotes from many suppliers and vendors with a telephone conversation. These preliminary quotes on matters such as the probable costs for major, commercially-available items such as basic materials, hardware, instruments, and software will allow the cost estimating team to have a ball-park estimate of these costs during the early work on the cost proposal. These procurement inquiries will also provide some information related to the time required to procure the high-value items and information about the changes likely in certain items.

Very few, if any, manufacturers or developers of high value items will estimate the probable costs five years into the future, so plan to use costs for current or near future items only. You cannot expect suppliers or manufacturers of high-technology items to provide any long-term cost information in these days of rapid technological changes. So you will have to apply your own discount or escalation factors because they won't. Just remember that any cost estimate is better than no cost estimate.

17.7.10 ATTENDING TO SEVERAL CRITICAL ACTIVITIES

Coordinating with Proposal and Design Teams - It is imperative that the Cost Volume Leader and the Senior Cost Estimator begin coordinating their needs with the activities of the proposal team and the design team. This coordination effort is critical to ensure that the cost volume requirements are reflected in the work planning by these two teams. It is particularly important that the design team and the proposal team know what is required from them and when it will be required from them. The proposal and design teams must not neglect the substantial costing activities.

It is recommended that the Cost Volume Leader attend the early planning and scheduling efforts of the design and proposal teams so that the costing needs are recognized. It is also recommended that the Cost Volume Leader attend the short daily meetings of the proposal management staff and that the Senior Cost Estimator attend the daily design review meeting of the design team. Maybe it is not necessary to attend all of the daily meetings, but it is difficult to know in advance which meetings are not critical.

Identifying Cost Discriminators, Ghosts, Uh-Ohs - The Proposal Manager, Volume Leaders, Proposal Planner, and Senior Cost Estimator must begin identifying the major cost drivers, cost risks, cost discriminators, and cost ghosts as soon as possible. Cost matters should always be a major concern of these managers; because costs will be a major consideration by the Government for contract award. It is recommended that the proposal management team regard the cost matters in the same light as the technical and management issues that must be addressed in the proposal.

One major proposal decision is whether to address matters such as cost risks and cost risk mitigation in the Cost Volume only or whether to address those matters (discretely so) in the technical and management volumes and in the design documentation also. Costs and cost risks are so important that they must be addressed, without a doubt. Virtually all RFPs states in unambiguous terms that cost data must be included only in the Cost Volume, but that does not include cost matters such as cost reduction efforts, cost risk mitigation efforts, and cost estimating models and algorithms. Just be adroit in this matter.

Defining the Cost Realism Issues and Approaches - Since a cost realism section in the cost proposal can be a major proposal expense, it is imperative that two decisions be made as early as possible, namely: are you going to prepare a cost realism section?, who has the skills to prepare a cost realism section? If the answers are No and No One, then this is a moot issue. But if the answer is Yes and the You Are the One, then begin work and worrying.

17.7.11 Using IRAD Projects to Reduce Cost Risks

It is illegal to use Independent Research and Development projects that are funded totally or in part by the Government to accomplish tasks during contract performance. However, it is legal to use IRAD project results during contract performance if the IRAD project was completed prior to award of contract. It is also legal to use IRAD results if the Government has not provided any funding for the IRAD program. So, it is possible, under certain conditions, to use the results of IRAD projects to add value to the proposal, like:

You have developed a broad-based technology, partly or in whole using Government funding, that is applicable to a wide range of research and development efforts within the corporation, and then the results can be used to support specific issues associated with a proposal. Which cannot to be used to perform work after contract award.

You have used corporate-funded IRAD projects to resolve technical issues, to mitigate technical risks, and to develop a technology that will be a major discriminator in your proposal. The results of these IRAD projects can be used without any reservations both in the proposal phase and the contract work phase.

IRAD projects, even with Government funding, can be used with significantly less legal concern in efforts such as: an investigation into the state-of-the-art of emerging technologies, the development of technology-related data bases, development of technologies that are unrelated to work during contract performance. It is recommended that legal advice be obtained in the matter of using Government-funded IRAD results in the proposal by your corporation and by your subcontractors. Do not fail to interrogate the subcontractors about this matter.

17.8 PLANNING TO STAY LEGAL AND ETHICAL DURING COSTING

It is recommended that every person with a major responsibility for costing conduct themselves as if they were likely to become the target for a criminal investigation or the subject of an expose in the New York Times. This means that the costing effort and the costing staff must be able to withstand the severest of criticism if major cost overruns occur after contract award. I always prepared cost proposals with the view that I can take a lie-detector test with a clear conscience and both the corporation and I would come through completely legal and ethical. I highly recommend that all cost proposal personnel act similarly.

Document your costing assumptions, cost models, cost data bases, and cost-estimating relationships and the reasons for their selection. Document (in writing) the instructions issued to all proposal and design personnel related to their costing efforts, stressing the matter of personal and corporate integrity. Perform a realistic cost risk assessment and prepare a thorough cost realism section. Maintain a record of all costing decisions and cost data forms. CYA

The most common defense against illegal or unethical conduct during the preparation of the cost proposal is; "I did not know that I was receiving wrong information". To which I say; "Damn it, it is your job to know if you have received information that is in error or is patently wrong". You will find the courts very unsympathetic with the "I did not know" defense. Plan your costing effort with the highest standards for honesty, completeness, and accuracy.

Part IV

THE MAJOR PROPOSAL
MANAGEMENT ACTIVITIES

CHAPTER **18**

THE MAJOR PROPOSAL REVIEWS

18.1 THE IMPORTANCE OF THE FORMAL REVIEWS

The importance of the formal proposal reviews cannot be understated because these reviews contribute to winning proposals in so many ways. Every proposal review increases the chances of winning the competition measurably, so each review is more than desirable. The formal reviews are essential.

The subject of reviews may seem dull, but an overwhelming number of proposals with which I have been associated that failed to win a contract were ones that had not had formal reviews or had not conducted the formal reviews properly. Not all losses are attributable to poor reviews, because some proposals are destined to lose for other higher-level reasons. But given an true opportunity to win, proposals with good, complete, structured reviews are definitely more likely to win any competition.

The formal proposal reviews should receive the attention and support of high-level corporate officers who have a stake in the contract after contract award. These high-level managers normally are the ones who provide the money, personnel, and resources to the proposal, which is the highest form of commitment to winning.

18.2 THE GOLD REVIEW- THE CORPORATE REVIEW AT THE ONSET

The first formal proposal review is appropriately titled the Gold Review because the review team is comprised of high-level corporate officers (who either wear the gold braid or earn the most gold, pick your own definition). The Gold Review, which is usually held within seven days after the receipt of the RFP from the customer, typically, is comprised of the following elements:

First Major Topic - An overview of the procurement, which includes the marketing intelligence, a background discussion of the customer, the reason for the procurement, the key organizations and personnel associated with the procurement, the likely competitors, and other information acquired by the marketing specialists. This briefing is usually presented by the Acquisition Manager or the Marketing Specialist.

Second Major Topic - A top-level summary of the proposal, including: type of contract, types of work involved, types of deliverables, special procurement provisions, major risks associated with the work, special provisions in the procurement, estimated contract value (based on a should-cost analysis), personnel skills needed to perform the work, special procurements needed for the proposal and for contract work, top-level proposal schedule and milestones, documents governing the deliverables and work standards, estimated cost of the proposal, and win themes and discriminators. This briefing is usually presented by the Proposal Manager.

Third Major Topic - An overview of the hardware and software to be designed, developed, and tested; level of work required to develop the hardware and software designs, level of work needed to develop the systems after contract award, major items to be procured for work during the design phase and during contract performance, major risk areas associated with contract performance, special staffing needs of the design team; special facilities and key personnel needed after contract award, and role of subcontractors in the design work and during contract performance. This briefing is usually presented by the Chief Engineer.

Fourth Major Topic - A review of the special issues associated with the procurement and the contract work, such as: security requirements, place of performance, subcontracting goals, government monitoring, penalties for failure to meet contract requirements, ongoing efforts to minimize risks, and commitment of key project personnel. This briefing is usually presented by the Proposal Manager or the Proposal Planner.

Fifth Major Topic - A summary of the resources (money, personnel, facilities) required to: prepare a winning proposal, prepare the system design, demonstrate the system, meet the security requirements, and develop the supporting specifications and plans. This topic also discussed the proposal process to be used by the proposal team. This briefing is presented by the Proposal Manager during non-system design proposals and by the Proposal Manager and the Chief Engineer during system design proposals.

Last Topic –Is a summary of the critical matters that require support and commitments from the high level corporate managers, who are members of the Gold Team Review.

After the briefing has been completed and all the supporting documentation has been reviewed by the Gold Team members, an open discussion begins. Typically, the Gold Team Review requires most of a working day. The specific hard copy given to the Gold Team members includes all material presented in the briefings, plus additional material such as the requirements-driven outline and the detailed proposal schedule and milestones.

18.3 THE BLUE REVIEW - THE PROPOSAL MANAGER'S REVIEW

The second major review in the proposal process is the Blue Team Review, a review that includes the proposal management team, directed by the Proposal Manager. The attendees are the Proposal Manager, Volume Leaders, Plan Leaders, Production Coordinator, Senior Cost Estimator, Chief Engineer, and Proposal Planner. This review typically can be completed in one very long day, but two days may be required to complete this review when large procurements and major proposal efforts are involved.

The Blue Review initially focuses on the following matters: examining the entire proposal in a draft version, identifying missing elements, identifying weak responses, ensuring that all proposal requirements are being addressed, assessing the quality of the writing, identifying the need for more or less graphics, and assessing compliance with the editorial

policy. The principal results of the Blue Review are specific instructions to Volume Leaders, Plan Leaders, and the Production Coordinator in areas such as:

- identifying areas needing writing or editorial attention
- identifying proposal requirements that do not have responses
- committing proposal resources to get-well activities
- identifying areas in which volumes and plans need integration attention
- estimating resources needed to prepare a Red Review copy of the proposal

The major inputs to the Blue Review include: current version of the proposal text and graphics, latest list of proposal requirements and compliance matrix, and current proposal outline with requirements allocated to the page level.

18.4 THE RED REVIEW- THE IMPORTANT REVIEW BY OUTSIDERS

The most important review of a proposal is the Red Review, in which the near final version of the proposal, text and graphics, is subjected to detailed scrutiny by high-level corporate managers, consultants, and proposal specialists. The Red Team may request a less-than-one-hour briefing by the Proposal Manager that summarizes the customer, procurement, competition, types of work, key issues, win themes, proposal milestones, and similar top-level issues. The team is provided with a near final version of the proposal text and graphics, the latest list of proposal requirements, a compliance matrix, and the current proposal outline with requirements allocated to the page level.

The three most important activities of the Red Team are ensuring that: (1) the issue of the corporation being a competent bidder is answered, (2) the proposal is complete by responding to every proposal requirement, and (3) the proposal is compliant with the proposal instructions. Then the Red Team reads and evaluates the proposal, all volumes and plans included, from the viewpoint of the customer. The Government evaluation scheme is used in this process. The Red Team is obligated to take a harsh look at all risk management matters also.

The time at which the Red Team Review is conducted is a compromise between the time needed by the production staff to prepare the final version of the proposal and the time needed by the proposal writers to prepare a good version of the text and graphics. For smaller proposals for services and studies, the Red Review can be as late as five days before the delivery date of the proposal, provided the proposal is in good shape production wide. For larger procurements with a longer time to prepare the proposal and with many pages and multiple volumes, the Red Review should be completed ten days before the delivery date.

18.5 THE GREEN REVIEW- THE COST RELATED REVIEWS

In some companies, the Green Review Team is a high-level corporate effort to monitor the cost aspects of both the proposal and the design effort on a continuing basis after the Red Review has been completed. Typically, the Green Reviews are associated with major proposals that involve major corporate financial commitments, involve high dollar-value contracts, and have a long time, normally about three months, for the preparation of the Cost Volume. The Green Reviews reassure higher-level corporate managers that the corporation will be able to financially support the contract work, that the cost risks to the corporation are identified and are manageable, and that the corporation will not lose a large amount of money on the contract.

The essential inputs to the Green Reviews are matters such as the cost strategy, the should-cost analyses, the cost risk mitigation efforts, the cost realism requirements, the documentation required for costs estimating relationships, the major purchases and procurement schedules, and the short-term and long-term investments required by the corporation. When the Green Review Manager is unstructured and when the Green Review team does not have excellent, directly related costing estimating expertise, the corporation can lose bundles of money. It can rightly conclude that Green Reviews are absolutely necessary for major procurements.

18.6 THE OTHER REVIEWS

18.6.1 THE PURPLE REVIEW - THE FINAL MANAGEMENT REVIEW

If the Red Team feels that the proposal, at the time of their review, needs major revisions and additions, then the Purple Review is required. This review, when required, occurs between the Red Team Review and the final assembly of the proposal by the production staff. The Purple Team is comprised of several members of the Red Team who ensure that certain critical issues identified by the Red Review are addressed properly in the final draft of the proposal. This review is usually one in which several knowledgeable senior managers review and approve the final draft of the proposal without a formal presentation or meeting.

18.6.2 THE PINK REVIEWS - THE ONGOING HIGH-LEVEL REVIEWS

In some companies, the Gold Team can appoint a Pink Team as a high-level corporate effort to monitor the proposal effort and the design effort on a continuing basis after the Gold Review has been completed. Typically, these interim Pink Reviews are staffed by members of the Gold Team who are scheduled to be members of the Red Team later. The Pink Reviews are associated with major proposals that have a long time, normally about three months, for the preparation of the proposal. The interim Pink Reviews reassure higher-level corporate managers that the proposal effort is progressing well and that the Gold Team guidance is being implemented, plus they give high-level management an opportunity to provide continuing inputs and direction.

18.6.3 THE INTERNAL PROPOSAL VOLUME REVIEWS

The proposal team should conduct daily reviews directed to: verifying the status of the ongoing proposal effort, identifying major problems or issues, assessing the productivity of the proposal writers, and allocating additional resources to problem areas. These proposal-internal reviews, which begin after the Gold Review, are of two types:

The **daily proposal status review** which is conducted by the Proposal Manager, Volume Leaders, Proposal Planner, Plans Leaders, and hopefully, the Corporate Officer Responsible. In these brief reviews, twenty minutes maximum, each member of the proposal management team gives a two to three minute summary of the status of his volume and discusses problems encountered, need for more time or resources, risks newly identified, need for more pages, and personnel matters. After each such summary, the Proposal Manager schedules a subsequent meeting time with one of the management team to discuss and resolve the problems.

The **daily volume status review** which is conducted by each Volume or Plan Leader with his/her staff of writers. The results and highlights of the earlier proposal status review are presented to the writers, after which the writers have two or three minutes to discuss the status of their modules or units, the need for more time, the need for assistance or resources, the need for more pages, and the near-term delivery schedule. After each such summary, the Volume Leader meets with each of the writers (not as a group) to resolve his/her issues.

During the proposal for the Medicare Transaction System, the Proposal Manager had twice-daily status reviews in which every member of the proposal and design teams participated. At least 30 people had to commit at least 3 hours each day for meetings at which every person was expected to say something. This West Coast approach to proposal status meetings meant that we lost about 10 pages of text each day for two feel-good meetings. What an incredible loss of productivity.

CHAPTER 19

THE MAJOR PROPOSAL MANAGEMENT ACTIVITIES

19.1 CONDUCTING THE PROPOSAL KICK-OFF MEETING

The proposal kick-off meeting is one of the most important meetings in the proposal process because it sets the tone for the entire proposal team during the coming weeks. The meeting is attended by all members of the proposal management staff, proposal writers, subcontractor personnel assigned to the proposal staff, production staff members, Senior Cost Analyst, Corporate Officer Responsible, Acquisition Manager, and other interested parties.

The meeting is organized, planned, and conducted by the Proposal Manager, because the meeting belongs to him or her. High-level corporate officers and other big wheels are not needed.

The meeting begins with an introduction by the Proposal Manager, who must make a very good first impression on all members of the proposal team. If the proposal is for a system development contract, the Chief Engineer is introduced, and he/she must make a very good impression on the proposal staff. The Volume Leaders and Plan Leaders are introduced.

The agenda for the Kick Off meeting is not fixed in stone, but the

Proposal Manager must address the following items, at a minimum:

The Procurement - The requirements of the RFP and its associated or referenced documentation are summarized. The type of work to be performed or the system to be designed is described briefly. The customer and its procurement history are summarized.

The Competition - The likely competition, by name and reputation, are discussed, along with their strengths and weaknesses. The means by which the competitors will be beaten are highlighted.

The Proposal Win Themes and Discriminators - Are important matters that make your firm the logical winner of the competition and eliminate the competition. This is known as the real pep talk because it convinces the proposal staff that they are winners.

The Proposal Process - The systems, documentation, processes, and organizations associated with the preparation of a winning proposal are briefly summarized. The important activities and procedures in the proposal process are discussed.

The Key Interface Requirements - The ground rules, procedures, and protocols governing the interfaces between the proposal team, design team, production staff, and corporate support personnel are summarized.

The Proposal Schedule and Milestones - The Gantt chart for the proposal schedule and the milestone chart are presented, followed by a brief commentary on the activities in the critical path. The formal reviews are emphasized.

The Facilities and Resources Available - The facilities and their location (including offices, eating places, restrooms, safes/vaults) are described and the corporate resources (including library, office supplies, office services) are described.

The Security Requirement - Procedures for the receipt, handling, storage, and use of classified and proprietary information are stated in very firm terms, as well as the handling of magnetic media and the reproduction of classified text or graphics is addressed.

The Proposal Outline and Page Budgets - The list of proposal requirements, the requirements-driven outline, and the page budgets are presented is a summary form visually and in a detailed hard copy format for the writers.

The Project Team and Its Organization - The members of the project team (your firm, the subcontractors, and the consultants) are introduced. Their strengths and their roles in the contract are described.

The Special Issues and Requirements - This subject area covers a wide range of critical issues and special aspects of the procurement, the customer, and the work to be accomplished.

At the end of the kick off meeting, the proposal staff should know how you are going to win the contract and be convinced that your corporation is the best for the contract. The staff should also believe that you have the best team for doing the work.

19.2 ENSURING THAT ALL FINANCIAL MATTERS ARE RESOLVED

If it is true that the love of money is the root of all evil, then the lack of money must be the second-most cause of evil. This is particularly true in the matter of competitive proposals. Given all other factors (like market intelligence, contract experience, facilities, management tools) being equal, the proposal team with the most financial resources wins an overwhelming amount of the contracts. So, in spite of the beliefs of many high-level corporate officers, the proposal with the greatest financial resources wins.

The Proposal Manager prepares an estimate of the amount of money needed to prepare a winning proposal, based on his/her experience, understanding of the procurement, and the competition. The Chief Engineer prepares an estimate of the funding required to prepare a winning design and to meet the RFP requirements, based on his/her experience and understanding of the demands of a system design effort. The Volume Leaders and Plan Leaders prepare estimates of their money requirements as inputs to the Proposal Manager in the preparation of total proposal costs. The professional opinions of these managers and leaders are the most important opinions when defining the funding requirements for the proposal and design efforts.

When the higher-level corporate managers tell the Proposal Manager and the Chief Engineer how much funding will be provided (the Bid and Proposal budget, which is usually significantly lower than the required amount), then these two managers can plan their work. This funding must be agreed upon at the start of the proposal effort so that the proposal can be the best possible for that amount of money. Not necessarily the best proposal, but the best for the money.

Once the Bid and Proposal budget has been defined, the Proposal Manager can establish the budgets for proposal planning, management, writing, and production. Charge numbers are defined for personnel and for procurements, and time charging procedures are published. Without funding, the proposal work cannot really begin; if it does, the auditors from the Defense Contract Audit Agency will introduce some stress into your life.

When working on proposals, I charged my hours to my Proposal Center's B & P account number. But when I traveled to another proposal site, I charged my travel expenses to an overhead account from the group responsible for the proposal. Every quarter, the DCAA auditors checked my records and found that I was charging two different accounts, from two different groups simultaneously. I invariably had a pleasant meeting with the auditors every quarter for about ten years to discuss the reasons behind that difference and to point out that the DCAA-Corporate agreement on proposal-related time charging did permit such accounting procedures. I became so familiar to the DCAA auditors that frequently I would eat lunch with them.

19.3 PROVIDING A SECURITY BRIEFING TO THE PROPOSAL TEAM

One of the most neglected activities associated with the preparation of classified proposals and classified designs is failing to include a security briefing at the kick-off meeting. It is preferable to have a member of the Security Department conduct the briefing, so that they

THE MAJOR PROPOSAL MANAGEMENT ACTIVITIES ➤

are the black-hat people for a change. This security briefing is particularly important when special security measures are required for sensitive (SCI, Code Word, Black) proposals. Every member of the proposal team and the design team must attend a security briefing and sign attendance sheets.

As a part of the security briefings, the Proposal Manager must state the security requirements associated with proprietary information. Proprietary information can be provided by the corporation, by the subcontractors, and the vendors. Do not neglect this matter, because you really do not want to be giving depositions and participating in court cases.

19.4 ASSIGNING KEY PROPOSAL PERSONNEL TO LEADERSHIP ROLES

The recruitment and assignment of key proposal management personnel to leadership roles is one of the most important activities of the Proposal Manager. The manager should ensure that the Volume Leaders and Plan Leaders have extensive experience in proposals, have proven that they are excellent writers, and have leadership qualities. Without a good or excellent second echelon of managers, the Proposal Manager will have to assume their technical and management roles in addition to the demands of the overall proposal.

The two approaches to the assignment of key personnel to a proposal are: (1) If the Proposal Manager is inexperienced, non-aggressive, hesitant, then the Volume Leaders must be experienced and must assume the leadership role. (2) If the Proposal Manager is dynamic, aggressive, and experienced, then the Volume Leaders do not have to assume these roles or characteristics. Management is very important, but leadership is critical.

In the Navy, if the Commanding Officer aboard a ship is a pleasant, likable person, then the Executive Officer is the SOB; conversely, if the Commanding Officer is the SOB, then the Executive Officer is the patient, understanding, and likable type. This management style is probably applicable in proposals, but I prefer that all proposal leadership roles be given to SOBs.

Some of the most disastrous proposal efforts in my career were those in which the Proposal Manager was a line manager with no understanding of the leadership requirements associated with proposals. These line managers invariably selected project managers or senior technical personnel to work as the volume leader's people with no proposal know-how. The Proposal Manager thought that his job was to sit in his office, hold daily meetings, and brief management; the Volume Leaders thought that their jobs were to sit in their offices, hold daily meetings, and edit the text prepared by their writers. In every such instance, we lost, in spite of a lot of money being expended.

19.5 PREPARING AND ISSUING THE PROPOSAL WRITERS FOLDERS

The preparation of a Writers Folder is a very effective method for ensuring that the proposal and its supporting documentation meet the highest standards for quality. For small proposals being prepared by two or three key people, the Writers Folder may not be a necessity. When a large team of proposal writers is assembled, the Proposal Manager of the Volume Leaders must prepare the folders for the writers. A typical writer's folder will include the following items:

Proposal directive, RFP elements, proposal outline, list of proposal requirements, a requirements-driven outline, marketing intelligence, win themes and discriminators, editorial policy, security instructions, proposal schedule and milestones, review requirements, policy for dealing with the production staff, list of references in a reading room, approved list of acronyms and abbreviations, organizational structure of the proposal team, telephone numbers of key proposal personnel, telephone numbers of corporate support personnel, location of office supplies, limitations on dealing with subcontractors and vendors, examples of material from prior proposals, general information on corporate facilities, points of contact locally, personnel security clearance matters, and mailing and Email addresses.

If this list seems to be a burden, think about the time that a Volume Leader would expend telling each one of a twenty-person proposal writing team about these matters, personally. The time for talking and Xeroxing would limit Volume Leaders productivity and patience, be assured.

19.6 PREPARING THE SUBCONTRACTOR DATA PACKAGE

Many proposal team members seem to believe that the Contract Specialist or the Subcontractor Specialist assigned to the proposal staff will prepare the Subcontractor Data Package. These dreamers are destined for a major surprise, because members of the proposal team, and in some instances the design team, must prepare most of the material included in the Subcontractor Data Package. Essentially, the Subcontractor Data Package is a miniature (only in scope) version of the Request for Proposal data package that was received from the Government. The proposal or design team must prepare a bid package for the subcontractor. Good luck.

After the teaming agreement has been negotiated by the corporate staff and the subcontractor corporate staff, the work to be performed by the subcontractor (s) and the level of effort envisioned for the subcontractor(s) will be defined. Then the proposal management staff can begin the preparation of the following material for the Subcontractor Data Package.

Statement of work, list of deliverables (CDRL), references, extracts from the Government's RFP, list of references, proposal outline relative to their area of participation, list of proposal requirements for their area of participation, elements of the Writers Folder, proposal preparation instructions, proposal schedule, interfaces with the proposal management staff, mailing addresses, telephone numbers, Email addresses, WBS work packages, list of governing regulations and instructions, security requirements, and teaming agreement.

The Contracts Specialist and Subcontract Specialist will prepare the general information for the Subcontractor Data Package, which will include instructions for preparing and presenting the cost related data and directions for the submission (time, place) of their proposal for their share of the contract work. They will issue this material to the subcontractor(s) in sufficient time for their proposal to be incorporated into the final draft of the proposal.

This task of preparing the Subcontractor Data Package is a time-consuming endeavor and a significant amount of work is necessary to accomplish this matter. The Proposal Manager should assign one senior member of the proposal staff to the task of preparing the data (bid) packages for the subcontractors. And that senior person should start as soon after the corporate officers make a handshake agreement with the subcontractor. There is no time to spare in this matter. Do not neglect this critical matter, unless you enjoy the pain of crises.

19.7 ALLOCATING THE FACILITIES, EQUIPMENT, AND SUPPLIES

Prior to the arrival of the proposal writers, the Proposal Manager will (should?) already know what facilities, equipment, and services will be available to the proposal team and will have an idea how they will be allocated to the Volume Leaders, Plan Leaders, and other key proposal personnel. The Proposal Manager will have rented the computers, printers, and a proposal file server, and will have acquired the applications software needed by the writers. Note: all computer-related hardware and software will be in the same version. This equipment, along with a local area network dedicated to the proposal, should be installed prior to their need by the writers.

The Proposal Manager should know how many and what type of offices, conference rooms, work bays, and other facilities (security vaults, whatever) will be available to the proposal team. Such facilities can be at a corporate proposal center, a dedicated work area that has been leased specifically for the proposal, or spaces within the corporate groups involved in the procurement. It is very important that all such facilities be in one contiguous area. These facilities will be allocated to the Volume Leaders and Plan Leaders, based on their estimates for the number of writers to be assigned to the volumes/plans.

Supplies and services are provided by a dedicated proposal center, as part of their normal operating procedure. If not working in a corporate proposal center, the Proposal Manager must specify the means by which supplies and services will be acquired and establish charge numbers for such matters.

19.8 ENFORCING THE PROPOSAL POLICIES AND PROCEDURES

The Proposal Manager expends much time in the preparation of the proposal policies and procedures, but that time will be completely wasted if they are not enforced. The policies and procedures, which are always in writing, include such topics as:

- adhering to the proposal's editorial policy
- dealing with vendors or suppliers for price and delivery quotes
- adhering to the policy for classified material and proprietary information
- controlling the interface between the writers and the production staff
- controlling the baseline proposal text and access thereto
- recording labor-hours to the correct B&P numbers
- controlling casual conversations between the proposal staff and outsiders

- discussing division of the contract with subcontractor personnel

These policies are discussed in the proposal kick-off meeting and are included in the written material in the proposal writers' jackets. Occasionally, following a major compromise, the entire proposal team is assembled and the policies and procedures are presented again, in a very forceful manner.

19.9 MONITORING SCHEDULE AND COST PERFORMANCE

The Proposal Manager must always be aware of schedule and cost matters on a daily basis, more so than the average line manager. The proposal teams schedule performance is an extremely critical concern because so much work must be performed by so many different members of the proposal staff within a very short period of time. Basically, the Proposal Manager uses a milestone management system in which the proposal costs and schedule performance are monitored at critical milestones, like:

- Milestone 0   Bid decision by corporate management
- Milestone 1   Completion of the Gold Review
- Milestone 2   Completion of the Blue Review
- Milestone 3   Start of the Red Review
- Milestone 4   Release of the proposal for production
- Milestone 5   Delivery of the proposal to the customer

It is noted that these milestones are normally about 7-10 days apart during a 45-day proposal effort and that the corporate financial reports seldom are produced with such frequency. Therefore, the Proposal Manager must base his cost performance assessment on the number of days or hours that the proposal staff has worked. Using these hours and the average salaries for the proposal staff, used earlier to prepare the proposal budget, cost performance can be estimated with reasonable accuracy. An experienced Proposal Manager should know the time-phased cost estimates by heart and, relying on the daily proposal review meetings, know how well the costs are conforming to the estimates, based on the number of people on the proposal staff.

Schedule performance is usually assessed by comparing the number of pages scheduled to be ready for Blue Review, Red Review, or final production. At the onset of the proposal, the Volume Leaders and Plan Leaders prepare an estimate of the number of pages of text and the number of graphics in their volumes. Daily, the Volume Leaders report their progress toward this estimate, which is verified by the Production Coordinator who knows how many pages of text and how many graphics have already been processed. Second-level editorial and production milestones include: author approval, Volume Leader approval, and Proposal Manager Approval.

It is very easy for the Proposal Manager to lose track of the costs incurred, so the Volume Leaders must provide reliable updating information related to man-hours charged to their parts of the proposal. It is extremely easy to lose track of the cost and schedule performance of those personnel assigned to the supporting plans because they are seldom in the critical path. And the critical path is where the Proposal Manager should focus attention.

19.10 CONDUCTING THE DAILY PROPOSAL REVIEW MEETINGS

The Proposal Manager conducts a daily proposal status meeting that is attended by the Volume Leaders, Plan Leaders, Production Coordinator, and the Corporate Officer Responsible. The Proposal Planner and the Acquisition Manager may attend the Proposal Manager meeting, but their role is more passive because they really have very little, if anything else, to report. On special occasions, the Chief Engineer, Contract Specialist, Senior Cost Estimator, and Subcontract Specialist may attend the daily meetings, but it is usually better to limit the number of attendees at the daily meetings in order to keep the meetings short.

The Proposal Manager begins these meetings with a summary of any new matters, such as amendments to the RFP or answers to questions by the customer; the manager then provides a top-level assessment of the status of the proposal effort and the problems that he/she has noted. The Volume Leaders and Plan Leaders review the status of their writing effort and discuss the problems that they have encountered. Each member of the proposal management staff should limit his/her reports to three minutes or less. The daily status meetings should be no longer than 20 minutes.

19.11 DEALING WITH CORPORATE PERSONNEL AND OUTSIDERS

Every member of the proposal staff will probably deal with specialists working on the corporate staff at some time, in matters as diverse as: travel arrangements, travel advances, security clearances and vaults, office services and supplies, timecards and pay checks, company vehicles, personnel office support, procurement office, legal services, computer repairs and services, and weekend air conditioning. All proposal team members should be allowed direct access to these corporate personnel without approval or prior notice to the proposal management staff; after all, they are professionals and should be treated as such.

This liberal policy governing the proposal staff's dealing with corporate personnel does not extend to their dealings with outsiders, however. The Proposal Manager must state in his kick-off meeting the policies for dealing with people or organizations outside of the proposal team. Normally, proposal writers do not talk with vendors or suppliers about proposal matters, and writers are directed not to talk about the proposal effort with outsiders, whether employed by their corporation or by another corporation. Members of the proposal staff are reminded that, if they are being interviewed by other potential employers, they cannot discuss, or even acknowledge, their current or recent work on the proposal.

19.12 MAINTAINING THE PROPOSAL REQUIREMENTS DATABASE

It is very likely that the proposal requirements data base prepared in the initial planning effort will need additions because of factors such as:

- Amendments to the RFP issued by the customer
- Answers to questions issued by the customer
- Additional win themes and discriminators developed by the proposal team
- Additional material deemed essential by the Proposal Manager

These items will be entered in the proposal requirements data base and to the compliance matrix, after which they will be distributed to the Volume Leaders for inclusion in their volumes and in their outline for the volumes. These entire proposal requirements data base will be used by the Red Team to ensure that the proposal is complete and compliant.

19.13 SUPPORTING THE GOLD AND RED TEAM REVIEWS

The Proposal Manager is responsible for organizing and supporting the Gold Reviews and the Red Reviews, but the Proposal Manager is not a member of these review teams. Instead, the Proposal Manager ensures that all material, including drafts, notes, data bases, requirements, planning documents, and market intelligence are readily available for the reviews. It is important that such material provided to the subcontractors and consultants are returned and that all copies of the review material is accounted for. This is a very important responsibility that is usually shared by the Proposal Manager and the Production Coordinator.

19.14 OBTAINING CONCURRENCE ON MAJOR PROPOSAL PROMISES

The proposal team is invariably faced with two types of promises to the customer during the preparation of a proposal: (1) promises to deliver what is required by the RFP and its documentation, and (2) promises to deliver items not required by the RFP material. Since the proposal must provide the deliverables specified by the customer, the proposal team has few problems with these items. Management invariably approves such promises because they are necessary to win the procurement.

Sometimes it is necessary to make promises that are not required by the procurement documentation, so that your proposal will have features that are above that offered by any of the competition. These offerings are a high form of discriminators. These promises can include such matters as use of IRAD results, use of proprietary material or data, or use of enhancing software at no cost to the customer. The promises can also include special office support and facilities for government contract monitors, an upgrade of your computer system to handle new capabilities, the use of cutting edge technology beyond the RFP requirements, and the use of other corporate resources to enhance the contract performance.

All of these promises require the corporation to make moderate to substantial investments and to incur additional, non-reimbursable expenses. So it is imperative that the Proposal Manager obtain corporate concurrence on these promises. Do not neglect to obtain concurrence, or you may face the corporate equivalent of a firing squad.

19.15 ASSEMBLING TIGER TEAMS TO RESOLVE MAJOR ISSUES

There has probably never been a major proposal in which serious problems were not encountered, so it is more than likely that the Proposal Manager will need to assemble special work groups, named Tiger Teams, to resolve a problem quickly. Tiger Teams are usually comprised on senior technical and management experts who can address a specific problem and can develop a work-around plan in a very short time. The members of the Tiger Teams are like a Fire Brigade they put out proposal fires.

Tiger Teams are necessary when the RFP requirements are changed by amendments to the RFP or by answers to questions submitted by contractors. Such changes can include a drastic lowering of the man-hours that the Government thinks is needed for contract performance or a increase in the number and type of contract deliverables. Other changes can include areas as diverse as a need to infuse an emerging technology into your design, to provide computers and facilities to a contract monitoring team along with special software, and to use Government testing facilities instead of corporate facilities. These major issues must be resolved quickly, and that is the job of the Tiger Teams.

19.16 MAINTAINING THE STORYBOARDS ON THE WALL

One of the most effective management techniques used in many proposals is the use of story boards that are pinned on a wall for viewing by all concerned personnel. When the storyboards are posted, everyone can see how the proposal is organized, how the pages are allocated, and what will be addressed on every page of each volume or plan. The keen proposal person can readily determine the number, type, frequency of graphics and visual impact items, and determine where the integration issues (sections in a volume or volumes) are most critical.

The use of storyboards is a very effective method for ensuring that the writers understand what is to appear on every page in every volume. The storyboard is a one-page unit that depicts the text, graphics, and visual impact items to be included on the page. The storyboard includes a sketch of the graphics and notes on its contents and it identifies the subject of each paragraph on the page. Basically, every writer and the proposal management staff know what every page will contain when a complete set of storyboards has been prepared.

One of the most effective management techniques associated with posting of storyboards is to initially put blank pages, pink in color, on the wall, one for each page, with the titles from the proposal outline, the proposal requirements, and the writer assigned to that page printed on those pink pages. As the storyboards are approved by the Volume Leader, the storyboards, yellow in color, replace the pink pages. When the final text and graphics are approved, white pages replace the yellow storyboards, and providing a complete view of the entire proposal.

The reasons that I like the concept of using colored pages for the storyboards posted on the walls are quite simple. First of all, if a writer is behind schedule, the pink pages attract the attention of corporate managers instantly. Second, it is very easy to assess the general status of the proposal with one swift look at the wall and the colors of the pages. Third, inconsistencies, omissions, and integration issues are very apparent to the viewer.

19.17 MIGRATING FROM DESIGN TEAM TO PROPOSAL TEAM

In every proposal requiring a concurrent system design and demonstration, the Proposal Manager must work closely with the Chief Engineer to ensure an effective and efficient transfer of the system design staff to the proposal staff. Some of the system design personnel must work on the technical volume because they are the only ones who know well what is being proposed. In some proposals, the key members of the proposal team will attend some of the design review meetings to obtain a better understanding of the system being proposed. The advance knowledge is essential for the Volume Leaders to plan the migration and integration of the two staffs.

In most proposals, the systems architecture and systems engineering specialists are available to work on the proposal team earlier than those people doing the detailed design and the system demonstration. Fortunately, the system architect and system engineering skills are the most essential needed for the technical volume. Some of the detailed design personnel who prepared inputs to the design specifications are very effective when assigned to the technical volume because they have already written much about their design.

Since the Volume Leaders know a bit about the system design and the concept of operations, based on their attendance at certain design reviews, they can determine how the technical and management volumes should be organized and presented. Then they can plan for an orderly transfer of design personnel to their proposal staff. In every instance, this migration is a very complicated activity that requires the best of management skills.

19.18 PREPARING THE INPUTS TO THE COST PROPOSAL

The Proposal Manager is responsible for the preparation of the basic cost data that is used by the Contracts Specialist and Cost Estimator in the preparation of the cost proposal. This matter of preparing basic cost data is one of the most demanding aspects of preparing a major proposal. The proposal team and design team cannot prepare the basic cost data until a series of major activities have been completed, mostly by the proposal management staff, like:

- a WBS must be prepared to at least the fifth level, preferably to the seventh level
- position descriptions must be prepared for the labor categories to be used in costing
- the project organization must be such that it allows the collection of costs by WBS
- costing assumptions and cost estimating relationships must be identified
- should-cost estimates should have already been prepared
- estimates for a Standard Day and the modifying factors must be developed
- a concept of operations for work after contract award must be defined
- a vision of the entire proposal must have been developed
- a form must be designed for recording the detailed man-hour estimates

When my employer was working on a proposal for the development of a combat system for the Navy as a subcontractor to Martin Marietta, we had to prepare detailed data to a cost proposal from us to MM. MM had been assigned about 55 WBS items for our cost estimating, with instructions to prepare monthly cost summaries for a five-year work program. When we prepared twelve data sheets for each WBS work package for each year, we had 3300 data forms. Then, when MM wanted us to submit costs by calendar year and by government fiscal year, we had 6600 forms. When we had other requirements added for options, we had over 7000 data forms. After an intense effort to integrate the forms, our final cost proposal to Martin Marietta had over 1280 pages.

19.19 INTEGRATING THE SUPPORTING PLANS WITH THE PROPOSAL

It is imperative that the Proposal Manager, Volume Leaders, and Plan Leaders have an integration review in which each plan is examined in detail to ensure that it is consistent with the technical volume, management volume, cost volume, and other plans. In this review, the key proposal management personnel read the plans for consistency with their volumes and they identify areas in which the volumes and plans must be modified. Since the Plan Leaders usually work in isolation from the proposal team, the Plan Leaders frequently do not fully support the assumptions and algorithms used to prepare the cost data and the Cost Volume.

The greatest problems encountered in integrating volumes and plans are important matters as diverse as:

- the assumptions used in preparing cost data
- the use of different job titles and different facilities
- a misunderstanding over responsibilities and authorities
- purchasing instead of leasing (or vice versa)
- differing organizational structures and chain of command
- not including similar reports and reporting procedures
- naming the wrong personnel for important roles

This inter-volume review becomes more important when the standards, specifications, and plans prepared by the design team are to be integrated with the proposal documentation. For example, the Facility Plan associated with the Management Volume must reflect the special facility requirements that the design team will need after contract award. The Staffing Plan associated with the Management Volume must agree with the work schedule prepared by the design team.

CHAPTER **20**

THE MAJOR DESIGN TEAM MANAGEMENT ACTIVITIES

20.1 THE UNDERSTANDINGS NEEDED BY THE CHIEF ENGINEER

It is absolutely essential for the Chief Engineer to fully understand the work to be performed, the system to be delivered, and the services to be provided. He/she must be able to translate customer requirements into performance and design requirements and to formulate an approach that will fully satisfy these requirements. The Chief Engineer must have both depth and breadth in the key areas of experience, education, and skills in order to fully understand the system requirements. And the Chief Engineer must have the leadership skills needed to direct a team of engineers, scientists, analysts, and specialists in the preparation of a winning design that fully satisfies the customer's requirements.

The challenges facing the Chief Engineer can be due to stringent operational requirements, to the procurement documentation, and to the technologies associated with the system to be designed. Factors such as the delivery schedule, the design and development process, the requirement to reuse software, and lower skill levels dictated for operations and maintenance personnel are certainly stressing. Some of the more difficult concerns are not truly technical or engineering in nature; for example the requirement to install a new combat system and to transfer the operations of an existing operational system with no loss of service or data can be stressing.

There have been few, system design and development contracts that were easy and understandable from the onset. So the abilities and understandings of the Chief Engineer, as a leader, a manager, a technical specialist, and a problem solver, are critical to the success of the system design effort. When the proposal and system design start from a poor understanding of the work and system requirements both the proposal and the design are doomed.

On one major proposal effort to the HCFA, we began our proposal and our design efforts for the development of a major software system, after our marketing specialist assured us that the contract would be for an all-new system. After two months on the design and proposal, we received, in response to questions to HCFA, an estimate of the man-hours needed to develop this major software system. The Government estimate was about 15% of the hours that we had estimated. Immediately several of us knew that the lower man-hour estimate meant that the Government envisioned a re-engineering of an existing system, which I had been saying for two months.

Four of our competitors had developed software systems used by HCFA but they were proprietary items; unfortunately, we did not have an existing system. Basically, we had been working on a completely non-responsive proposal and an irrelevant design, and the corporation was faced with a decision: (1) Make a No Bid decision, or (2) prepare another type of proposal and a design based on a re-engineering approach. High-level corporate management decided to bid anyway and the proposal and design efforts became something of a Bataan Death March. Of course, we lost. I did not blame the Chief Engineer too much, but he should not have followed the promises of the Marketing Specialist blindly.

20.2 DEFINING THE ORGANIZATION OF THE DESIGN TEAM

The Chief Engineer is responsible for organizing the system design team so that the personnel resources are used in the most efficient manner. The organizational structure of the design team will depend upon whether the contract will be for a hardware system with embedded software or for a software system applicable to one or more hardware systems. If the contract is directed to the development of hardware, the design team's organization will emphasize the architecture of the system to be developed. If the contract is directed to the design and development of a software system, then the design team will be organized with major emphasis on software design, software development, and software testing.

While the Chief Engineer's actions will be tailored to the requirements of the procurement, there will always be certain organizational structures that are similar in all system development proposals. For example, virtually every design team has a Team Leader who directs the:

- Software Design Team
- Systems Engineering Team
- Systems Demonstration Team
- Data Management Team
- Hardware Design Team
- Logistics Specialty Team
- Systems Documentation Team

The logistics specialist team will include those with skills in logistics engineering, training, technical documentation, maintenance and operations, spare parts and outfitting, and with a Logistics Engineer heading the team. The systems engineering team, in addition to the systems engineers will include specialists in areas as diverse as interface control, human factors, EMI-EMC, configuration management, and system safety.

Hopefully the Chief Engineer will ensure that the structure of the design team meets the general criteria for good management. The team will be organized so that at least three Team Leaders, but not more than seven Team Leaders, report to him/her.

20.3 ASSEMBLING THE FACILITIES, EQUIPMENT, AND RESOURCES

The Chief Engineer and his chief henchman must assemble a wide range of facilities, equipment, and resources for use by the design team. The complexity of this requirement is apparent when faced with the following:

Offices, Conference Rooms, Work Bays, Utility Areas, Administrative Areas - These facilities should be collocated in an area with good working conditions. Several conference rooms, one large and two or three small ones are needed. Offices are needed for the Chief Engineer, Project Manager, and about five of the leadership cadre. Work bays are completely adequate for the majority of the design team, but many desks, chairs, lamps, chalkboards, and file cabinets will be needed. Storage and utility areas are also needed.

Computers, Printers, Software, Networks, Internet Access - These computer-related items are needed, one computer per member of the design team. All computers must have the same operating system and the same applications software. A design team local network should be installed, with a few computers having access to larger area networks. A minimum of two printers should be available in the design facilities.

Administrative Resources, Special Features - These items include the office supplies, office equipment, office services, reproduction machines, facsimile equipment, and binding equipment. They also include food service items such as a refrigerator, a microwave oven, a coke machine, and an eating area. Voice mail, E-mail, USPS mail services are essential.

Corporate Resources and Capabilities - These items include resources such as: the corporate library, local transportation, security support, purchasing office, personnel services, and travel support.

20.4 ASSIGNING KEY DESIGN PERSONNEL TO LEADERSHIP ROLES

The Chief Engineer is responsible for assigning the right people to the leadership roles within the organizational structure of the design team. This means that the proposal team must not be comprised of what the press gang found wandering around the halls and playing computer games. The proposal team must have the exact skills needed to prepare a winning design and to prepare that design within 60 to 70 days. And the team must be directed and managed well in order to be productive and effective at all times.

Hopefully, the Chief Engineer will already know most of the design team before the design work begins. So, the general experience, years of experience, special skills, and work ethic will already be known. Otherwise, the design team may have a tendency to spend more time thinking about problems than the time spent solving the problems. Whereas the Proposal Manger relies on his Volume Leaders and Plan Leaders, the Chief Engineer must rely on the heads of his hardware design, software design, system engineering, logistics, and engineering groups for his second tier of leaders.

20.5 INTEGRATING SUBCONTRACTORS INTO THE DESIGN TEAM

Some subcontractor personnel assigned to the design team merely show up and watch the activities around them. But most subcontractor personnel assigned to design team are very professional and they work long and hard to prepare a winning system design. The general rules for the integration of the subcontractors into the design team are:

- they work at your design team facilities and use your resources
- they work under the supervision of your managers and leaders
- they can work together on design matters in their area of expertise
- they can work in small groups with other subcontractors

Probably the most important matter associated with the integration of engineers, specialists, scientists, and writers from your subcontractors is; their labor contribution must at least equal the share of the contract proceeds that they will receive. Twenty-five percent of the money means that they develop twenty-five percent of the design by providing twenty-five percent of the staff on the design team.

If a subcontractor will be responsible for a major configuration item after contract award, then that subcontractor will provide the skilled personnel to the design team to develop the design for that item. No free rides.

20.6 BRIEFING ALL DESIGN PERSONNEL ON THE REQUIREMENTS

In the first major meeting of the design team, the Chief Engineer must conduct a briefing that emphasizes the design requirements, the proposal requirements, the risks, the deliverables, the demonstration requirements, the schedule and milestones, and the risks that have been identified. Further, the Chief Engineer summarizes the Proposal Directive, the organizational structure of the design teams, the procedures and interfaces, security requirements, and the documentation requirements. The design process and the design review requirements are summarized. At the end of this briefing, all members of the design team should have a broad base of understandings, with all members having the same understandings.

It is helpful for the Chief Engineer to describe the team members, to introduce the key subcontractor personnel, and to specify the design requirements that they will be concerned with. The leaders of the design team are introduced and their responsibilities and authorities are summarized. The briefing ends with an enthusiastic pep talk that encourages all members of the design team to work together.

20.7 PREPARING THE DESIGN SCHEDULES, MILESTONES, AND DEADLINES

The Chief Engineer must have exceptional skills in the preparation of the schedules, milestones, networks, and deadlines needed to manage, monitor, and control work performed by the design team. This requirement is particularly stressful because of the limited time available to prepare a hardware and/or software design, to prepare the specifications and technical documentation, and to conduct a system demonstration. The need to transfer design personnel to the technical proposal later in the design process imposes severe scheduling demands that cannot be ignored.

Ideally, the development of the design team's schedules begins with a top-level Gantt chart in which timelines indicate the time allocated to each major activity. This top-level Gantt chart is the basis for the identification of the important milestones associated with each major design activity. With the top-level Gantt chart and the major milestones, the preparation of the planning network can be done. After this top-level effort, the schedules, milestones, and networks are resolved to more details, and then to even more details. The critical path in the design activity can be readily seen and monitored by the Chief Engineer and his leaders when these management tools have been prepared.

The graphics associated with the schedules, milestones, deadlines, networks, and deliverables intrinsic to the design effort are posted in a central location so that every member of the design team can readily see where their efforts fit into the overall system design. The use of diamond-shaped icons that are not filled in to denote those milestones not achieved and filled-in (blackened) diamond icons to denote milestones achieved has a hell of a visual impact to those managers viewing the networks and to the designers who did not meet the milestone.

20.8 CONDUCTING THE DAILY DESIGN REVIEWS

The Chief Engineer must schedule daily design reviews in which members of the design team present the results of their work to other members of the team. In these reviews, the designers will present the results of their work since the last presentation. Typically, a team will present the results after the following milestones: completion of the design analysis, completion of the design, and completion of the integration of their work with other design teams. During a Martin Marietta proposal for a Navy combat system, the daily design reviews went as follows.

The leader of an element of the design team made a formal presentation to the entire design team, beginning with the analysis of the requirements for the display used by the operators of the tactical system. The designer reviewed the customer requirements and the performance requirements and then evaluated three available display units against these requirements. Three displays (Hewlett Packard, Aydin, and Techtronics) were considered in the evaluation, and the design analysis results were; each of the three displays fully satisfied the requirements, but the Aydin was selected as the display on its technical merits.

When the design leader's presentation was over, the Chief Engineer asked for comments from the design team. The logistics engineer stated that the Aydin display was not in current inventory, and the costs to the Navy for establishing a new set of spare parts and repair parts would mean the Navy would add at least $7,000 for each part of the Aydin display to our bid costs. The training specialist stated that only the Hewlett Packard display has existing training manuals and training aids, and that the Navy would experience higher costs for training with the other displays. The human factors specialist stated that there are no differences in operator productivity between the three displays. The technical documentation specialist stated that only the Hewlett Packard display had technical documentation for its system that met Navy standards.

As a result of this one design review, the Chief Engineer, with the complete concurrence of the design team, selected the Hewlett Packard display. The design team leader was in complete agreement because he had not considered factors other than technical performance

Having design reviews each day, virtually all of which are

completed in less than 30 minutes, has proven an amazingly effective technical management technique. By this process, all factors associated with a design element are considered, and all members of the design team were informed of design decisions at an early date. As the design reviews continued, the reviews became more effective. Every Chief Engineer should schedule design reviews daily.

20.9 PREPARING THE SYSTEM ARCHITECTURE AND DESIGN

The Chief Engineer and his senior technical staff, which should include an engineer with system architecture skills, prepares a system architecture and a top-level systems design before turning the detailed design and analysis work over to the technical staff. The system architecture effort begins with a review of the overall system requirements and the identification of the major subsystems. When the major subsystems are identified, the system requirements are organized by subsystem, then allocated to the subsystems, and the interfaces between the subsystems are identified.

When the subsystems are identified and the requirements have been allocated to the subsystems, then the system architecture is extended to the next level, and namely the equipment group for hardware and configuration item for software. The subsystem requirements are then allocated to the equipment groups or to the configuration item. At this point, the system engineers take over the process and extend the system design to the next two or three levels of detail, allocating specific requirements to specific equipment, components, units or whatever the levels may be.

While assisting a project manager preparing a presentation on a corporate design effort associated with an ammunition handling robot, it was apparent that he and his staff were at a loss. I stepped in, at the suggestion of a higher-level manager, and supported the effort, drawing on my systems engineering experience on the High Energy Laser Weapon System. I began with an analysis of the requirements and it was apparent that the systems architecture included the following subsystems:

- *the frame subsystem which included the suspension and mounting features*
- *the electrical and hydraulic subsystem that powered the robot*
- *the propulsion subsystem that moved the robot*
- *the navigation and guidance subsystem that piloted the robot*
- *the forklift subsystem for lifting and lowering ammunition pallets*
- *the computer subsystem that controlled the overall robot*

I then allocated the system requirements to these subsystems and identified the next level of the architecture to the technical staff. Seeing the structure and approach, they took over and quickly prepared an excellent presentation for the aerospace manufacturer's review team.

20.10 IDENTIFYING TECHNICAL AND SCHEDULE RISKS EARLY

It is imperative that the design team identify every risk that is associated with their design, their technical approach, and their technical management style. Rest assured, there has never been a system that, during its design and development phase, did not have any technical or schedule risks. Some of the risks can be controlled by the contractor, but some risks cannot be controlled by the contractor, no matter how well they manage risks. Examples of technical risks that are beyond the control of the winning contractor include:

Risks Associated With Manufacturers, Vendors and Suppliers

Ceasing production of an essential hardware item, discontinuance of support for a commercially-available CASE tool, failure to deliver critical items on-schedule, failure of hardware and software to perform as promised.

Risks Associated with Government Provided Items

Non-availability of test facilities, failure to provide equipment, inadequacy of technical information and documentation, changes in the Government funding schedule, and changes in technical direction and requirements.

Risks Associated with Subcontractors

Small firms going out of business, small firms being unable to obtain skilled personnel, large firms undergoing reorganization, conflicts of interest between differing contracts, firms being barred from Government contracting.

The risks associated with outside organizations are usually minor when compared with the risks that the prime contractor faces in the contract, because the prime contractor is responsible for most of the contract work and for the most difficult aspects of the contract work. Very few contractors are willing to have a subcontractor responsible for most of the risks or the most serious risk, because the prime contractor will be the firm held liable for fines and contract cancellations.

The Chief Engineer, his staff, and his consultants must make a diligent effort to identify the technical risks that are associated with the system design that his team has prepared. It seems to be a rule that half of the design team members state confidently that their part of the design has no risks and that the other half of the designer state that their work involves unknowns which means risks. If the design team does not actively engage itself in a risk identification, risk analysis, and risk control effort during the proposal phase, they are going to be roasted alive during the Gray Beards review.

The one rule to remember in the area of system design and development is; every new system has technical risks and every technical risk certainly has a schedule risk and probably has a cost risk.

20.11 PREPARING PERFORMANCE AND DESIGN SPECIFICATIONS

As part of the proposal and design effort, the Government requires the bidder to prepare design specifications, and sometimes performance specifications to be submitted as part of the proposal. The design specification, known as a "C Spec" or a "Design-to Spec", presents the details of the hardware and software design in a format specified by the Government. When the C Spec is completed, any other competitor, or even some Government laboratory, could build the system that you have proposed. This means that you have reduced the risks, prepared the design, and provided a technical roadmap that could be used by another organization. This situation is akin to cowboy who, on being told that the roulette wheel was crooked, stated "But it is the only game in town".

The Chief Engineers assign the task of developing the text and graphics that describe each specific unit or component of the system design to members of the design team, the ones that developed, tested, and validated the unit or component. The preparation of the design specification will invariably require a bigger effort than the writing of the technical proposal or of any of the supporting plans. Without a doubt, the preparation of a design specification will be a major effort for the design team. Particularly since engineers and scientists are notoriously poor writers.

It is imperative that the Chief Engineer allocate the time, personnel, and resources to the preparation of the specifications during the planning of the design effort. Remember that few people write more than one page per day and that a design specification can entail over 300 pages.

20.12 PLANNING AND CONDUCTING THE SYSTEM DEMONSTRATION

Virtually all proposals for the design and development of software systems require a systems demonstration prior to contract award in which the essential functions of the software system are shown to the Government technical personnel. The system demonstration requires the bidder to assemble a hardware system on which the proposed software system will be shown to meet the customer's essential requirements. The hardware suite will be a close replica of the hardware system that will ultimately be used with the software being developed. The demonstration software will include the critical elements of the system being proposed to the Government.

These demonstration requirements mean that the bidder must assemble a computer-based hardware system that has the essential capabilities and the same operating system required by the software that the bidder is designing. A dedicated computer site must be established and be fully operational for the demonstration. Computers may be purchased or leased; when the computers are military types, such as the AN-UYK-34 are required; the equipment must be loaned by the Government to the contractor.

The Government will specify the requirements for the system demonstration, including the features of the software system that must be demonstrated. The Government directions for the system demonstration will state what capabilities must be demonstrated, the sequence in which the features of the software system will be demonstrated, and what data must be collected as proof that the system meets the performance and design requirements.

The Chief Engineer designates a team of computer hardware specialists and operating system specialists to assemble the demonstration system; this team will select the site, acquire the hardware, integrate the hardware, and test the hardware. The team will handle the routine aspects of the software demonstration, while the design and test personnel perform the demonstration and collect the data.

20.13 PREPARING THE DATA NEEDED FOR COSTING

If there is one task that every design engineer and every software specialist detests and avoids as much as possible, it has to be the preparation of the detailed cost data needed for the cost proposal. Basically, the cost data preparation includes major items and activities such as:

- **The Make or Buy Decision -** in which the designers determine if you will fabricate a hardware item or if you will buy that item.
- **The Procurement Specifications -** in which the designers prepare a formal statement of the equipment to be purchased so that manufacturers or vendors can prepare their bids.
- **The Fabrication Estimates -** in which the engineers prepare a

detailed statement of the types and amounts of work needed to fabricate hardware items.

- **The Lines of Code Estimates -** in which the designers estimate the total lines of code, the complexity of the code, the source of the code, the use of existing code, and the amount of code to be developed.
- **The Materials, Supplies, and Services Estimates -** in which the designers estimate the amount of materials and supplies to be used, the supply inventory and supply services needed, and the level of maintenance to be used.
- **The Test and Integration Estimates -** in which test engineers prepare a complete description of the test facilities, activities and resources needed; logistics specialists define the integration activities needed for the overall system.
- **The Facilities and Logistics Estimates -** in which the designers prepare an estimate of the personnel and procurement requirements associated with facilities, test equipment, training, maintenance support, spare parts, storage, and materials handling.
- **The Operations and Maintenance Services Estimates -** in which the designers estimate the number of operating and maintenance personnel required by the system, the skill levels of the O & M personnel, and the supervisory personnel required to manage the system.

It is very likely that many more costing items will be prepared by the design team, because many additional cost items will be identified when preparing documents or conducting analyses such as: Level of Repair Analysis, Configuration Management Plan, Maintenance Plan, Training Plan, and Spare Parts and Test Equipment Analyses. Many cost items will be identified when preparing the Project Work Breakdown Structure and the system architecture and design. As a conservative estimate, the preparation of the essential cost input data will require almost every member of the design team working full-time for at least two weeks.

20.14 DEALING WITH OTHER KEY PERSONNEL

The Chief Engineer and the design staff will deal with many other organizations, individuals, and activities during the design effort. Some of these dealings and interfaces will include:

Proposal Manager - The senior manager of the overall proposal effort who provides overall direction and advice to the Chief Engineer, Volume Leaders, and Plan Leaders; coordinates the responses in all volumes, issues the top-level planning efforts, and win strategy papers.

Cost Volume Leader - A member of the proposal team who prepares the outline for the Cost Volume and determines what material is required from the design team, management team, and other teams. This leader specifies the type and amount of documentation required for the cost volume for the design team.

Senior Cost Estimator - A member of the cost proposal team, who deals with the design team in areas such as: should-cost analyses, detailed cost data, cost estimates, manpower estimates, costing assumptions, costing models, costing documentation, and costing instructions.

Production Coordinator - The senior production manager from the proposal center who coordinates and integrates the publication of material prepared by the design team, serves as the interface between the design team and the production staff, and maintains the master file of all proposal related material.

Subcontracts Specialist - A senior member of the proposal team who deals directly with management of the subcontractors, coordinates the preparation of the subcontractor data package, and works frequently with subcontractor personnel on the design team.

20.15 MEETING THE SPECIAL SECURITY REQUIREMENTS

When a classified system is being proposed, the Chief Engineer must ensure that the security requirements for the design team are presented in a forceful, authoritative manner to all of the staff. This briefing should be conducted by a member of the corporate security staff at the onset of the design effort. The briefings must be followed with daily checks by members of the design team and with random checks by the security office personnel. And the Chief Engineer must support the checking personnel without hesitation.

When the design team is working on a system that falls within the special security category (SCI, Code Word, Black, or whatever), the security procedures, controls, and activities become even more restrictive. And the Chief Engineer must be even more stern in these matters. If a company has a violation of a special security requirement, the Government will likely decide that the company does not have the safeguards and discipline to meet the special security needs of the contract. And you will lose because of security.

20.16 SPECIAL DESIGN TEAM ACTIVITIES

The Chief Engineer and the system design team are burdened with many other critical responsibilities, such as:

- preparing questions to the customer regarding the technical matters in the RFP
- requesting requests for deviations or exceptions to the system requirements
- performing risk analyses to identify risks to their company
- identifying inconsistencies in the procurement documentation
- preparing for the technical presentations following proposal submittal
- reducing risks associated with the system by analyses and breadboards

CHAPTER 21

THE PROPOSAL WRITING ACTIVITIES

21.1 THE TOP-LEVEL REQUIREMENTS FOR PROPOSAL WRITING

A proposal effort can have the best planning, best management, best production, and the best reviews, but these proposal activities cannot compare in importance to the work of the proposal writer. The proposal writing, without a doubt, is the most important activity in the preparation of a winning proposal, because the Government and customer must evaluate what you have written in order to award the contract to you and your corporation. Every other activity in the proposal process, however essential, is subordinate to the importance of the proposal writers.

The text in a proposal is so important because Government Contract Officers deal in words and select winners based on words. The Contract Officer is probably unaware of such matters as detailed planning, high-level reviews, and great printing. The Contract Officer is required, by law, to execute a contract of words, not graphics, not magnetic media, not briefings, not viewgraphs, not talk, just the written word.

The Proposal Writer must be a very structured, disciplined person who deals regularly in the written word. No sales people with their spoken words, expensive suits, and arm waving. Writers belong to the reading-writing class, not the talking-listening class. They are successful when they:

- understand their role in the proposal process
- respond well to their leaders and managers
- have a good command of the English language
- comply with the proposal's editorial policy
- write about subjects that they know something about
- write in response to the proposal requirements
- meet their page budgets and deliver their material on-time
- write in a confident, convincing, formal style
- rely more on words than on graphics

In one of the greatest books ever, "Ogilvy on Advertising" Ogilvy, of the largest, most successful advertising agency in the world, Ogilvy and Mather, states emphatically, that the ad writer is the most important person in the advertising business. The account executives, the marketing specialists, the administrators, who outnumber the professional ad writers by about 5 to 1, are not as important as the ad writer. So it is in the proposal process the writers are the most important personnel in the proposal effort.

21.2 MANAGING THE PROPOSAL WRITERS AND THEIR WRITING

It is critical that the Proposal Writers work in a structured environment, in which their instructions are simple, unambiguous, and documented. Such an environment means that the Proposal Manager and the Volume Leaders must provide written material to the Proposal Writers. Remember; Proposal Writers are writers because they are not talkers. One must communicate with them by way of written instructions in order to be effective.

Managing the Proposal Writers is much like the normal project management activities, in which the manager plans the work, organizes the workers and resources, assigns work to people, monitors the work in progress, provides management direction, and reviews the ongoing work at regular intervals. Basically, one only needs to change the words "work and workers" to "writing and writers", and the essential elements of managing the proposal writers becomes clearer.

The single most important activity in the management of the Proposal Writers is to provide the Proposal Writers Folder to each of the writers; this folder, which is normally prepared by the Volume Leader, basically provides the following information to the Proposal Writer:

- the proposal requirements
- the writing style
- the review activities of the volume
- the editorial policy
- the resources available

- the proposal schedule
- the graphics standards
- the formal reviews
- the overall proposal process
- the proposal outline

I have found the following management approach to be most effective in the preparation of a proposal volume:

Assigning the Writing to Writers - As the Volume Leader, I always make assignments to writers in small packages, in which the easiest writing efforts are done first. These writing assignments are in units of one or two pages at a time, never a complete section to be prepared by a writer on a single assignment. I specify the number of pages and the time at which a final draft must be completed; normally, I allow a maximum of three days for a unit of two pages.

Reviewing Work in Progress - Each day, I hold a review of my volume with all of the writers assigned to that volume. I require each writer to state their progress since the prior day. I try to never let a day pass without an assessment of progress. Remember, writing assignments normally last for only one or two days, so the volume reviews must be on a daily basis.

Controlling the Writer's Outputs - When the writer has prepared a draft of his unit, I review and comment on their material within a couple of hours. After reviewing my comments, the writers modify their unit and return it to me for approval. They then can turn their material over to the Production Coordinator. Then I give the writers a new assignment of one or two pages in another unit.

Probably the most important aspect associated with the management of proposal writers is that the Volume Leader must display a thorough knowledge of the writing process and train their writers to become better writers. You can easily and quickly tell when the Volume Leader is incompetent, because that person sees his/her role as that of an administrator or a proofreader.

I have observed that when writers are not managed well, proposal writing is accomplished in three steps. In the first step, people write about what they know best and like to write about and to Hell with the proposal requirements. After their tail feathers are burned a bit, those people write about what they believe the customer should really have asked for. Then, after another burning of the tail feathers, they become proposal writers and write about what the customer wants to know. As a Proposal Manager or Volume Leader, you must make each writing assignment a one-step process. This is called leadership.

21.3 PREPARING STORYBOARDS AND PAGE LAYOUTS

One of the most effective techniques used to plan, coordinate, manage, and produce a winning proposal is the use of storyboards. Basically, a storyboard depicts the layout and presentation for a specific page in proposal volume; the page layout can depict text only, text with visual impact items, text with graphics, or graphics only. The topics of each paragraph are identified, the type and size of graphics are depicted in a sketch, and the placement of text and graphics is illustrated. When the storyboard is completed, the writer knows what each page will look like.

Sometimes, during rush efforts, a page layout technique is used instead of storyboards to depict the layout of each page in a section (or even a volume). The Volume Leader normally prepares a page layout sheet for each section in the volume, depicting what the pages will look like, with text and graphics being presented in a macro style.

The value of storyboards and page layouts is three-fold. First, the writers know exactly how much text and graphics is to be prepared in each unit or module; this knowledge means that the writer will be very focused and very productive. Second, other proposal writers can see where their units and modules fit into the overall volume and can integrate their writing with that of the other writers. Third, corporate managers can view the storyboards and page layouts and see what the proposal will look like when completed.

When working as a Volume Leader or Proposal Manager, I incorporate storyboards into the proposal process in the following general sequence, which is based on a volume limited to a maximum of 25 pages:

- I post 25 blank sheets of paper on the wall, with one sheet for each page to be prepared
- I use the outline and page budget to determine the subjects for each of the 25 sheets
- I then partition the 25 pages into smaller groups that match the page budgets for sections
- I print each of the major titles from the outline onto the pages (blank no longer)
- I block out space on each page for paragraphs and/or graphics
- I then denote the topic for each paragraph and prepare a rough sketch of each graphics
- I post the 25 pages with sketches, titles, and paragraph topics back onto on the wall

21.4 WRITING THE TEXT IN A CONVINCING STYLE

The Proposal Writer must believe that our proposal will be a winner because we offer the best buy to the Government and we are committed to providing quality services and products. This attitude permeates the writing of the text and the preparation of the graphics, believe me. If a writer is not convinced that we are going to win, he/she will be unable to write in a convincing style. Remember that confidence radiates from the text and lack of confidence casts a dark shadow on the text.

The single most important method for writing in a convincing style is to write with personal pronouns like. "We have the best staff because we have been a leader in the field of laser technology for over 15 years". Hopefully, the editorial style guide will accommodate this technique for aggressive writing. Of course, if personal pronouns are not used, strong statements such as "SAIC has been a leader in laser technology for over 15 years" are almost as good.

Never waffle or equivocate on any important statement in a proposal. Write as if you will be the person to perform the work or develop the product yourself. Let your personality come through to the Government evaluator who will become more enthusiastic about your statements and will probably give your proposal a higher score.

Remember that it is much easier to tone down the text than it is to boost the text late in the proposal writing effort. My advice is, from the first sentence, write with an aggressive, confident style, and then let the Red Team or the Volume Leader decide how to make the proposal more like pabulum later.

During a proposal to the Ships Parts Control Center in Mechanicsburg, PA, our marketing specialist, our designated Project Manager, and the Corporate Officer Responsible would not make a firm decision on where we would perform the work and where our office facilities would be located. The customer wanted an office in Mechanicsburg to ensure responsiveness, but the Project Manager wanted to stay in his McLean, VA office suite. The corporate manager did not want to risk offending his designated Project Manager, so, in the management volume, we had to waffle the matter of the main office's location. The SPCC proposal evaluation team recognized this non-decision and we lost miserably; proof that you cannot write in a wishy-washy manner.

21.5 WRITERS' DEALINGS WITH THE VOLUME LEADER

While the structure of the proposal team means that writers are assigned to and work under the supervision of the Volume Leader. The Volume Leader is responsible for the overall volume, and the writers are responsible for specific sections or modules within that volume. But, in fact, the proposal writers and the volume leaders work as a team, with the writers following the instructions and schedules of the Volume Leader. When a writer is uncertain about the scope or content of a section, module, or unit within the volume, the Volume Leader is obligated to clarify the matter and provide guidance on all such matters.

The Volume Leader should meet at least once each day with the writers' assigned to his/her volume; actually twice a day is preferable. Such team meetings should last less than 20 minutes. In addition, the writers must have direct, informal access to the Volume Leader at all times for matters such as receiving writing assignments, discussing approaches and problems, and delivering text and graphics. Basically, the writers work as a team with the Volume Leader.

21.6 WRITERS' PREPARING THE COST INPUTS

Proposal writers are usually required to prepare detailed cost data for inclusion in the cost volume, largely because they are the most aware of:

- the concept of operations
- the key personnel requirements
- the skill levels and experience required by the work
- the project/program schedule
- the major technical and management activities
- the facilities and resources needed for the work

21.7 WRITERS' DEALINGS WITH THE REVIEW TEAMS

As a general rule, the Proposal Writers seldom have contact with the Gold Teams and seldom participate in the Blue Team Reviews. However, all proposal writers are required to attend the debriefing of the Red Team. The most important instructions governing the Proposal Writers' participation in the Red Team debriefing are: "Shut up and listen. Do not argue with the Red Team. Let the Volume Leader take the heat. Make copious notes on comments related to your writing assignment. Remember that the Red Team will have many nitpickers. Keep the faith because the Red Team will go away very soon".

21.8 INTEGRATING THE TEXT WITH OTHER PROPOSAL ELEMENTS

While the Volume Leader is responsible for integration of the overall volume with other proposal volumes, the writer is responsible for integrating his/her text and graphics with other elements of his/her volume and the related plans. This requirement means that each writer assigned to a volume must be aware of the material prepared by the other writers. As an example, the titles of the key personnel in the personnel section must agree with the titles in the resume section and in the staffing plan. Fortunately, this integration effort is facilitated by the meetings of writers assigned to the management volume and the supporting plans so that writers do not work in isolation.

21.9 WRITING THE SUPPORTING PLANS AND SPECIFICATIONS

The Proposal Writer may be required to prepare a supporting plan or a specification that must be submitted along with the proposal. When assigned to a supporting plan or specification, the writer must ensure that the plan is supportive of the proposal in every respect. Basically, this means that the plan must meet four important requirements:

- It must be completely believable and must be documented.
- It must follow the format specified in the CDRL or the AMSDL.
- It must be consistent with the concept of operations and the system design.

- It must not commit the corporation to activities or deliverables not addressed in the proposal.

In procurements, the supporting plans must be "selling" documents, similar to the proposal itself. Therefore, the writer must convince the Government evaluators that the corporation is committed to satisfying the provisions of the plan during the contract. Examples of the many types of plans associated with the management volume of the proposal include the: staffing plan, facilities plan, quality assurance plan, data management plan, security plan, and make or buy plan. In virtually all procurements, such plans are as important as the text in the management volume itself.

Specifications to be submitted in system design proposals must be prepared by members of the design staff because of the technical nature and the system-specific aspects of the hardware and software. Invariably, in major system procurements, specifications must be prepared and must be consistent with the system itself, the engineering approach to the system development, and the facilities committed to the contract.

The writing style associated with supporting plans and specifications is rather formal and very terse. Excessive text is not appropriate, but good English is certainly required of the writer. Just remember that the plan or specification must be written better than the Government's instructions and examples which any good writer can do with little effort.

21.10 ADHERING TO THE PROPOSAL STYLE GUIDE

The Proposal Writer is obligated to comply with the Proposal Style Guide, the writing instructions, and all elements of the Proposal Writers Folder. The titles specified in the proposal outline must be used in the writing of the sections, modules, and units. The guidelines for the writing style, use of personal pronouns, graphics callouts, and references, for example, are firm requirements, and the Proposal

Writer must adhere to these guides and directions. Remember, one of the most important features of a proposal is its consistency and lack of deviations. The proposal must appear as if it was written by a single author, and this objective can be achieved only when all writers adhere to these instructions.

21.11 PREPARING THE COMPLIANCE MATRIX AND OTHER ITEMS

Proposal Writers must be prepared to make entries to the compliance matrix for the text that they have prepared in response to the related proposal requirements. Such action requires the writer to designate the exact part of the proposal where the responses to the requirements are located and to enter those locations in the compliance matrix. While this activity requires a minor effort on the part of the writer, other personnel may find it difficult to locate all of the responses. So, the writer fills in his/her part of the matrix when the response has been completed.

Proposal writers should prepare a list of figures, a list of titles, and a list of references cited in their writing assignment. These lists, which accompany the final draft of their section, modules, and units, are used by the Volume Leader and the Production Coordinator to locate all items, assemble the final outline, to prepare the final list of figures, and to insert the references into the volume. Under no circumstance should the writer force others to compile these lists.

CHAPTER 22

THE PROPOSAL COSTING ACTIVITIES

22.1 WHAT YOU MUST KNOW TO PREPARE COST PROPOSALS

This subject is what you must know to prepare cost proposals could be the subject of an entire book. Nevertheless, this section will attempt to provide some direction on the minimum essentials that someone on the cost proposal team must know.

22.1.1 THE CONTENTS OF THE COST PROPOSAL

Almost every cost proposal requires the following items, with more cost-related items being required in larger procurements:

- SF-33 The Standard Form that is the cover page of the Request for Proposal
- Representations and Certifications (cited and referenced)
- Costs by Contract Line Item Number (and possibly by CDRL Number)
- Standard Contract Clauses
- Cost Realism Response
- Work Breakdown Structure and Cost Breakdown Structure
- Detailed Cost Data, including costs by WBS, by Month, by Phase

For procurements that require cost reporting in accordance with the provisions of a Cost Schedule Status Report or the Cost Schedule Control System, the cost proposals must include additional costing efforts to prepare Estimates at Completion and Budgeted Cost of Work Scheduled. This type of costing is a major effort, so the best cost estimator in the corporation must be assigned to the effort.

22.1.2 The Type of Contract Being Bid

The type of contract being bid is a major consideration during the planning and preparation of the cost proposal. For example:

- For fixed price contracts, costs must be estimated accurately (within 5 percent).
- For cost reimbursable contracts, costs must be estimated closely (within 7 to 10 percent).
- For system design contracts, cost for hardware and software are usually significant.
- For technical services contracts, wage and benefit costs are always significant.
- For construction contracts, subcontracting and material costs are always significant.

22.1.3 The Documentation Need for Costing and Cost Planning

The team developing the cost proposal has a requirement for massive amounts of specific documentation from the proposal and the design team members. This documentation includes items of great importance such as:

Cost Documentation from the Proposal Team - work breakdown structure, project schedule and milestones, major work activities, key personnel, labor grades for project personnel, staffing schedule/plan, cost realism response, man-loading forms and charts, subcontracting and consulting agreements, special security requirements, project facilities, Subcontractor Data Requirements Package, results of risk analyses

Cost Documentation From the Design Team - procurement specifications, facility requirements, system architecture, detailed cost estimates, design schedule and milestones, agreements on subcontractor roles and assignments, additional facilities and leasehold improvements required, detailed A&E design documentation and drawings, bill of materials

Cost Documentation From Higher Level Management - results of should-cost analyses, guidance on acceptable risks, availability of key personnel, commitment of IRAD funds to reduce risks and costs, commitment to developing or acquiring additional facilities, place of performance for contract work

22.1.4 THE RESULTS OF SHOULD-COST ANALYSES

When the costing team begins its work on the cost volume, the team should already be provided with the results of a thorough should-cost analysis. The should-cost analysis can be comprised of the following:

For a technical services, SETA support, or O&M proposal, the average fully-burdened labor rates that will be bid in the cost proposal should have been defined by the marketing specialist or the Acquisition Manager prior to the start of costing. The management volume team is responsible for developing position descriptions and selecting personnel for the project staff with the right hourly rates; the costing team is responsible for defining the overhead rates and profit level. Together, they develop the should-cost estimates.

For a proposal to design, develop, test, and install a new system, the marketing specialist or Acquisition Manager should define the winning cost for the contract. The overall winning cost is then broken down and allocated to elements of the system architecture (like System Testing, Quality Control). The management volume team, the design team, and the procurement specialists then work together to develop should-cost objectives for the system and the project.

For a proposal to build a new structure or renovate an existing structure, the RPF usually specifies a Not to Exceed cost for the contract. The A&E staff and the construction staff, with the Cost Estimator, then allocates the total NTE cost to each major element of the construction work including: design, materials, labor, sub-contracting, equipment. These elements are then broken down by discipline, product, or activity; for example, NTE design costs are broken down into architectural, civil, mechanical, electrical, and structural design costs.

Proposals should never be started until a cost estimate or an educated guess about the winning contract value has been made. Invariably, a disaster results when the proposal is in its final phases, and management decides that the costs are too high. At that late date, there is seldom time or resources to completely revise the staffing, the procurements, the design, the facilities, and to prepare a new cost realism section.

22.1.5 The Strategic Costing Decisions and Strategies

One of the most frustrating times in the planning for a proposal is for a high-level manager to make an over-simplified statement like; "We will prepare the best technical and management approaches and bid the lowest costs". It may be easy to prepare a superior, maybe even winning, technical approach and a great management approach, but it is very difficult to reconcile those two items with lowest cost. Particularly when the proposal team is not told by the arm-waving cheerleader manager what the lowest cost should be and how they can reach the lowest costs.

The high-level line managers, the Acquisition Manager, and the marketing specialists would be better appreciated if they made decisions and specified strategies such as:

- Bid a technical staff in which all personnel has the exact set of skills, expertise, and experience needed to perform the work. Do not compromise, but do not select personnel who are over-qualified and very expensive. We intend to win by providing the customer with a qualified staff that has excellent credentials and is paid a fair, commensurate salary. We will rely on our cost realism section to support this approach.

- Bid an overhead rate based on a dedicated cost center that is tailored to the exact requirement of the contract. Ensure that overhead items are consistent with the Cost Realism section. State that you do not intend to exploit the staff by reducing their fringe benefits or their salaries when you transfer them to the new cost center.

- Bid subcontractor personnel with both lower salaries and lower overhead rates to perform the lower-skill work. We will not use our own personnel with their high salaries and high overhead costs except in management or specialist roles. Note: it is difficult to find a small business subcontractor with lower salaries and lower overhead/G&A rates.

- Bid a work program that will exceed the customer expectations, RFP requirements, and provide significant long-term advantages to the Government. Bid the best personnel, within reasonable salary limits, that are well-known to and valued by the customer. We intend to win this contract because we are the best and we offer the most. Note: This is the way that AT&T beat IBM at a $250 million higher cost.

- Bid the contract using your personnel who are currently working for the customer and who are valued by the customer. Develop a staffing plan based on a normal turnover rate and on the replacement of incumbent personnel with lower cost personnel on a gradual basis. Place great emphasis on the importance of continuity and understanding. State that the corporation intends to employ all incumbent personnel on other corporate contracts so that they will not be available to other contractors.

During the competition for a major SETA support program for the Navy, in which my corporation was the incumbent contractor, the Project Manager for the Navy stated, without reservation, that winners hire losers. Further, the proposal evaluation process by the Government was taking an inordinately long time, during which our competitors were making overtures to our staff members. The outcome of the procurement did not look good for us.

After securing approval from high-level corporate managers, I visited with that Navy officer, who I knew from my prior work on the ongoing contract, and told him that our corporation intended to retain every employee assigned to the ongoing SETA contract. I also commented that a new, incoming contractor would have to provide an all-new, inexperienced engineering and scientific staff without any background or understanding of the program or its technologies. I assured the Navy Project Officer and his deputy that we needed our skilled personnel for other contracts. They knew that I was a corporate messenger, without a doubt.

I will never know whether the corporate message that I delivered entered into the decision process of the Source Selection Authority, but we won the competition and kept the contract and our staff for another five years.

22.2 THE TOP-LEVEL MAKE OR BUY DECISIONS

When working on a contract that requires the delivery of hardware or software, one of the first activities in the preparation of a cost proposal is to conduct the make-or-buy assessment, in which you decide if you or a member of your team are going to make an item, or if you are going to buy the item from some other source. These decisions are required primarily when the Government is contracting for hardware, software, and system development programs. However, in certain O & M contracts and construction contracts, the make-or-buy process is required also.

This activity, deciding whether to make something or buy something, may seem rather simple at first glance, but the make-or-buy decision on an item by item basis can be very time consuming. When deciding to make something yourself, it is implied that you must compute the total costs for labor, materials, and services. When deciding to buy something from another source, you must prepare procurement documentation and solicit bids from qualified sources. So the make-or-buy decisions will have a measurable impact on almost every aspect of the cost proposal preparation.

Fortunately, the overall decision-making can be simplified a great deal when a structured approach is used in the make-or-buy process. For example:

- Hardware Items - For supplies, materials, tools, hardware, equipment that are routinely available from many commercial sources, and buy decision is mandatory.
- Software Items - For systems software, applications software, and special software-related items that are available from commercial sources, and buy decision is mandatory.
- For Hardware and Software Items - For new systems and equipment that must be developed during the contract, and make decision is virtually mandatory.
- For Specialized Services - When special services or capabilities are required during contract performance, the bidder can perform the services or buy the services

22.3 MAKING THE TOP-LEVEL COSTING DECISIONS

Prior to any other activity in the preparation of the cost proposal, it is extremely important to define the assumptions, instructions, and make a series of very important decisions that will guide the overall costing activities. Never start the compilation of cost data or the use of costing models and algorithms until the assumptions and instructions are prepared and the major decisions are made. This is true for all cost proposals, whether for technical services, system development, construction, or A & E design.

Decisions Required For All Cost Proposals

Escalation Factors - Define the duration of the contract in terms of the start and completion dates and determine the escalation factors that will be used to increase the costs for wages, supplies, equipment, and travel during that period.

Labor Rates - Decide if the labor rates will be based on the specific personnel described in the Management Volume and Staffing Plan or if average labor rates will be used, based on the results of the job-skill analyses.

Overhead Rates - Decide if special overhead rates for taxes and fringe benefits, payroll-related costs, indirect overhead, and G & A costs will be bid on the basis of a dedicated cost center or will be bid from the fully burdened rates used on most contracts.

Special Contract Requirements - Determine if the requirements for special contract reporting, special security facilities, place of performance, office support for customer personnel, and test or laboratory facilities will increase the contract costing effort.

GFI, GFE, GFM - Decide if Government-furnished information, equipment, facilities, and materials are available and if their use would result in a lower-cost contract.

Additional Decisions Required for System Development Proposals

Costing Approach - Define the systems and procedures to be

used, including the cost models, data bases, and cost estimating relationships to be used. Define the general guidelines to be used in the development and justification of costs. Prepare rationale for inputs for the cost realism section.

Hardware and Software - Determine the availability of existing, usable code. Determine if GFE can be used to reduce hardware costs. Determine the optimum schedule for procurement of commercially-available hardware and software. Determine the optimum strategy for the design and development program.

Additional Decisions Required for Other Procurements

General - Determine if: Government-dictated labor rates must be used, if the Service Contract Act is applicable, if foreign labor can be employed, if dedicated cost centers will be allowed, and if subcontracting goals will dictate much of the staffing.

22.4 RELATING COSTING TO THE CONCEPT OF OPERATIONS

It is imperative that the Proposal Manager develop a concept of operations for the work to be performed after contract award. This concept of operations is especially critical because it is the foundation for the integration of the contract work in every area organization, staffing, facilities, management, approaches, resources, activities, tools and systems, and documentation. This concept of operations provides the entire proposal team with an understanding of the program after contract award. At a minimum, the concept of operations is essential to the costing effort in the following areas:

- the skill levels of the personnel required to perform the work
- the number and type of personnel required over the life of the contract
- the facilities needed by the work and the location of those facilities
- the management tools, data bases, and models used by supervisors

- the types and complexity of the contract deliverables
- the general schedule for performing the work and the associated milestones
- the resources required during the contract and the utilization of those resources
- the engineering and technical activities to be completed
- the major quality initiatives, organizations, and schedules
- the major risks associated with the contract work
- the major operational and environmental issues to be accommodated
- the security systems, resources, and facilities needed by the work
- the logistical requirements associated with the design effort

During competitions in which the Proposal Manager has very little time to prepare the proposal, it is not likely that he/she will have time to write a concept of operations. In such instances, the Proposal Manager must have the concept of operations in his/her mind and must brief the proposal team on that concept, so that all proposal writing efforts will be based on a single, unifying vision of work after contract award. If time is available, the writing of the concept of operations should require less than four pages, as a general rule.

On major system development competitions, the Proposal Manager and the Chief Engineer must find the time to prepare a concept of operations that will guide the proposal staff and the design staff. This concept of operations will probably require two or three man-days and six to ten pages for preparation. The concept of operations is provided to the proposal team and the design team and is an integral part of the Proposal Writers Folder.

When tasked to prepare the concept of operations for a proposal for a small technical study, I responded with several short paragraphs, like:

The Customer - The customer is the Ballistics Research Laboratory, Aberdeen Proving Ground, MD. The specific office associated with the contract will be the Weapons Effects Department, Laser Radiation Effects Group.

Scope and Objective of the Contract - The objective of the procurement is the development of algorithms for predicting the effects of laser radiation on a variety of aerospace materials. The study will be based on currently available experimental data from Navy, Army, and Air Force laboratories and contractors. The effects of electric lasers, chemical lasers, and gaseous discharge lasers will be included.

Facilities - The contract work will be performed by the Electro-Optics Department of the Military Sciences Group at its main facilities in Crystal City, which will be the place of contract performance. The project staff will use the offices, library, security facilities, storage areas, reproduction equipment, utilities, and the existing office furniture and equipment. No new facilities or resources are required.

Staffing - The project staff will be drawn from the current technical staff located at Crystal City, augmented by personnel currently working in the West Palm Beach office. At peak times, the project will include three scientists and engineers, including the Project Manager, supported by a part-time secretary. No new hires are required.

Schedule and Man loading - Work on the contract will begin within three days of contract award and will be completed within five months. The total man-loading will be in the order of 10 man-months for all scientific and technical personnel. Part-time secretarial support, estimated at two person-months, will be in addition.

Organization - The Project Manager, who will be located full-time in Crystal City, will report to the Manager of the Electro-Optics Department, who is also located in Crystal City. The Project Manager will be the principal interface with the Army customer throughout the contract. There will be a Contracting Specialist assigned to the contract.

Deliverables - The contract will result in the delivery of two major technical reports. The first report will summarize the data collected from a wide range of sources. The final report will summarize the analytic procedures used and present the algorithms for predicting the effects of laser beams on aerospace materials.

During proposals for major construction projects, large SETA projects, and system development contracts, preparing the concept of operations is much more extensive and difficult. For these larger proposal efforts, the concept of operations must reflect the needs associated with major facilities, special tools, security constraints, complex schedules, staffing requirements, use of subcontractors, quality initiatives, high-value deliverables, fluctuating man-loading, GFI-GFE, special management activities (such as risk management), dedicated cost centers, should-cost guidelines, and dozens of other important factors. In these types of proposals, the concept of operations has required about 20 to 30 pages.

22.5 ISSUING COSTING INSTRUCTIONS TO SUBCONTRACTORS

As an essential element of the subcontractor data package, the costing instructions must be issued to the subcontracts at least two weeks before their cost proposal is due to be submitted to your corporation for inclusion in your cost proposal. The costing instructions should include the following items, as a minimum:

WBS work packages for which the subcontractor is solely responsible
WBS work packages in which the subcontractor will support your
WBS items
Approved guidelines for organization and presentation of cost data
Instructions for the preparation of the subcontractor cost proposal
Descriptions of cost models, data bases approved for use in computing costs
Descriptions of labor categories for bidding personnel
Project schedule, project milestone, project organization
Instructions for delivery of subcontractor cost proposals
Descriptions of the deliverables required from the subcontractor

These costing instructions must be consistent with the teaming agreements between your corporation and the subcontractors in every respect. You can specify the level of effort to be bid for work performed in support of your WBS activities and you can specify the cost budget for WBS activities that are the sole responsibility of the subcontractor.

I had a policy that I cited to all prime contractors prior to preparing my cost inputs; "If you tell me the manning level, I will tell you the costs, if you tell me the budget, I will tell you the manning level". When dealing with subcontractors, observe this policy and they will respect you. When dealing with a prime contractor, insist on this policy or you will be abused later.

22.6 PREPARING THE DATA FORMS AND PROCEDURES

22.6.1 DATA FORMS AND PROCEDURES FOR PERSONNEL COSTS

The development for the form on which to tabulate the detailed personnel cost data is very simple in theory and in practice. Basically, the upper part of the form must begin with headings that identify the activity being costed. The identification material should include: WBS Work Package Number, Title of the WBS Work Package, Year and Month, Special Concerns. The form should have 13 columns; one column for the labor category (ies) and 12 columns for the months. At least five rows should be available for inserting five labor categories for personnel performing the work on that WBS item. The bottom four rows of the form are used for certain expenses (like art/graphics support, computer time, ODCs, and travel).

When the forms have been prepared, the Cost Volume Leader must issue a set of instructions and procedures for entering the detailed cost data onto the forms. This material must also include the overall project schedule, project WBS, RFP requirements, labor categories, position descriptions, productivity guidelines, major milestones, and deliverables. The instructions will include information on the cost strategy, costing algorithms, cost guidelines, and the should-cost results. Some of the instructions that I issued included:

Example 1. When preparing man-hour estimates for software development, use the NRL estimate for Design, Coding and Debugging, and Testing of 40:20:40.

Example 2. When preparing man-hour estimates for writing the various plans, use a production rate for writers of one page per day.

Example 3. When preparing the travel estimates, use government per diem rates and assume one car rental for each three people.

Example 4. When preparing the art-graphics costs, assume an average cost of $90 for each graphics item. Assume one graphics item per 16 hours by writers.

When preparing the detailed cost data forms for labor, I always used the position descriptions and labor categories instead of the name of a specific person. My reason was that I prepared cost proposals based on my employer assigning the right level (or pay grade) employee for the work to be accomplished. I let the corporate officers fight the duel over the actual salaries versus the salaries needed to do the work. Remember this axiom in a cost-competitive proposal:

YOU CAN BID REAL PEOPLE AT THEIR ACTUAL SALARIES, OR YOU CAN BID THE SALARIES REQUIRED TO DO THE WORK. BUT DO NOT CONFUSE THOSE REAL SALARIES WITH THE LABOR COSTS YOU SHOULD BID TO WIN THE CONTRACT.

22.6.2 Data Forms and Procedures for Non-Labor Costs

The non-labor costs during contract performance are the costs that are not included to the overhead rates and G&A rates. These non-labor costs will include two major areas:

- The purchase or leasing of major items of hardware, software, facilities, materials and supplies, computer time, local area networks, and contract-specific resources.
- Those costs associated with the labor-hour estimates which will include travel, art/graphics support, consulting fees, reproduction/printing, and other Direct Costs.

The forms used for the travel costs are not complex. The travel cost form begins with headings similar to the labor-hour forms so the travel cost can be related to a specific WBS and the month in which they will be incurred. This simple form basically answers the following questions so that the travel specialist or the travel office can prepare a cost estimate. How many people will be traveling? How will the people be traveling? On what dates will the people be traveling? How many days/nights will the people be traveling? Will a rental car be needed by the people? Are there any special travel costs involved? (tolls, taxi, etc.)

The documentation and forms associated with the purchase or leasing of major items are much more complex and require a very formal procurement activity. The forms will include: procurement specifications, invitations for a bid, reports on surveys of vendors, purchase orders, quality reports, delivery schedules, and special requirements. These forms and matters are discussed in detail in the corporate Purchasing or Procurement Manual. Refer to these key references before starting the costing effort.

22.7 ORGANIZING AND MANAGING THE COST ESTIMATING EFFORT

22.7.1 ORGANIZING AND MANAGING THE COST ESTIMATING TEAM

The cost estimating team will include personnel from the proposal team, the design team, and, at times, personnel from the subcontracting, procurement, and contracting offices. The planning and integration of the work by the cost estimating team will be coordinated and managed by the Proposal Manager (on small costing efforts), the Cost Volume Leader (on medium-size costing efforts), or the Senior Cost Estimator (on large system development proposals). Usually, the design team members on the cost estimating team will work in their design offices; the proposal team members will work in an office within their proposal facilities.

The manager (Proposal Manager, Senior Cost Estimator, Cost Volume Leader) directing the cost estimating effort must hold short status meetings each morning to identify problems, to review work status, and to assess the productivity of the cost estimating team. When problems are identified, the manager may schedule a separate meeting with the personnel who have identified the problems if the problem is minor. When a major costing problem is identified, the entire team may attend a subsequent meeting and work toward problem resolution.

It is almost an axiom that when one cost estimator encounters a problem in preparing the cost data forms, estimating the detailed costs, or finding the necessary data for the cost models, every member of the costing team will be facing the same problems. The first step in the resolution of such problems may be to have a short group meeting in which the opinions and observations of all cost team members are presented. It would be ideal to reach a consensus decision at that meeting; in real life it is usually necessary for the cost team leader or a tiger team to resolve the problem after due consideration.

22.7.2 Assigning Personnel to Specific Costing Efforts

Perhaps this is a platitude, but it is imperative that the cost estimating personnel work in areas where they have technical knowledge and an understanding of the contract work. Examples of assigning personnel to specific costing areas include:

- System Engineers and Systems Engineering Specialists who have assisted in the preparation of the detailed WBS should be assigned to costing in the areas such as quality assurance, reliability analyses, and configuration management.
- A Management Specialist who has assisted in the preparation of the Management Volume and the detailed WBS should be assigned to costing in the areas such as plans and planning, financial reporting, subcontractor management, and WBS maintenance.
- Software specialists who have assisted in the software design and in the preparation of the related WBS should be assigned to estimating the costs for software design, coding, testing, and documentation.
- A Logistics Specialist who has worked extensively in related logistics efforts, such as training, documentation, maintenance, installation and checkout, and has assisted in the development of the detailed WBS should be assigned to this costing effort.
- A Senior Cost Estimator with extensive experience in design contracts, construction contracts, has knowledge of both the WBS, and the project should be assigned to cost estimating for A & E proposals and construction proposals.
- A Senior Analyst or Study Specialist who has worked on similar research studies and has assisted in the preparation of position descriptions, technical approaches, and the WBS

should be assigned to costing in the technical areas specified in the proposal.

- Several <u>Technical personnel</u> with knowledge of the proposal and the design and have assisted in the preparation of the WBS should be available to the cost estimating team to work in many different areas as utility infielders.

- A corporate <u>Procurement Specialist</u> with knowledge of the hardware, software, materials, and supplies to be purchased should be assigned to prepare the cost estimates for such items, based on quotes from suppliers and vendors (A short-term effort, at best).

- A corporate <u>Facilities Specialist</u> with knowledge of the facilities to be acquired, developed, or allocated to the project and the costs for such facilities should be tasked to provide costing support in these areas.

- A corporate <u>Personnel Specialist</u> with knowledge of the local labor market should be tasked to prepare average salaries and benefit costs for the position descriptions provided by the management specialist.

In summary, the cost estimating team must include a wide range of specialties and resources in order to develop accurate, defensible, realistic cost estimates. Also, remember that very few technical or management personnel have all of the skills necessary to perform every task in the cost estimating effort. So a team effort is essential.

22.7.3 PROVIDING SPECIFIC GUIDANCE TO THE COSTING TEAM

It is imperative that those members of the design team and the proposal team who have been transferred to the costing effort be provided with very specific guidance by the Cost Volume Leader or the Senior Cost Estimator. This general guidance must include:

- definitions of the terms used in the costing effort

- contents of the detailed cost data forms
- major assumptions regarding the cost estimating effort
- use of approved cost data bases and cost models
- guidelines for estimating other direct costs (ODCs)

In addition to the general guidance, the cost team must be provided with other critical documentation, including: the Work Breakdowns Structure, the Cost Breakdown Structure, the project schedule and milestones, the project planning networks, the cost budgets allocated to major WBS items, the schedule for preparing the detailed cost data forms, and the forms for recording the lower-level assumptions associated with the compilation of cost data. Other matters such as the inter-relationships and the inter-dependencies between the various WBS work packages must also be noted.

It is important for the costing team to concentrate on the technical, logistical, and engineering activities, leaving the project management WBS work packages to a management specialist. The person responsible for preparing the detailed cost data forms for those WBS work packages related to project, engineering, logistics, and other management activities must provide the detailed schedule, milestones, and networks to the other costing team members. This person is the one responsible for the integration of the management activities with the other activities.

The specific guidance to the cost team members should include solutions to specific problems; such as the need to integrate all of the task schedules with the overall project schedule. Example: Software QA audit and inspection activities must be scheduled immediately after the WBS work package for hardware testing has been completed. Example: High-level project reviews by the customer, a normal project management activity, requires the support of engineering and logistics personnel working under related WBS work packages in their functional areas.

It will probably prove impossible for the Cost Volume Leader or the Senior Cost Estimator to issue a complete suite of instructions and guidance to the costing team at the onset of the costing effort. This condition means that much of the guidance, of necessity, must be provided on an as-necessary basis.

22.7.4 Costing Reviews, Assessments, and Audits

The cost estimating team, which will include people with many skills and diverse areas of expertise, must conduct periodic reviews, assessments, and audits to ensure that all aspects of the cost estimating effort are accurate, complete, and consistent. This management initiative by the leader of the cost estimating effort ensures that:

Daily how-goes-it reviews by the costing team will result in quick recognition of problems and the development of remedies or solutions. These very short meetings allow an exchange of ideas between the team members and their discussions will ensure that all costing personnel are working from the same set of assumptions, data bases, and models.

Daily audits by the costing team of the cost data forms posted on a wall will provide insights into the progress achieved by all team members. The audits of forms on the wall are supplemented by very brief discussions by the preparers of the forms. Most of these audits are folded into the daily costing team reviews with a major audit on a weekly basis.

Daily Assessments of the progress of the overall cost estimating effort is an activity accomplished by the leader of the cost estimating team on a continuing basis. The leader views the postings on the wall about four times each day and ensures that the cost data from the various proposal, design, and corporate personnel meets the master cost estimating schedule.

It should be apparent that the cost estimating team have the same general requirements for reviewing, auditing, and assessing progress as do the proposal team and the design team. The costing effort must be managed and the usual management tools are applicable.

22.7.5 COMPILING AND VERIFYING THE DETAILED COST DATA FORMS

When all of the detailed cost data forms have been completed, the cost estimating team must compile the many forms by their WBS number. This compilation must verify that all WBS work packages have been addressed, either by the prime contractor or by the subcontractors. Or the missing cost data forms must be located or prepared anew. Just remember that in major, multi-year contracts, the WBS will require cost data sheets for over 1000 work packages for each year. So the task of compiling and verifying the forms can be a major paperwork assignment.

In major system development proposals, the compilation and verification of forms is a major undertaking, because hundreds of cost data forms from the subcontractors must be integrated with the thousands of cost data forms from your corporation. Of course, in the costing for small proposals, such as technical services or O & M support, the compilation and verification of forms is a significantly less demanding task. Instead of thousands of cost data forms, there may be only 100 detailed cost data forms for your corporation and less than 20 such forms from the subcontractors.

When the cost data forms are posted on a wall, it is much easier to spot major and minor problems, such as the man-hours for Configuration Management not being consistent with the completion of hardware or software work packages that are ready to be placed under configuration control as baselines. Some technical personnel may make an argument for keeping all of the detailed cost data solely in a computerized data base, but a computer display does not provide the broad overview of the costing effort that is so essential. After the review of the detailed cost data forms on the wall has been completed, then the information should be entered into a computerized data base. It cannot be stressed too strongly the need for posting the forms on a wall for review by all personnel.

22.8 PREPARING PROCUREMENT SPECIFICATIONS

The technical staff assigned to the design team must prepare the procurement specifications that will be used by Procurement Specialists to solicit quotes for hardware, software, materials, supplies, and support services. These specifications support the purchase or leasing of major items, ranging from raw materials to finished products, to special services. As a general rule, these specifications must be available for issuance by the procurement staff at least five weeks prior to the date at which the responses are required for inclusion in the cost proposal.

Technical Equipment Procurement Specifications - The procurement specifications for technical equipment (such as computers, tape drives, motors, displays, etc.) must describe either: (1) the specific equipment (source, name, model number, paint color, whatever) to be purchased or leased, or (2) the capability (speed, storage capacity, weight, size, whatever) of the equipment to be purchased or leased. These procurement specifications must also include the requirements imposed by military standards and specifications and by FIPS standards.

Software Procurement Specifications - These specifications for system software systems and applications software must describe the specific items to be procured. Like Microsoft Word or Adobe

Illustrator. It must be noted that all software procurements are for commercially available systems that are well defined. Normally, these specifications are easy to prepare.

Materials and Supplies Procurement Specifications - These specifications are associated with major procurements of high-dollar value items, such as the steel to build a ship, cement to construct a building, rivets for aircraft construction, and aluminum for panels and mats. As a general rule, these procurement specifications reference the Government Type D or Type E specifications governing the characteristics of materials and supplies.

Major Equipment Procurement Specifications - These specifications are associated with large, commercially-available equipment such as vehicles, forklifts, cranes, graders, cement mixers, office trailers, air handlers, pumps, and food service systems. The procurement specifications describe either the specific item to be procured or state the capabilities and characteristics of the item to be procured.

Note: procurements for military hardware, weapons systems, aircraft, ships, landing craft, and other major items of equipment are covered in special Government procurements, i. e., research and development procurements and production procurements. Procurements of these items are not made by contractors; the Government buys these items directly. If any of these tactical or logistical systems are required by the contractor, the Government will provide them to the contractor.

22.9 NEGOTIATING WITH SUBCONTRACTORS AND VENDORS

Negotiating with subcontractors, consultants, vendors, and suppliers is rightfully the responsibility of managers, contract specialists, subcontracting specialists, and procurement specialists. These personnel have the skills, expertise, and understandings associated with the procurement process and, probably, the organizations associated with the negotiations. Under no circumstance should negotiations be entrusted to engineers, scientists, analysts, or other technical personnel who, because they know the items being procured better, think that they are best qualified for negotiations.

In a major procurement of computer hardware, the manufacturer's representative called our lead design engineer and discussed the availability of a newer, faster, neater CPU, for a slightly higher cost. This engineer gave the manufacturer permission to substitute a different CPU which did not satisfy the procurement specification, varied from the purchase order, and exceeded the previously negotiated cost. When the new CPU arrived, the Quality Control and Procurement staff rejected the unit. The manufacturer cited the design engineer's concurrence with the change. Although we accepted the CPU as delivered, but the work to change all the procurement documentation was demanding.

22.10 DEALING WITH THE DESIGN TEAM

22.10.1 THE DESIGN TEAM AND COSTING TEAM INTERACTIONS

The Design Team plays a major role in the preparation of the cost proposal because they are the ones who prepare the procurement specifications that describe the hardware and software that are needed in a system development contract. The Design Team knows the design and performance characteristics of the hardware and software, so they provide the documentation needed by the Procurement Specialists who solicit quotes and delivery schedules from vendors, suppliers, and manufacturers.

It is essential that the technical personnel on the Design Team work closely with the cost proposal staff and that they meet the harsh demands of the procurement schedule. The Design Team should define the system architecture early, followed by the definition of the design features and performance capabilities needed in the hardware items. Normally, this assistance to the cost team should be completed at least five weeks before the cost proposal is due, since major hardware procurements will require that much time in order for a manufacturer to prepare a quote for items to be delivered two to five years in the future.

It is highly recommended that the Senior Cost Estimator attend all major design reviews to assess the status of the overall design effort and to collect information that is used in the should-cost analyses. It is imperative that the Senior Cost Estimator convince the design team of the importance of minimum costs and the need not to overdesign the system, a requirement best achieved by working closely with the design team.

22.10.2 MAJOR COSTING INPUTS TO THE DESIGN TEAM

The Senior Cost Estimator must provide a wide range of cost-related information to the Design Team so that your system design is consistent with the funding limitations and profiles of the customer. These critical costing inputs will include:

- recommended costs for project work to conform with Government funding profiles
- recommended cost limitations for major hardware and software activities
- recommended cost limitations for logistical matters such as training and documentation
- recommended means for lowering overall costs by use of GFI, GFE, GFM, GFF

The costing inputs will be based on the information collected from the customer and from competitors plus information accumulated in the cost log, should-cost analyses, and cost data bases. These inputs to the design team will also be based on the outputs from cost estimating algorithms and related cost models. Ideally, the costing inputs will provide the designers with extensive guidance on the scope of the work, the complexity of the system, and the probable development schedule.

22.11 DEALING WITH OTHER COST VOLUME MATTERS

The Supporting Plans - Probably the painful oversight in the preparation of a cost proposal is failure to read the supporting plans, some of which can represent major costs. If the cost proposal team has not read and understood the Facilities Plan, Staffing Plan, Security Plan, Installation and Checkout Plan, Training Plan, Maintenance Plan, and the other plans, they are destined for a major trauma. It is highly recommended that the Cost Volume Leader arrange for a briefing by each Plan Leader and for an advance copy of the plans for review. If you overlook the contents of the plans, your costs may escalate radically after contract award.

The Production Staff - The Cost Volume Leader must deal with the Production Coordinator to ensure that the services of the production staff will be available for word processing, art-graphics, proofreading and editing, printing, and binding. Some system must be used to minimize or eliminate any errors in the Cost Volume, which means that the best personnel in the production support staff must be assigned to the work on the Cost Volume. It is a critical activity, the preparation of the cost volume for submission to the Government.

The Marketing and Acquisition Staff - It is imperative that the Cost Volume Leader employ the skills and knowledge of the people who know the customer best, the Marketing Specialist and the Acquisition Manager. But this does not mean that these specialists know the procurement best or understand the proposal. These market intelligence personnel must be used in their area of specialization and they should not be allowed to meddle in the detailed cost estimating effort.

The Project Planning Specialist - It is an axiom in the proposal process that the Project Planning Specialists have a unique vocabulary, in which words commonly used by other proposal personnel have a different meaning when used in project planning. It is important for the Proposal Writers and Volume Leader assigned to the management volume fully understand the meanings of these common words. For example, the word **completion** can mean: an activity is completed, an activity is terminated, a deliverable has been prepared, a major milestone has been achieved, a contract deliverable has been made, and work on a task has been canceled. Beware the jargon of specialists.

The Integration of Subcontractor Costs - If the Proposal Manager has been very structured and very thorough in giving cost proposal directions to the subcontractor, the integration of costs is simple. This means that the proposal team has prepared a Work Breakdown Structure that defines the work to be performed and has allocated specific WBS work packages to the subcontractor. If this discipline has not been an integral part of the proposal process, the effort to integrate cost will be very difficult and painful. Remember, the subcontractors must use your schedules and assumptions, and they must use costing models and data bases that your previously approved.

22.12 CONTRACTING, SUBCONTRACTING, AND PROCUREMENT PERSONNEL INVOLVED IN THE COST VOLUME

Dealing With The Contracting Specialist - In most competitive proposals, your corporate Contract Specialist is the Cost Volume Leader. However, during major system development proposals with complex costing requirements, the Senior Cost Analyst could be the de facto Cost Volume Leader in the early phases of the proposal process. But ultimately, the Contract Specialist will almost certainly be the Cost Volume Manager in the final phases of the proposal process.

The cost estimating team must work closely with but separate from this Contract Specialist, because this team is completely absorbed by the preparation of the detailed cost data sheets while working under the direct supervision of the costing team leader. In such instances, the Contract Specialist is responsible for the completeness and quality of the overall Cost Volume. There may be instances when the Senior Cost Analyst appears to be the best qualified for the Cost Volume

Leader role, but it is difficult to envision such a condition.

Dealing With The Subcontracting Specialist - In many, if not all, proposals for the development of a major system, the Subcontracting Specialist is a member of the Proposal Management Staff. This is necessary since the subcontractor personnel will be working at the prime contractor's proposal facility and because only the Subcontracting Specialist is authorized to deal with the subcontractors on business matters. It is noted that the Subcontracting Specialist is a long-term member of the corporate staff who is temporarily assigned to the proposal team.

Members of the proposal team seldom, if ever, deal with the Subcontracting Specialist except when their assistance is required in the preparation of the Subcontractor Data Package. Subcontractor lead personnel deal with the Subcontracting Specialist on a very frequent basis.

Dealing With the Procurement Specialists - It is almost a fact of life that every proposal requires the services of a Procurement Specialist at some time during its preparation. The Procurement Specialist requests and receives quotes for facilities, materials, supplies, equipment, and other items identified by the proposal staff or the design staff. The Procurement Specialist negotiates with vendors, suppliers, and manufacturers, using the procurement specifications prepared by the proposal team or the design team. Note: the proposal staff and the design staff must not attempt to act as Procurement Specialists.

22.13 PERFORMING THE COST RISK ANALYSIS

The bidder must perform a cost risk analysis that will be an integral element of the cost proposal. Why? Because the Government will perform its cost risk analysis, in which its risk specialists will determine the additional costs that will be added to your costs to arrive at a probable cost to the Government for the contract work. If you do not address the matter of cost risks, you will be faced with cost risks identified by an outsider. And I have never found an instance in which the Government's cost risk analyses did not seriously impact on our costs.

The cost risk analysis should begin with two major endeavors: (1), evaluate those risks associated with costs that you can control, and (2), evaluate those risks associated with costs that you cannot control. It is important that you identify these two types of risks as early as possible in your cost risk analysis and that you address these risks in a structured approach. It is recommended that cost risks be organized into the following categories:

Cost Risks Associated With Government Contracting Actions

Includes: failure to deliver contract required information, late delivery of contract required material, late delivery of comments on critical documentation, changes in design or performance specifications, delayed approval of major contract purchases, and delays associated with test facilities or ranges.

Cost Risks Associated With Vendors and Suppliers

Includes failure to deliver hardware or software on schedule, failure of hardware or software to meet advertised performance, changes in hardware configurations, cessation of maintenance support for software, termination of a product line, unforeseen price increases, closing of a product line, and new national labor wage agreements.

Cost Risks Associated With Contractor Factors

Includes: failure to procure hardware and software on schedule, failure to provide the necessary facilities when required, inability to recruit key personnel when required, new technical risks not previously identified, severe and adverse environmental conditions, labor strife and strikes, underestimating the extent of the required work, poor scheduling, and programming failures.

Cost Risks Associated With Outside Factors

Includes new environmental or workplace regulations, new international agreements and trade restraints, major national crisis such as terrorism, and closing of military bases to contractor personnel.

It is highly recommended that the cost proposal address these four types of risks since they can have a measurable impact on the overall contract costs. In most instances, responses to those cost risks associated with Government performance and outside factors can be addressed in paragraphs in which the types of risks are identified and the fact that you, the contractor, has no control of these sources of cost risks and cannot be accountable for such cost risks. Such a response may be as simple as:

We have identified those cost risks that are beyond our control and must be considered as risks to the Government. These cost risks fall into two categories:

Cost Risks Associated With Government Contracting Actions -We are prepared to adjust our work program to accommodate the impact of these risks, but we certainly have no control over these risks. These cost risks can include such diversity as: failure to deliver contract required information, late delivery of contract-required information; late delivery of comments on critical documentation, changes in design or performance specifications, delayed approval of major contract purchases, and delays associated with test facilities or ranges. We will reschedule our work when these customer-concerned risks are encountered.

Cost Risks Associated with Outside Factors - We are prepared to reschedule and reorient our work program to accommodate the impact of these factors which are beyond our control. These cost risks can include matters such as: new environmental or workplace regulations, new international agreements and trade restraints, major national crisis such as terrorism, closing of military bases to contractor personnel, and severe and adverse environmental conditions. We have built into our project schedule the time to offset unpredictable environmental conditions, up to five days in each year.

We have identified those cost risks associated with our sources of materials, supplies, equipment, software, and the cost risks associated with our contract performance. Our cost risks mitigation efforts fall into two categories:

Cost Risks Associated With Vendors and Suppliers - We include the possibility of cost risks associated with vendors and suppliers into our planning efforts. We are prepared to change our procurements and our work schedule in event that we experience matters such as: failure to deliver hardware or software on schedule, failure of hardware or software to meet advertised performance, changes in hardware configurations, cessation of maintenance support for software, termination of a product line, unforeseen price increases, closing of a product line, and new national labor wage agreements. While most of these risks are beyond our control, we can minimize their impact through planning, work-around plans, vendor-supplier monitoring, and frequent risk assessments.

Cost Risks Associated With Contractor-Controlled Factors - We have prepared a realistic schedule for our project and have completed an intensive cost risk assessment as part of our normal management activities. We believe that we can control these cost risks through special activities such as work-around plans, constant monitoring, get-well tiger teams, and commitment of management reserve. We believe that our risk mitigation efforts will minimize, if not eliminate, cost risks associated with: failure to procure hardware and software on schedule, failure to provide the necessary facilities when required, inability to recruit key personnel when required, new technical risks not previously identified, and labor unrest and strikes.

In summary, the best instructions that I can give to the person on the proposal team concerned with the cost realism responses to the two cost risks that are controlled or somewhat controlled by the contractor will include:

For Procurement Risks - Provide a verbal statement of the procurement actions taken to reduce the cost risks associated with the vendors and suppliers; this statement should include the rationales for selection of each vendor or supplier that are presented. Since delivery and performance risks are an essential element of the selection process, this information should be readily available. Statements about the performance of vendors and suppliers in past procurements and the statement about the availability of alternative sources will help in this matter. Contract specialists can help in this matter. **Use Words.**

For Contract Performance Risks - Provide a synopsis of the risk analysis presented in the management volume. The cost risks associated with all identified schedule and technical risks must be addressed, and the risk mitigation actions must be cited. This cost risk activity should be performed by an outsider who is not a member of the design team or the technical volume team. Remember that contract cost risks are largely driven by technical and design related matters that they are ever-present. So you must assign numbers for items such as the probability of occurrence, severity of impact on schedule or performance. **Be Quantitative.**

22.14 WRITING THE RATIONALE FOR MAJOR COST DECISIONS

The Government evaluators will perform their own cost risk analysis, but the bidder can influence that analysis by including a statement of its reasons for and rationale behind its major cost decisions. Such major cost decisions will include: the cost estimating relationships used, the cost data bases used, the major costing assumptions, the sensitivity of the costing results to the assumptions, the cost breakdown structure used for compiling costs, and the results of the risk management plans.

Basically, the bidder must provide compelling reasons for the Government costing personnel to use its assumptions, models, and methods. If the bidder does not provide this information, it is likely that the Government will use data from previous procurements or, worse, use the cost information provided by one of the competitors. Remember, you want the Government to use your costing decision.

It is important that the bidder provide an explanation of its cost risk information and provide a rationale for its risk information, models, and approaches being the best. Convince the Government to use your models, assumptions, approaches, data bases. The Government analysts should arrive at your results.

22.15 FACTS OF LIFE ABOUT COSTING

One of the major realities that the cost proposal team must accept is that the proposal presents a concept for performing the work specified in the RFP. In major system procurements, the proposal presents the best approach to designing, developing, testing, and installing a system. Both the concept and the approach should be the best estimate of the proposal and design team at the time of the submission of the proposal. You must make your best effort at describing how the work will be performed, how the system will be developed, and how you will manage the overall project work. But you must remember the description of the work and the system is not cast in stone, because:

- After contract award, the Government will issue instructions (and amend the contract, in some instances) that reflect their better understanding of the project and the system.
- As the work progresses, the Project Manager will realize that there are better, more efficient ways to manage the project and perform the technical tasks.
- As the risks are overcome and the uncertainties eliminated, the technical approach and engineering work can become more focused and streamlined.
- The work program may unexpectedly require additional facilities and personnel to integrate an emerging technology into the system design.

In essence, the cost proposal presents a snapshot of the costs that would be incurred if the work began immediately, if the approach and design is unchanged after contract award, and if all risks and unknowns have been identified and quantified.

CHAPTER 23

PREPARING THE COST REALISM SECTION

23.1 THE IMPORTANCE OF THE COST REALISM SECTION

If you prepare the best cost realism section to the cost proposal, it will mean that only your costs are realistic and that the costs of all other competitors are unrealistic. Clearly, the cost realism section in the cost volume is the "Win All or Lose All" part of your entire proposal effort. There is no second place in the matter of cost realism. Just pray that the Government does not require a cost realism section.

Preparing the Cost Realism section is one of the most difficult tasks in the entire proposal process, and only the most talented, experienced, and committed person should be assigned to that task. If you use a less qualified person, you must face the fact that you can only win if the other competitors are as dumb as you are.

23.2 COST REALISM IN TECHNICAL SERVICES PROCUREMENTS

When working for a company bidding a technical services contract at Fort Monmouth, I prepared a cost realism section that the Army declared as "the only real cost realism response that they had ever received". Basically, my work included:

1. An analysis of the statement of work to determine the skills,

education, years of technical experience, years of management expertise, and special efforts required by each activity
in the statement of work.

2. The preparation of detailed position descriptions for all engineers, scientists, analysts, and technical personnel that
defined the necessary qualifications for the staff that was
qualified to accomplish the tasks in the Statement of Work.

3. The use of Department of Labor Wage Surveys for northern
New Jersey to determine the average salaries for personnel
fitting the position descriptions. At this point, I knew the average salary that should be bid.

4. The use of Government information on the fringe benefits (annual leave, sick leave, holidays, tuition refund, etc.) provided
to technical personnel employed by medium-size and large-
size companies. I then computed realistic direct overhead
rates for fringe benefits and, at this point, I know the fringe
benefit rate to be bid.

5. The computation of the taxes, which by law, must be paid by
all companies; these taxes covered such items Social Security
and state/federal unemployment taxes. At this point, I knew
the tax rate to be bid by all companies.

6. A review of Government publications related to the General
and Administrative rates associated with defense contractors
that indicated that the bidder had a G&A rate slightly lower
than the average for the defense industry. I decided to use
the actual G&A rate for the bid. Note: most G&A rates for
Government contractors range from 10% to 12%.

7. It was apparent that there were no overhead costs associated
with the workplace for the employees, because the personnel
were going to work in Government facilities (offices, laboratories, etc.), using Government equipment and supplies.

8. Using historical data, I computed the escalation factors associated with labor rates during the next five years. This activity
involved a review of the COLA increases during the past ten

years and computing the average for such increases. I then multiplied the COLA rate by 0.70 to reflect that wages only increase at 70% of the COLA increase. Then I could adjust the costs for the entire five year period of performance.

9. The weighted guidelines for profits and fees, as published in the Code of Federal Regulations were used to determine the percentage to be bid for profit/fees.

10. Then I performed two additional analyses, based on Government publications. First, I examined publications that documented the turnover rates associated with personnel who were not paid a fair, average salary. Second, using the Government salary data and Government position descriptions, I noted that a 10% percent lower average salary meant that the personnel were not qualified to perform the work required by the contract.

This effort required about eight long days of my time, which included working with the firm's accounting department for almost two days.

During a proposal for the support of a Navy logistics center in California, I argued that it was imperative to prepare a cost realism response as an integral part of the cost proposal. I noted that the RFP stated a requirement for cost realism in the cost volume. The Group Manager did not want to pay me for six days of support, saying that since we were the incumbent contractor, we had realistic costs. And that was our response to the requirement. A competitor bid a total contract cost well less than our cost, without any cost realism response, and WON. We had to fire over 350 long-term, loyal employees and close a major operation with very short notice, all because the Contract Specialist and Group Manager did not understand cost realism.

23.3 COST REALISM IN SOFTWARE DEVELOPMENT PROCUREMENTS

The approach to cost realism in software development procurements begins with estimating the man-hours required for software design, development, and testing using the COCOMO cost estimating model, or if still in use, the RCA Price cost estimating model. COCOMO is the preferred model, so this discussion will be directed to this method since most Government procurement officials will accept the man-hour estimates generated by the COCOMO model.

The COCOMO model requires specific inputs related to the estimated number of lines of code to be developed and the source of those lines of code.

- The estimate of the lines of code to be designed, coded, and tested requires the skills of senior technical personnel who have developed similar software systems and have already defined the architecture and top-level design of the software system.

- The three sources of lines of code includes: existing code that requires no revision or very little revision, existing code that requires moderate to extensive revision, and all-new code to be developed by the contractor. A complexity factor for each source of code is needed.

- With these inputs (total lines of code, complexity of the code, and sources of the code), the COCOMO model will predict the total man-hours required to develop, test, and document the software system and present a probable schedule for accomplishing the work.

- The man-hours required to develop the software must be increased by factors that reflect the need for a system demonstration, for system documentation and training, and for the management and administration of the project.

At this point, the person responsible for the cost realism section knows how many man-hours will be required and how much time will be required for the technical efforts. But this is only the first step in the cost realism effort. Next, the cost realism specialist must perform the same ten tasks described in the previous **section 22.2,** to ensure that the labor rates are realistic. At this point, over 50 percent of the total costs for a software development contract are accounted for and proven to be realistic.

One additional effort is necessary in the matter of personnel costs proving that the much larger direct overhead costs are realistic. The additional overhead costs will include items such as offices, office supplies and services, office furniture, laboratory spaces and equipment, computer hardware and software, security services, computer mainframe hours, art-graphics support, and library charges. You must estimate these costs, preferably using historic data from cost data bases; and then you must support the realism of the costs by comparing them with the average costs shown in Government publications.

It will be necessary to document the costs for other items, such as those associated with the purchase or leasing of equipment, supplies, computer time, special security systems, guard services, and similar items with vendor or supplier quotes. These quotes can be used to establish the fact that these costs are realistic. If you cannot document the costs, the Government analysts may prepare a much higher cost risk estimate.

23.4 COST REALISM IN TECHNICAL STUDY PROCUREMENTS

Proving that your proposed cost for a technical study is realistic is an extremely difficult endeavor because technical studies are so difficult to categorize. Perhaps the best way to address this matter is to cite several instances in which we developed what we considered realistic costs. Later the Government officials stated that our arguments about the realism of our costs were very helpful in their considerations.

Example 1. The Government provided an estimate of the man-hours to perform the work associated with the

Statement of Work. In our proposal, we prepared a staffing plan that provided that number of man-hours and a technical plan that proved that we could do the work. We then used the steps in Section 22.2 to prove that our proposed costs were realistic. In this effort, labor hours accounted for over 90 percent of the total contract costs.

Example 2. The Government did not provide any guidance on the level of effort required for the work, leaving all the decisions related to labor-hours to the bidders. In our market research and marketing intelligence efforts, we learned what the customer had paid for similar efforts in the past, and how much funding the Government agency has for the project. Not coincidentally, our proposed costs were within the funding level of the Government and close to the costs for other comparable, completed studies. That was enough to establish the realism of our costs.

Example 3. The Government did not provide estimates for the man-power requirements, we could not determine the funds available, and the Government had not contracted for similar work in the past. So, in the absence of all information, we had to address the cost realism from a different, creative perspective:

We prepared a thoughtful estimate of the man-hours and skill levels required to perform the activities and to prepare the deliverables as described in the RFP, using our best judgement. We cited our many years of experience on similar study efforts and the man-hours associated with those efforts to establish a realistic staffing level. We then used the steps described in Section 22.2 to establish the realism of our costs

We prepared a very low estimate of the man-hours and skill levels required to perform the activities and prepare the deliverables as described in the RFP. We explained the lower staffing requirements by our existing data bases, our proven models and simulations, and the results of our IRAD program that improved our technology. It required the skills of a superior proposal writer to prove that these resources would enable us to perform the work at a lower staffing level. We then used the steps described in Section 22.2 to establish the realism of our costs.

We prepared a work breakdown structure and a cost breakdown structure in which we defined every activity down to weekly periods and costs down to less than $1,000 items. We then described every activity in every WBS work package in extreme detail, including the man-power required to accomplish the activity. Our final costs were based on a summation of the detailed staffing levels for each activity. We overpowered the Government with detail and stymied them in any effort to cut out any activity. Having established realistic staffing levels, we used the steps in Section 22.2 to establish the realism of our costs.

There will be instances in which the proposal must not adhere blindly to the information provided by the Government. One of our divisions wanted to bid on a contract from the Bureau of Standards related to computer security, shortly after this Government agency was given responsibility for this field. Our Proposal Manager (who was also the Division Manager) had great concern about the Government's estimate of the man-hours needed to accomplish the work required by the contract. The Government, because of its inexperience in this field, had prepared an estimate that was less than one-third of the staffing level needed to accomplish the tasks in the Statement of Work. Our proposal manager stated emphatically that the work could not be done at that manning level, and my supervisor and I agreed with him. Our advice was to bid the man-hours needed to do the job, without concern with the Government's estimate.

We prepared the best technical and management proposal in the competition. Shortly after we had submitted the proposal, the NBS technical and contracts staff requested a meeting with our Division

Manager so that they could explain that our proposal was good but non-compliant. When they shut up, our Division Manager, who had recently retired and was involved in the National Security Agency activities that was at the cutting edge of computer security, then told the NBS staff how much they did not know about computer security, how trivial was their understanding of the current technologies, and how they did not understand what they were asking for. In a 45-minute lecture, he explained why our approach was the only realistic way to accomplish the work. The awed NBS staff decided to award the contract to our corporation and we won a contract in which we were well beyond the staffing levels (Please note that this is a high-risk method to win a contract).

In a proposal to the Ballistics Research Laboratory, we proposed to develop models for estimating the effects of laser radiation of metals of various types. In the RFP, the Government had provided a detailed description of the work to be accomplished and the deliverables to be submitted, but it had not provided any guidance on the matter of staffing levels. Several weeks after submitting our proposal, the Government directed all bidders to submit revised proposals based on the Government's estimate of the man-days needed to complete the work. It appeared that all contractors had submitted cost proposals with total contract values well in excess of the BRL budget.

The BRL instructions directed all bidders to describe what part of their work as described in the original proposal would have to be deleted. We really wanted this study contract, so we bid the same number of man-hours as the Government had specified, and we stated that we would still perform the same work as originally proposed. I explained that our continuing IRAD efforts, our ongoing contract work for the Navy, and our better understanding of the BRL requirements meant that we could do the same work as originally proposed at a lower staffing level. We won the contract.

If I had to summarize the matter of cost realism in the matter of study contracts, I would state without reservation that cost realism is a black art and that a creative, disciplined mind, combined with a superior ability to write convincingly is an imperative.

23.5 COST REALISM IN HARDWARE DEVELOPMENT PROCUREMENTS

The most complex hardware procurements are probably those required for advanced technology fighter aircraft, in which major engineering and production efforts are required over a period of eight to ten years. These procurements require major efforts in fields as diverse as applied research, engineering design, technology development, fabrication and manufacturing, testing, and logistics planning and support. But for every one of these major system procurements, there will be over a hundred contracts for the development of computer-based hardware systems. This section **(22.5)** is directed to cost realism associated with the development of small hardware systems, beginning with the planning activities and ending with the validation of the costs.

The first major activity in addressing cost realism for hardware development is to develop three baseline systems: (1) the architecture and top-level design of the system, (2) the work breakdown structure associated with the tasks to be accomplished, and (3) the cost breakdown structure used for reporting costs to the Government. The three documents define what will be developed, how the work will be organized, and how the costs will be reported.

The second major activity related to cost realism is the review and selection of cost models, cost estimating relationships, and cost data bases related to the system to be developed. Hopefully, these items will be readily available and current, in addition to having been validated recently. If not, the cost realism effort may be in deep trouble.

Assuming the corporate resources for estimating hardware development projects are not available, are not applicable, or are not current, then the cost realism effort must begin a bottoms-up effort to provide that all costs are realistic. This approach means the bidder must secure quotes for components from at least three vendors, perform a job task analysis to determine the personnel skills and experience needed to perform the work in the WBS, validate the man-hours needed in each work package of the WBS (down to the sixth and seventh level, as a rule).

It is possible to use the comparability approach to establishing the realism of costs for hardware being developed. This approach uses the costs for comparable hardware systems that the corporation has already developed as a baseline for determining the probable costs for the system being developed. This approach uses cost estimating relationships based on factors that range from the weight of the system, the number of component or items in the system, complexity of the designs for the systems, and the impact of emerging technologies on system performance. Essentially, this approach requires the cost realism specialist to develop and validate cost estimating relationships anew.

23.6 COST REALISM IN DESIGN AND CONSTRUCTION PROCUREMENTS

23.6.1 CONSTRUCTION CONTRACTS COST REALISM

Cost realism is seldom a consideration required in construction contracts because all construction contractors use the same documents for estimating the man-hour required for each element of the construction effort. The Means cost estimating manuals have estimates for every imaginable activity, from laying floor tile to installing windows, from laying concrete to roofing, from installing guttering to hanging doors. So, if all contractors use the same references for estimating the man-hours required for construction, the differences in the costs will be associated with the fully-burdened hourly rates for the personnel.

The costs associated with the construction man-hours when working on a Government construction contracts are usually driven by the hourly rates specified by the Government in accordance with the Davis-Bacon Act. The Davis-Bacon Act requires all workers to be paid at a certain minimum hourly rate. Of course, contractors can bid at rates higher than those specified by the Davis-Bacon Act, but in practice, most contractors bid the hourly rates specified by the Government in the RFP. It is recommended that, if bidding higher labor rates than those presented in the RFP, the bidder somehow prove that the work will be done faster and better when higher paid employees do the work.

The fully burdened rates, which are computed for each labor category, will include the employees hourly rate, overhead, taxes and fringe benefits, general and administrative expenses, and profit. Any differences in the rates charged to the Government or to the customer will be largely driven by these additional costs. And it is here that costs begin to make a difference in the cost proposals submitted for construction contracts.

23.6.2 A & E Design Contracts Cost Realism

Cost realism has not been a matter of concern to architects and engineering companies until recent years, because A&E design contracts have always been open-ended. Firms employing professionals (architects and engineers) have been treated differently from all other types of firms, in that they have not been required to compete on the basis of costs. Supposedly, the Government picked the most qualified firm to prepare a design; the contractor worked until the job was done, billing the Government whatever the costs were.

In recent years, the Government has been soliciting bids from A & E firms in which the firms are required to present a cost proposal with a final "Not to Exceed Cost". Any costs incurred by the A & E firms in excess of the NTE costs will not be reimbursed except by a contract amendment associated with a change in scope. Someday, A & E firms will be required to prepare cost proposals based on factors such as:

- Number, size, type, and complexity of engineering or architectural drawings
- Number, type, and size of design analysis documents
- Number, type, and size of specifications and supporting documents

Note: The book *Cost Estimating* by Ron Stewart, includes a table that estimates the man-hours required for various types and sizes of drawings; this data could be used if the bidder has not developed a cost data base of its own.

23.6.3 Summary Observations

A & E firms and construction firms have never had to worry about cost realism in their proposals, but it is likely that Government contracts will require this section in future cost proposals. The biggest differences in the costs cited by these bidders will be driven by whether the work is performed by employees of the contractor, by subcontractor personnel, or by consultants.

CHAPTER 24

THE MAJOR PRODUCTION ACTIVITIES

24.1 THE MAJOR PROPOSAL PRODUCTION ACTIVITIES

The customer knows that the best document that it will ever receive from your company will be the proposal that wins the contract. The customer believes that every document delivered after contract award will not be as good as the proposal that won the contract. So, when you prepare your proposal, you are showing the customer the best document that your company can prepare and that all contract deliverables will be of lower quality. Therefore, your proposal must be of great editorial quality in order to impress the customer with your high standards for publications.

The production activities that are essential to a quality proposal that will impress the customer and increase your chances of winning the competition are:

- Proposal Coordination
- Word Processing
- Printing and Binding
- Artwork and Graphics
- Proofreading and Editing

Proposal Coordination Activities - The Production Coordinator, who happens to be a key person in the proposal team organization, ensures that the following activities are accomplished in the

most efficient manner possible:
- serving as a member of the Proposal Management Staff
- serving as the interface between the proposal staff and the production staff
- defining the production requirements and schedule
- maintaining the current version of the proposal, plus files of earlier versions
- notifying the proposal writing staff of serious matters
- reporting daily to the Proposal Manager and Volume Leaders
- ensuring that the copyright, proprietary, and security markings are proper
- controlling all versions and drafts of the proposal
- coordinating the security reviews of the final proposal

Artwork and Graphics Activities - The Art-Graphics Specialists are responsible for preparing high quality graphics for the proposal text, preparing the design for the cover and tabs, recommending improvements to the proposal writers, maintaining a file of all proposal graphics for possible future use, preparing the initial layouts for review, and then preparing the final version of the artwork and graphics.

Word Processing Activities - The Word Processing Specialist receive draft text and tables from the proposal writers by a variety of means: hard copy, magnetic media, network files, and previous proposals. These specialists are responsible for preparing a smooth draft for review by the writers and a final draft for printing; they consult with the production coordinator on matters such as style and formatting, and identify potential problems such as not meeting page budgets. They prepare the final version of matters such as; the Table of Contents, List of Abbreviations and Acronyms, and List of References. They ensure that the text is consistent with the proposal style guide and the proposal editorial policy.

Proofreading and Editing Activities - The Editors and Proofreaders are responsible for ensuring that the text and graphics are integrated into an editorial correct publication. They check the text for spelling errors, make recommendations regarding changes to improve editorial quality, and ensure that the proposal style guide and editorial policies are fully satisfied. Routine matters such as correct graphics callouts, proper use of abbreviations and acronyms, and writing style are handled. They are the final effort to ensure that the text is consistent with the proposal style guide and the proposal editorial policy.

Printing and Binding Activities - The printing-binding specialists are responsible for printing the draft versions of the proposal for the reviews and the final version to be delivered to the customer. They print the final versions of the proposal, design documents, supporting plans, and specifications; this task includes black-white printing of the text, color printing of special pages and covers, and binding the proposal in accordance with the editorial policy.

24.2 SELECTING THE PROPOSAL PRODUCTION ORGANIZATION

At the onset of the proposal, during the early planning phases, the Proposal Manager, the Corporate Officer Responsible, the Production Coordinator, and the Manager of the Production Department, make the decision regarding the organization of the proposal production effort. As discussed previously the production organization can be of several types in which the production staff works in one of the following roles:

- a member of a separate cost center providing direct support to the proposal
- a member of a support organization located remote from the proposal team
- a member of the line organization responsible for the proposal providing general support
- a member of the proposal team who is attached for the duration of the proposal
- an outside contractor in general support of the proposal

The most effective proposal production organization is to have the services of a service center that has a full array of production skills and great depth in production specialists. This type of organization can respond to a wide range of workloads, provide support by highly qualified personnel, and meet the harsh deadlines and schedules. This type of production organization is probably the lowest cost approach to production.

24.3 THE MAJOR TIME FACTORS ASSOCIATED WITH PRODUCTION

Typically, the Proposal Manager, Proposal Planner, Chief Engineer, Volume Leaders, and Plan Leaders prepare schedules for the design efforts and for proposal writing before the Production Coordinator is brought into the planning process. These key personnel know what publications must be prepared, what text and graphics will be required in the publications, and the general schedule for preparing drafts for release to the Production Coordinator. **Then**, the Production Coordinator will tell the other members of the proposal management staff what the real schedule must be for the production of those documents.

Some of the major time factors to be used in planning the proposal production activities include the following:

- proofreading and editing the hard copy of the proposal - 3 to 6 pages per hour
- printing and binding the Blue Review copies of the proposal - 1 day lead time
- printing and binding the Red Review copies of the proposal - 2 days lead time
- printing and binding the final version of the proposal - 2 days lead time
- preparing a full page graphics item without color - 4 to 6 hours
- preparing a half-page graphics without color - 2 to 3 hours
- preparing a full page graphics item with color - 4 to 8 hours
- preparing a four color cover for the proposal - 1 day

- typing from hand-written text inputs - 8 to 10 pages per hour
- formatting the text from magnetic media - 1 hour per 20 pages
- scanning text and proofreading that text - 20-25 minutes per page
- checking the security and proprietary markings in the hard copy - 4 hours

Note: some of these activities can be conducted in parallel.

24.4 THE KEY PERSON IN THE PRODUCTION PROCESS

Without a doubt, the Production Coordinator is one of the most important individuals in the proposal management staff. Artists, graphics specialists, proofreaders, editors, printers, and other production personnel can be augmented or replaced by other skilled personnel, either in-house employees or free-lance specialists with little loss of production capability. But not the Production Coordinator, for he or she will always be a key proposal person in every respect.

24.5 KEY MATTERS ASSOCIATED WITH THE PRODUCTION PROCESS

Writers Preparing a Complete Package for the Production Staff - Every Proposal Writer must deliver a complete package to the production staff when the writing assignment is completed. This package is submitted to the Production Coordinator, not the production people themselves. This complete package includes the text and the graphics, with instructions on the insertion of the graphics into the text. The package also includes an outline for the package, a list of figures with exact numbers and titles, a list of references, a list of abbreviations and acronyms with definitions, and any special instructions. I always prepared these items and found that the complete package made life easier for all concerned.

Keeping the Writers Away From the Production Staff - The Proposal Writers must submit their draft material to the Production

Coordinator, and the Production Coordinators must keep the writers away from the production staff. If a member of the production staff needs to deal with the author, such a meeting will be at the office of the writer, not in the production center. Writers have bad habits, such as trying to up the priority for their material, inserting material late in the process, and telling the production specialists how to do their job. It is a miracle that more writers are not killed by members of the production staff.

Preparing and Maintaining the Proposal Master Copy - The Production Coordinator is responsible for maintaining the master copy of the proposal, the plans, and other related material. Basically, the activity ensures that a current baseline copy of the proposal is available for review by the Proposal Manager and Volume Leaders at any time; this baseline version of the proposal and plans is the true measure of progress in the preparation of the documents. The Production Coordinator, upon request, is responsible for providing the Proposal Manager and Volume Leaders with a hard copy of the current baseline.

Reporting the Status of the Proposal and Plans - The Production Coordinator is charged with the responsibility for assessing the status of the proposal, the plans, and for reporting the status to the Proposal Manager and other key proposal personnel at the daily meetings. The Coordinator is the best person for identifying those chapters and sections that are behind schedule.

Controlling the Copies of the Proposal and Plans - The Production Coordinator is responsible for controlling the copies of the proposal and plans. This responsibility means that all draft copies used by the Blue Team and Red Team in their reviews must be accounted for and that no copies are to be released to any other personnel. Uncooperative personnel are identified and reported to the Proposal Manager and the Corporate Officer Responsible.

Destruction of Draft Material - The proper destruction of drafts of the proposal and plans is an absolute necessity for many very good reasons, like: (1) classified draft material must be destroyed by an approved organization in accordance with the Proposal Security Plan or the Corporate Security Plan, (2) proprietary draft material must be destroyed as if it were classified information in accordance with the Proposal Security Plan, (3) proposal planning material and versions of the text must be destroyed by burning. In no instance should the ordinary trash procedures be used for this material.

Preparing the Lists (References, Graphics, Abbreviations, Etc. - The word processing specialists in the Production Center are responsible for preparing the structural items of the proposal and the plans. These structural items include the final version of the: table of contents, list of figures, list of references, footnotes, glossary, and list of acronyms and abbreviations. Hopefully, the Proposal Writers will provide much of the material needed to prepare these lists.

Dealing with the Cost Volume and the Contracts Staff - The Production Coordinator may be tasked to support the preparation of the cost volume, although this activity is usually managed by the Cost Volume Leader. Since the production staff is ready to provide editorial, graphics, word processing, printing support to the Cost Volume, their services should be used whenever practicable and efficient. Normally, the Cost Volume Leader does not deal with the Production Coordinator in the matter of production support.

Preparing An Estimate of Production Costs - The Production Coordinator is responsible for preparing an estimate of the costs for the production support provided by a cost center. In this role, the coordinator collects information about the volumes and plans from their leaders, such as number of pages, number and type of graphics, security classification, type of binding, printing system used, and similar items. Then with the manager of the production center, an estimate of the costs for the production support is prepared. This estimate is submitted to the Proposal Manager.

24.6 SPECIAL PROBLEMS ENCOUNTERED DURING PRODUCTION

Security - Members of the production staff have a tendency to pay little attention to the security requirements that govern the preparation and production of a classified proposal or plan, especially after having worked on unclassified proposals for a long time. The Proposal Manager, although not the line manager for the production center, must make a major effort to ensure that the production staff members observed the provisions of the Proposal Security Plan.

Only persons with DOD security clearances are allowed to process, handle, receive, and store classified material. Only those production personnel with a security clearance, a certified need to know, and special approval by a client will be allowed to work on a special security proposal. All draft material within the Production Center must be handled properly and stored in an approved security container; all hard drives with classified material must be removed and stored in an approved security container when not under the immediate control of a cleared person.

The transfer of draft material, text or graphics that has a security marking from the Production Center to the Production Coordinator to the Proposal Writer is a continuing problem. It is recommended that each person in this chain of custody keep a personal record of the receipt and transfer of classified material and keep the classified material in an approved container. It seems that most security violations during the proposal process is associated with this transfer and handling of classified material in this review and approval activity.

Editorial Policy - The Editorial Policy is one of the first proposal planning documents issued by the Proposal Manager, and it has always been a critical matter in every proposal in which I have been involved. This policy is used by the writers, the Production Coordinator, and the production staff so that the proposal and plans are prepared in a single consistent style. Changing the Editorial Policy during the later phases of the proposal is almost a sure ticket to the on-earth version of Hell.

It is very important, if not critical, for the production staff to review the Editorial Policy immediately after its draft copy is ready. This is the time to make suggestions and to improve the policy. Not later.

Styles and Formatting - It is only natural that the word processing specialist will want to use a style or format that they have already defined and installed on their computers. If an existing style satisfies the wishes of the Proposal Manager, then it should be used, because the word processing staff is already familiar with the style and formatting matters. If, however, the Proposal Manager decides that a different style or format is required for the proposal, then the word processing staff should enter that style or format onto the computer. And use them during the preparation of the proposal.

In my earlier days in the proposal business, the word processing staff had a style of one carriage return between lines and two carriage returns between paragraphs, which they really enjoyed using. So this became their standard style. As a Proposal Manager, I was faced with severe page limitations and did not want to waste four or five lines per page for extra carriage returns between paragraphs. So I directed a new style with only one carriage return between paragraphs, which the word processing staff rejected summarily. I reminded them in no uncertain terms that; when I am paying for their services, they will do what I tell them to do; otherwise I would outsource the word processing support to someone that would do what I paid them to do. Care to guess who won out on this matter?

Stopping the Writing - The Production Coordinator is responsible for informing the Proposal Manager and the Volume Leaders when the Proposal Writers must stop writing and stop preparing new graphics. The Production Coordinator knows when the last moment at which new material can be entered into the Blue Review copy, the Red Review copy, and the final version to be delivered to the customer. This knowledge is based on the coordinators many years of experience and on discussions with the production staff.

When the Production Coordinator says "stop the preparation of any new material and stop the revision of existing material", the Proposal Manager must issue unambiguous orders to the Proposal

Writers and Plan Writers. Otherwise, the proposal may not be delivered on time. And that is cause for the guilty to be lined up at the wall and shot.

Overtime Hours - Never has there been a proposal that was prepared without overtime for the production staff, or so I believe. The need for overtime can be attributed to many causes, such as: poor estimates of productivity, poor scheduling, poor discipline among writers, extensive changes, technical redirection, management indecision, late receipt of material from subcontractors, and dozens of other excuses. Without a doubt, overtime for the production staff is a fact of life.

When estimating the production costs for a proposal, it is wise to include some allowance for overtime pay. According to federal law, overtime must be paid to all non-exempt employees for all work in excess of eight hours in any one day and all time in excess of 40 hours in a week. Further, the law requires that overtime pay for non-exempt employees for weekday and Saturday overtime shall be 50 per cent higher wages than the normal hourly wage for a 40-hour week. Plus the law requires that overtime work on Sundays and holidays by non-exempt employees must be paid at twice the hourly rate paid for a 40-hour week.

Overtime pay for non-exempt personnel can greatly increase the costs for the preparation of a proposal, so the Proposal Manager and the Production Coordinator should include some overtime factor in estimating the production costs.

CHAPTER 25

THE END-GAME ACTIVITIES

25.1 ATTENDING TO THE FINAL SECURITY MATTERS

One of the final activities in the preparation of a classified proposal is the review and approval of the classification markings of the various volumes. The security markings will include the following items:

- the security statement and the security markings, top and bottom, on the title page
- the security markings (like SECRET) on the top and bottom of each classified page
- the security denotation (S) of each classified paragraph
- a statement regarding the downgrading date for the proposal
- security markings, top and bottom, on the front cover and back cover
- identification number for copies on front cover and title page

The classified proposal must be processed, recorded, and handled by the Security Department after it is in the final format. Then the packages with the copies to be delivered to the Government are wrapped twice. The inner wrapping has the security level of the proposal stamped in numerous places and has the receipt attached to it.

The outer wrapping is plain, with no security markings; a simple mailing label can be attached to the outer wrapping to remind the courier where it is to be delivered.

The copies of the proposal that are to be retained in the line divisions having approved security containers are issued to the manager of the division, with a signature. The line manager can use the copy to prepare for the post-submittal activities, while providing the required level of security handling dictated by the Industrial Security Manual and the Corporate Security Manual.

25.2 HAVING A SENIOR CORPORATE OFFICER SIGN THE COVER LETTER

The Contracting Officer who receives the proposal is a high ranking official in the Government's procurement office. It is only fitting that the cover letter for the proposal, which is addressed to the Contracting Officer, be signed by someone who is also a senior member of the corporate staff. We had a very simple policy on the signing of the cover letters:

- The President of the corporation must sign the cover letter when submitting a major proposal, a must-win proposal, or a special proposal.
- A high level corporate officer who is well known by the Contracting Officer and the Government technical staff must sign all proposals in their area of expertise.
- A corporate officer who is at least a Vice President must sign all of the other cover letters.

Under no circumstance did we ever have a low-level manager, a Contract Specialist, a technical specialist, or whoever happened to be available to sign the covering letter.

Make no mistake, Government officials note who signs the cover letter, and they may form a negative bias against your corporation if you do not have someone of importance sign the cover letter.

25.3 DELIVERING THE PROPOSAL TO THE CONTRACTING OFFICER

It may seem a very simple task, the delivery of the proposal to the Contracting Officer, but it is a task with many pitfalls. Too often a proposal fails to be delivered because of poor planning, adverse conditions, or plain dumb decisions. Every plan for the delivery of a proposal must have a backup element and adequate time must be scheduled for the backup to be executed.

With classified proposals, the delivery is especially critical and requires more management actions and planning. First of all, the courier for a classified proposal must have the required security clearance, a very important consideration on Special Security matters. The courier must be briefed on actions to be taken when unforeseen problems are encountered and must have a letter from the Security Department designating him/her as a classified courier. Lastly, the courier must have the telephone number of local FBI offices to notify in case of problems.

The Proposal Manager must ensure that the typical unclassified proposal is delivered on time through actions of the Proposal Manager such as:

1. The Proposal Manager delivers the proposal.
2. A reliable senior person delivers the proposal
3. A backup proposal is prepared in case of delivery problems with the original set.
4. When delivery by airline is required, never take the last flight available
5. When making a local delivery by private vehicle, have two vehicles make the trip
6. Adequate time is available to deliver a second set of proposals
7. An out-of-town facility where the classified proposal can be stored must be identified

Some problems have been encountered during the delivery of unclassified and classified proposals. After the fact, the problems seem a bit humorous, but at the time, they were not laughing matters.

25.4 DEBRIEFING THE PROPOSAL TEAM AND DESIGN TEAM

Upon completion of the design effort and the proposal effort, the design team and the proposal team must be subjected to a debriefing by the Proposal Manager, the Chief Engineer, and the Security Specialist. This debriefing must include:

Security Debriefings - The Corporate Security Specialist must brief the proposal staff and the design staff on the continuing requirements in the areas of security and perform the security debriefings. The matter of destruction of classified draft material is emphasized.

Office Services Debriefing - The Office Services Specialist, who is responsible for the shutdown of offices, test sites, computers, and special facilities, must brief the proposal staff and the design staff on the procedures for closing, disposition, and return.

Technical and Financial Debriefings - The Proposal Manager and the Chief Engineer must brief their staffs on the need to control all discussions related to the proposal, both within the corporation and outside the corporation.

25.5 SHUTTING DOWN THE PROPOSAL EFFORT

The final activities of the proposal and design teams during the closing down of the facilities used during their work efforts should include:

- returning all leased computers, printers, and other equipment
- destroying all drafts of the proposal and all draft design documentation
- destroying all proposal planning material except for a master copy
- erasing all hard drives, CD-ROMs, and magnetic media
- restoring all facilities to their original or initial condition
- ensuring that all classified material is properly stored or destroyed
- reviewing and approving the final financial accounting records

- signing all time cards and approving all travel vouchers for payment
- preparing thank-you letters to subcontractors and vendors
- preparing letters of appreciation to the proposal and design team members
- acknowledging the efforts of the production staff specialists
- writing a Lessons Learned paper for management

If there is any money remaining in the proposal or design budget, have a short social event.

When delivering a special security proposal to the Denver Technical Center of the Government, I was stopped at the airline gate by several guards who declared that they had to search the plain brown wrapped package that I was carrying. They had received a bomb threat that morning for the flight I was taking and were diligently searching all packages. I stated that I was a classified courier, that I had the security letter, and that they did not have the clearance to even see the title of the proposal, much less inspect the contents. I stated that I was required to contact the local FBI office in the event of a security com-promise. After talking to a series of security supervisors, I was allowed to board the plane, after the package went through an X-ray machine.

When delivering that same special security proposal to the Contracting Officer at the Denver Technical Center, I was stopped by guards at the DTC gate and told that they had to inspect all incoming packages. They too had a bomb threat that morning. I stated once again that I was a classified courier, that I had the security letter, and that they did not have the clearance to even see the title of the pro-posal, much less inspect the contents. After talking to the corporal, sergeant, and officer of the guard, I was allowed to enter the Center, sitting in the middle seat of a pickup truck with guards on both sides. The Contracting Officer, a friend of mine, assured the guards that I was delivering a bona fide package. The guards left, relieved, and I had to hitch-hike back to the gate where my rental car was parked.

After completing a very difficult proposal to the Army Missile Command for a large, must-win contract, we sent the proposal in a brown-paper wrapped package via the airlines, in a counter-to-counter mode, from Washington, DC, to Huntsville, AL. We delivered the package to the airline counter at Washington National Airport, and were guaranteed that the package would be on the next flight out. I called a Huntsville representative and told him that the proposal was being shipped by air, counter to counter, and he assured me that he would handle the delivery. That night, I received a call from my contact in Huntsville, asking where the proposal was. It seemed that he expected it to be delivered to a counter in his kitchen. I immediately recruited a courier and sent the courier and the backup copies of the proposal on the earliest possible flight the next morning. We made the delivery on time and won the contract. Moral: never assume that all people know what counter-to-counter means.

A subsidiary of my employer prepared a proposal that had to be delivered to the FAA offices in Atlantic City. Just to be sure that the proposal was delivered on time; our manager sent the proposal for delivery a day early, with a low-level clerk being employed as the courier. The clerk stopped in the Philadelphia area to visit an old girlfriend for two days, failing to deliver the proposal on the day that he was sent and on the subsequent day. So, being the creative type, he had his girlfriend sign the receipt for the proposal, and he ditched the proposal. He returned to our offices with a signed receipt and, within a week, he resigned to take a better job; his manager wrote a glowing letter of reference for him. About 60 days after the supposed delivery date for the proposal, our Contracts Specialist called the Government office about the schedule for contract award. The Government Contracting Officer asked why we were concerned since we did not submit a proposal. Moral: always send a reliable person as the courier.

There is a legend in the Washington area about a courier who was going to be late with the delivery of a proposal to the Navy. Being a very creative person, he called the NAVELEX building with a bomb threat, precipitating the evacuation of a large office building in the

Crystal City area. The evacuation lasted about two or three hours and the courier arrived about the time that the Civil Service employees were returning to their offices. The contracting officer allowed delivery of proposals after the closing time because of the crisis. So help me, it was not me.

CHAPTER 26

THE POST SUBMITTAL ACTIVITIES

26.1 THE ORAL PRESENTATIONS

Many Government agencies require the bidder to make a series of oral presentations in which key personnel cited in the proposal have to address specific problems, issues, and technical matters. The reason behind such oral presentations is to allow the Government's staff to meet and listen to their counterparts with whom they may have to work in the future. Possibly another reason is look and listen to the people for whom glowing resumes have been presented in the proposal.

During the oral presentations, the Government staff decides whether they will be able to work effectively with the bidder; frankly, they do not like to work with SOBs any more than you do. It is also at this time that the key project personnel make an oral commitment to work on the contract after award; they give their word on their availability. Finally, at the oral presentations, the Government staff can ask questions, many on surprise subjects, and evaluate the judgment of the presenter by his or her response. Ad hoc responses are a quick method to separate the briefer-only person from the briefer-worker person.

When required to make an oral presentation, a special effort should be made in the matter. Off the cuff presentations are a sure way to eliminate your corporation from a competition in which they are in the competitive range. Remember, the oral presentations are requested only from those bidders that have been determined to be in the competitive range. Therefore, it is imperative that the oral responses to the questions be practiced in-house many times before the real presentation is made to the Government staff. It would be doubly effective if the bidder had personnel who had been Government COTRs to act as the Government staff during the briefing and to ask questions like they did when working for the Government.

It is imperative that the oral presentations be made by personnel who show respect to the Government employees, who dress similar or slightly better than the Government employees, and who use proper English and Government terms. The presenters must not use acronyms, jargon, superfluous words, and must avoid lecturing to the Government staff. Remember; rehearse the presentation, many times before many audiences before making the real presentation. Also remember that you can lose a contract very easily when you flunk the oral presentations.

In the engineering design and construction business, it is a well-known fact that the proposal is primarily the means by which the bidders make the "short list". Those bidders for Government contracts who make the "short list" must then make an oral presentation to Government specialists from the contracts, technical, management, and administrative offices. These presentations are usually limited to one hour, with additional time reserved for clarifications and responses to questions from the Government. Every construction company and every A & E firm knows that it must win the contract in the oral presentations.

I have always tried to impress Project Managers with the importance of making a very professional presentation, one in which he/she is perceived as being a very competent manager supported by an outstanding technical staff. I also make a strong effort to impress the key project personnel with the fact that the Government staff is qualified in their work areas, even though they may not be as strong technically as the presenters. In every instance, the oral presentations must be based on the recognition that the Government personnel are good listeners and that they can detect the slightest sign of a presenter "talking down" to them.

In a major procurement The Flour Corporation, with my company as a major subcontractor, submitted a superior proposal, after which we were directed by the Foreign Building Office, Department of State, to make an oral presentation that was limited to 45 minutes. We were directed to respond to 17 tough questions related to our understanding of the work and the issues. We diligently practiced the presentation, even with a stand-in acting as the President of Flour, and we were able to respond to the 17 questions in exactly 45 minutes. But when the presentation was made at the DOS conference room, the Flour president exceeded his two minutes by 12 minutes, during which time he had his yes man talk also. We were unable to present our responses to the 17 questions, and we lost the $ 25 million contract. The DOS managers said to our representatives; "if you cannot manage a 45 minute presentation, you cannot manage the contract work." We lost a contract that we had every reason to believe we had worn.

26.2 THE TECHNICAL CLARIFICATION MEETINGS

Many Government agencies use technical clarification sessions to discuss technical and management matters with the bidders after they have completed their evaluation of the proposals and have determined which firms are in the competitive range. Virtually all of the technical clarifications meetings in which I have participated fall into one of the following classes:

- The Government evaluators realized that their RFP could be interpreted in more than one way, and that all bidders should bid with the same understanding so that they can be ranked. In these meetings, you discover where you were misdirected by the RFP. After the meeting, you can submit your clarification responses based on the real intent of the Government.

- The Government evaluators were intrigued with our technical approach, but they could not assess the risks associated with the innovations proposed. The Government technical staff wanted further information, largely so that they can determine the types and levels of risks associated with that innovative approach.

- The Government contracts and technical staff had decided to engage in "technical leveling", in which all bidders are assisted in reaching the same proposal evaluation ratings.

- Then the Government could decide the winner of the competition on the basis of cost only. Note: this tactic is prohibited, but it exists in many agencies.

- The Government technical staff may have realized that their Statement of Work should have been revised to reflect current understandings and needs. They did not want to start the procurement over, so they provided technical direction to all bidders, who in turn, could modify or expand their proposals.

- The Government technical staff realized that its estimate of the probable costs for the contract were significantly different from the costs proposed by all of the bidders. This meant that they had to obtain more money (a solution that is most painful) or provide technical direction that limited the scope of the work. A lower-cost justification was always required in this instance.

- The Government technical staff or management staff wanted to provide additional guidance to the bidder, in touchy areas such as the replacement of a key person in the proposed project organization with whom they have severe difficulties or the replacement of a subcontractor with whom they have had contractual performance problems in the past.

- The Government personnel wanted to discuss the impact of changes in the facilities, materials, information, and equipment that it was scheduled to commit to the contractor. These changes could include less being provided or more being provided. Such changes were largely related to the costs being proposed and do not require major proposal revisions.

- The Government financial and contracting personnel wanted to discuss the impact of changes in the availability of their year-to-year funding for the procurement. Such discussions are directed to probable changes in project schedule, milestones, reporting requirements, and deliverables to fit the funds available in the Government five year financial plan.

26.3 THE GRAY BEARDS SESSIONS

During the Middle Ages, the Spanish Inquisition subjected thousands of people to cruel and inhumane torture in an effort to make the guilty and the innocent confess to heresy, after which the unfortunate souls were mercifully put to death. During the late 1900s, the Government resurrected the inquisition, calling it the Gray Beards review of contractors. While no contractor personnel were executed, the verbal torture is well known in the community.

Basically, the Government assembles a group of very senior technical and management personnel who have extensive credentials in many diverse areas. Most of the personnel assigned to the Gray Beards review are normally employed in Government offices, laboratories, and research center; in Federal Contract Research Corporations, in industrial or commercially organizations, and in some instances by Government contractors. Together, the members of the Gray Beards group represent some of the finest technical and scientific personnel in the nation.

The Gray Beards sessions begin with a relatively brief presentation by the bidder, followed by an excruciatingly-long question and answer period. The questions from the Gray Beard members can cover topics as diverse as:

- How would you handle a certain risk if it arose during contract performance ?

- When do you anticipate the emergence of a new technology ?
- How do you intend to hold your project staff together ?
- What is the basis for your innovative approach to a design problem ?
- What is the basis for your estimate of the level of work associated with documentation ?
- What is your philosophy regarding get-well plans ?
- What will you do if a major subcontractor defaults in its performance ?
- Will you change your approach if Government-furnished support is not available ?
- How will you acquire the facilities and resources needed for get-well plans ?
- What is the rationale for the amount of money in your management reserve ?
- How will your corporate TQM Program impact on quality in this project ?

It is highly recommended that the key project management staff be very skilled in dealing with tough questions and who do not become irritated when faced with tough questions. Just remember that the other bidders are undergoing the same exorcism and that your session will end soon. Also keep in mind that there are very few instances in which the Gray Beards group requested follow-up sessions. And pray for deliverance from the torture.

When I was employed by the Johns Hopkins University's Operations Research Office, we had the equivalent of the Gray Beards group, which was appropriately called the Murder Board. The Murder Board was comprised of very senior, very experienced technical personnel who reviewed draft copies of all publications before they were allowed to be printed and distributed. The Board prepared written comments and questions for the study team and then had an oral review of the publication in which the researchers-writers were subjected to great professional pain.

Every assumption that I had made and every analysis that I had conducted had to be defended in an inquisition. Some reviewers wanted to know why I did not investigate other approaches and others asked if I had performed analyses to determine the sensitivity of my results to factors that I had not considered. After my first Murder Board review, I was prepared to submit my resignation. After all, who would want anyone of their professional staff that was as inept and as unenlightened as me

26.4 THE BEST AND FINAL OFFERS

After the proposals have been evaluated by the Government, all clarification sessions are completed, the Gray Beard reviews are thorough, and technical redirection has been provided to the bidder, the Government usually requests a Best and Final Offer. This opportunity is provided to all bidders still in the competitive range, in writing, with specific guidance for the format and detail associated with the BAFO. In all procurements, the Government will require the bidder to justify any reduction in costs proposed in the BAFO, which makes the lowering of the original bid price a lot more difficult.

The Section L requirements in the RFP, which are the Instructions to the Offeror, still govern the general format for the Best and Final Offer. The BAFO format is driven by the same Contract Line Item Numbers (CLINs), the same work packages associated with the WBS, and the same format of the CSSR/CSCS systems, all of which can be affected by new directions from the Government regarding the BAFO. This means that the proposal team must review all cost accounts and work packages when preparing the BAFO response.

One of the most important matters to consider in the Best and Final Offer phase is the distinct possibility that the Government is using the BAFO to accomplish technical leveling. Each offeror is provided with a unique set of questions or requirements to which they must prepare a response and to which they probably have to prepare a new cost volume. When the offerors in the competitive range reply to their questions or requirements, it is almost a certainty that all offerors will have the same evaluation score. This is called Technical Leveling. Never forget this term.

During technical leveling, the Government strives to have all proposals reach the same evaluation score on technical and management matters, so that the selection of the winning offeror can be based solely on cost. Since all other matters are the same, costs rule. It is wise to assume that all BAFO efforts involve technical leveling and to work diligently to avoid such a situation by constantly upgrading all aspects of the technical and management volumes with each BAFO. Note: technical leveling is prohibited in Government procurements but it does happen.

In a major procurement when I was the proposal manager, we had to submit three Best and Final Offers because, I will always believe, the Government was involved in technical leveling. But I did not play the game and I never allowed the Government to raise the evaluation scores of my competitors to the level of my proposal. I kept upgrading the technical approach, skills of the project personnel, facilities and resources committed to the project, and other aspects of both the technical and management volumes with each Best and Final Offer. We were advised by the Government that our proposal was satisfactory and did not need any changes; if we had believed them, we would have lost the competition. Basically, I outlasted the Government by improving the quality of our proposal so that we stayed well ahead of our competitors. Finally, the Government gave up and awarded the contract to my corporation

26.5 THE FACILITY INSPECTIONS

When the availability of facilities is a very critical consideration in the selection of the offeror for contract award, a Government team will conduct a site inspection of each offeror in the competitive range. This inspection will examine the offices, laboratories, engineering centers, workshops, production lines, storage areas, and other corporate resources cited in the proposal to verify that the facilities described in the proposal do exist, that the facilities are adequate for the work to be performed during the contract, and that the facilities will be available when required, to determine their availability, special features, and staff quality. Note: Facility inspections are relatively painless to the contractor, because the Government inspectors do not ask penetrating questions.

The Government will issue a letter to each offeror that is subject to a facility inspection, informing the offeror of the purpose, date, and scope of the inspection. The inspection team will normally complete their inspection within two days, after which the team will prepare a Pass-Fail report to the Contracting Officer and the Source Selection Authority. The contractor is not given a chance to comment on that report. If you failed, you will be told so in the debriefing given to the losing contractors when the contract has been signed with the winning offeror.

Just remember, if your company does not have the facilities needed to perform the work required during the contract, you will not be awarded the contract. I have never won a competition in which we made a promise to the Government to acquire or develop the necessary facilities after contract award. And I do not think that anyone else can win with such promises.

Part V

WRITING THE EXECUTIVE SUMMARY, COVER LETTER, AND OTHER ITEMS

CHAPTER 27

PREPARING A WINNING EXECUTIVE SUMMARY

27.1 THE IMPORTANCE OF THE EXECUTIVE SUMMARY

Who Reads the Executive Summary - One of the most important considerations for every writer are the people to whom the Executive Summary is being directed. Specifically, the writer of the Executive Summary must recognize that the readers will likely include: the Contracting Officer, the Head of the Source Selection Evaluation Board, members of the Source Selection Advisory Council, Contracting Officer's Technical Representative, and likely, members of the Source Selection Authority Council. Other potential readers of the Executive Summary could include members of the Source Selection Evaluation Board, the Gray Beards group, the Small Business Subcontracting Advocate, and key personnel who work in areas such as risk management, cost analysis, and automated planning systems. It can be safely concluded that the majority of the senior personnel responsible for selecting the winner of a competitive procurement are the potential readers of the Executive Summary.

The Importance of the First Page - The first page of the Executive Summary must summarize the overall volume and the most important parts of the proposal (and the critical features of the system design). This one-page unit tells the customer why our proposal is best, what special features we offer, and how our proposal (and design) is the "best buy" for the Government. In the space of four, maybe five, paragraphs you must convince the customer that you are the best contractor. Ideally, the first page should provide the Contracting Officer with the material needed to justify the selection of your corporation, making the job of the Contracting Officer easier. A word of caution, do not attempt to put all key points of your proposal on the first page because it just cannot be done.

The Design of The Executive Summary - Three of the most important inputs associated with the design of the Executive Summary are the number of pages allocated to the summary, the method of binding, and the editorial dictates of the Government. The next most important input is the outline of the overall proposal, because the Executive Summary must have a parallel structure, and must use the same titles that are used in the body of the proposal. Finally, a list of the win themes and discriminators is an essential input to the writer, who can then develop a vision of the Executive Summary and begin a page-by-page layout of the volume. Do not undertake the writing of the Executive Summary until you have this vision.

Writing the Executive Summary Late in the Proposal Process - Most Proposal Managers prefer to write the Executive Summary when the overall proposal has been completed in a draft form. The strength of this approach is that the writer has a better understanding of what the corporation is offering to the customer. This approach to preparing an Executive Summary is driven by what we are selling, and you must hope that what is being presented in the proposal is what the customer is buying and what is important to the customer. Using this approach to the preparation of the Executive Summary, we can cover all issues, concerns, and we have not overlooked any essential requirement.

Writing the Executive Summary at the Start of the Proposal Process - A few Proposal Managers prefer to write a preliminary draft of the Executive Summary at the start of the proposal, with revisions being inserted as the overall proposal moves toward completion. The strength of this approach is that the Executive Summary is driven by almost entirely what the customer is buying. Another strength of this approach to preparing the summary is that the entire proposal team knows how we intend to win the procurement and what they are required to prove in their portions of the proposal. I have always preferred this approach.

27.2 PLANNING AND WRITING THE EXECUTIVE SUMMARY

27.2.1 PLANNING THE EXECUTIVE SUMMARY

The front-end activities during the planning of the Executive Summary, in chronological sequence, include:

- determining the number of pages to be allocated to the Executive Summary
- determining the method for binding the Executive Summary
- allocating pages within the Executive Summary to specific topics
- preparing a layout for the Executive Summary prior to writing

Defining the Page Budgets for the Executive Summary - The Proposal Manager or the Proposal Planner prepares an initial estimate of the number of pages allocated to the Executive Summary. Normally, the Proposal Instructions, Section L of the RFP, specify the page limitations of the various proposal volumes (assuming the proposal is page limited). When the Proposal Instructions specify the maximum number of pages to be included in the Executive Summary, then that determines the page budget for that item. No more pages than the RFP says.

If the RFP Proposal Instructions do not specify any limitation on the number of pages in the Executive Summary, then the number

of pages allocated to this item is somewhat arbitrary. Consider the
following:

- If the Executive Summary is a standalone volume using sad-
  dle-stitching, the . sheets used for the printing are 11" by 17"
  in size and each such sheet results in four pages of 8.5" by
  11" dimensions. This method means that the number of pages
  in a saddle-stitched volume will be some multiple of 4, with
  the most common sizes being 12 and 16 pages.

- If the Executive Summary is a standalone volume using three-
  ring binders, GBC binding, Velo binding, or stapled with
  binding tape, each of the pages, except for possible foldouts
  (I do not recommend foldouts in the Executive Summary).
  will be 8.5" by 11". While the total number of pages in this
  volume can vary over a wide range, 8 to 20 pages seem to
  favored.

- If the Executive Summary is integrated into the Technical and
  Management Volume, then the page size will be 8.5" by 11",
  and the total number of pages can range from 8 to 12 pages,
  as a general rule. Note: it seems that standalone. Executive
  Summaries invariably entail a few more pages than those
  Executive Summaries that are integrated into and bound with
  the Technical and Management Volumes, particularly when
  the Technical and Management Volume have severe page
  limitations.

- When defining the number of pages within the Executive
  Summary for a major proposal for the development of a
  hardware or software system, the number of pages can range
  from 50 to 100 pages, with foldouts being quite common.
  These larger Executive Summaries normally use either three-
  ring binders or are stapled with binding tape. An Executive
  Summary for this type of procurement quickly becomes a major proposal volume that requires an extensive planning and
  writing effort.

Allocating Pages Within the Normal Executive Summary - The number of pages allocated to the various topics in the Executive Summary are driven by the total number of pages in the volume. Typically, the number of pages allocated to the various topics in a 16 page volume is generally twice those in an 8 page volume. The following page allocations can be used as a guide for planning the Executive Summary.

The Major Topics Page Budget for Page Budget for In the Executive Summary 16-page Volume 8-page Volume

- Introductory Letter Always a one-page unit One page maximum
- Problem Understanding Normally a two page unit One page maximum
- Technical Approach Normally a two-page unit One page maximum
- Management Approach Normally a two-page unit One page maximum
- Personnel Qualifications Normally a two-page unit One page maximum
- Contract Experience Normally a two-page unit One page maximum
- Organizational Structure Normally a two-page unit One page maximum
- Facilities and Resources Can be one or two-page unit Half-page maximum
- Related IRAD Projects Normally a one-page unit Half-page maximum

Note: In the above table, the number of pages allocated to major topics in the Executive Summary is not a direct function of the weight assigned to those topics in the Evaluation Criteria (Section M of the RFP). It is more important to cover all major topics in the Executive Summary with a structure of one or two pages than it is to vary the

number of pages allocated to the topics according the their evaluation weight.

Selecting the Method for Binding the Executive Summary - While
the selection of the method of binding for the Executive Summary
may seem a minor decision, the method of binding has a major impact on the layout of the Executive Summary. The six major methods
for binding include:

- Saddle-stitched format with facing pages
- Three-ring binder with or without facing pages
- GBC plastic binding with many punched slots*
- Velo plastic binding with many pierced holes*
- Perfect binding with a cover over the spline
- Stapled with binding tape over spline

* These bindings are not normally used for facing pages

Each of these six methods has their advantages and disadvantages,
and I have worked with all methods during my 25+ years of proposal
work. My observations relative to binding include the following:

Saddle-stitch binding must be some multiple of four pages; it cannot be more than 48 pages total. This method requires great structure,
and it requires trimming of the volume to eliminate ragged edges to
produce a very neat document. It cannot accommodate. foldouts.

Three-ring binding can have any number of pages although it is
difficult to have facing pages. This method is the easiest and fastest
method for binding. It provides a hard cover for the document, can
accommodate foldouts, and both printing and page changes are easy.

GBC binding can have any number of pages. Assembly of the
volume is a pain, because it requires special supplies and unique
equipment for punching and assembly. It can accommodate foldouts,
but it is difficult to keep plastic bindings from snagging or sagging.

Velo binding is a difficult binding method which can handle any
number of pages. It can accommodate foldouts and the bound volume can stand erect. It requires special equipment (drill, heating unit)

and it is difficult to assemble pages onto 20+ plastic posts.

Perfect binding is the method used with commercial printers. It looks very professional, the volume can stand up without sagging, it is easier to handle than most bindings, but the effort is more expensive and labor intensive.

Stapled volume with binding tape is a very effective method of binding the Executive Summary. It looks professional, the volume can stand up, it is easier to handle than other bindings and it is more difficult for the Government to zerox your proposal.

Note: Do not even consider the **Smythe-Sewn binding** used by professional book binders for textbooks and high-cost, hard-cover books because of the great expense and the long lead time.

In many RFPs, the customer specifies the method for binding the various volumes of the proposal. The binding requirements are invariably contained in Section L, Proposal Instructions of the RFP. Because three-ring binding eases the evaluation effort and because Government personnel can remove and Xerox pages of interest, the long-term trend in Government procurements seems to be headed toward three-ring binding. But remember that saddle-stitch and perfect binding produce the most professional-looking volumes.

Preparing a Layout for the Executive Summary - When writing the Executive Summary, it is imperative that the writer prepares a planning sheet in which every page of the Executive Summary is depicted as a rectangular box. Sixteen boxes for a 16 page Executive Summary. Then the writer must sketch what the text and graphics will look like in the final version, with the topics of paragraphs being noted and sketches of graphics being inserted. It can be seen that I am planning a volume with sixteen pages and that I have sketched in the layout and format for the material planned for each of the pages. Note: If material is to be included on the inside of the front cover and the inside of the back cover, then I would have prepared an 18 page layout.

After the planning/layout sheet has been completed and the writer has made all the preliminary decisions related to the content of the

Executive Summary, he or she prepares a set of 8.5" by 11" sheets, one for each page in the Executive Summary, in which the final layout is shown. These mockups, normally about 16 of them, show all interested managers what the Executive Summary will look like when completed. Once the writer has decided what will be put on each page of the Executive Summary, the preparation of these full-size layout sheets should be completed in less than two hours.

The layout and mockup effort for the Executive Summary is a critical element in the proposal process because: (1) it ensures that everyone associated with the proposal will know what the Executive Summary will look like and what will be included, and (2) it defines the writing effort while providing basic inputs to the graphics and word processing personnel in the production shop.

When working on the Chemical Demilitarization Proposal to the Army, I was responsible for the preparation of the contract experience sections for six volumes, one for each of the task areas. This assignment was critical because we intended to win the competition based on our previous five years of work for the Army Chemical Center. In this effort, I prepared page layouts within three days of the start of the proposal effort for all six tasks and I posted the pages, about 36 pages total, on the wall. When the proposal was printed and bound, my six sections looked exactly like the page layouts that I had sketched over two months earlier. You can do the same.

27.2.2 Writing the Executive Summary

The Importance of Writing Skills - The greatest advertising firm in the world is Ogilvy and Mather, and this organization under the leadership of Ogilvy. In his stellar book, **Ogilvy on Advertising**, he states that the most important person in the advertising business is the writer. This is also true in proposals, and it is doubly true with Executive Summaries.

An effort to tell anyone how to write a winning Executive Summary must begin with some very basic assumptions, such as: (1) the writer should have at least the equivalent of two to four semesters of college-level English classes, (2) the writer should have worked on many proposals, (3) the writer should have a technical education and have worked in a related technical field, (4) the writer should have an aggressive and convincing writing style. And it helps if the writer has a stake in the work to be done after contract award.

I will attempt to provide guidance to a good writer so that he or she can become a skilled writer of Executive Summaries. Basically my guidance focuses on the structured approach to deciding what will be included in the Executive Summary. I believe that once a good writer decides what to write about, the rest is routine. So in the topics that follow, I try to assist the writer in determining what should be in the Executive Summary and how it should be presented. Remember, that this part of the proposal is the "hard sell" document.

Some Rules Governing Text, Graphics, and Visual Impact Items - One of the most important rules related to persuasive writing is; words are more important than graphics. This means that the graphics, which include artwork, schematics, drawings, data tables, photographs, and sketches should never occupy more than 50% of the pages. The second most important rule is that every page of text without a graphic must have some visual impact items, such as bullet listings, titles, bold or underlined words, shadow boxes, shading, changes in lines per inch or margins, changes in fonts, and use of special symbols.

In summary, ensure that the ratio of text to graphics is somewhere between 3 to 1 and 1 to 1, and that visual impact items must be on every page of text. This matter of text versus graphics is best addressed by preparing a layout or mockup of every page. Layouts and mockups allow you to see that the general rules cited above are observed. You may rest assured that writing the text and sketching of the graphics will become routine once these general rules and procedures are observed.

Identifying The Subject of Every Paragraph - The first step in writing the text for a great Executive Summary is to decide the topic of each paragraph. The principal sources for the topics on each page are:

- For the introductory letter, the paragraphs must be based on the most important win themes, which in turn, must be based on the most important evaluation factors. The most important paragraph in the cover letter must be directed to the most important evaluation factor, preferably one in which we make statements that other bidders cannot make, statements that offer great advantages to the customer.

- For the one-page and two-page units following the cover letter, the topics for paragraphs must be based on the evaluation factors and sub factors, the more important proposal instructions, and the more important win themes. The topics of the paragraphs in the cover letter should be covered in more detail in the following one- and two-page units.

- For all units, the writer must decide which topics are important enough to merit inclusion in the Executive Summary and leave the other topics, which are also important, to the Technical Volume or Management Volume. Remember, you cannot put everything important in the Executive Summary, just the most important.

Identifying the Graphics - The selection of the graphics to be included in the Executive Summary is based on the need to present information that is better in a graphical format than in a textual format. Typical graphics are for the units related to Personnel, Contract Experience, Management Approach, Technical Approach, Problem Understanding, Facilities and Resources, and Organizational Structure. It is likely that proposal graphics in the Executive Summaries for design and construction contracts and for major system development contracts will include an additional, different array of graphics, such as:

For design and construction proposals - The graphics can include sketches of buildings proposed, photographs of buildings constructed in previous contracts, system architecture drawings, construction schedules and milestones.

<u>For system development proposals</u>- The graphics can include photographs of hardware developed in previous contracts, photographs or drawings of development facilities, listings of special test equipment and special facilities.

The most important guidelines to remember when identifying the graphics to be included in the Executive Summary are:

Graphics occupy at least 25% of the space and less than 50% of the space.

Graphics are used when words cannot adequately present the information..

Graphic are used to ensure that the volume has a more appealing format

Graphics are used to condense information and save pages of text.

Writing the Paragraphs - The writing of the paragraphs in the Executive Summary is the most important element of preparing a winning volume. The paragraphs must present compelling reasons for why your corporation should be awarded the contract. This is the acme of persuasive writing.

I recommend that the writing of each paragraph begin with the theme sentence, the first sentence, and that a concurrent decision be made as to the type of paragraph to follow the theme sentence; remember, chain structure or daisy structure. Some proposal experts recommend writing the first sentence of every paragraph before completing any of the paragraphs; some experts recommend writing one paragraph complete to develop the writing style early. This decision is best made by the writer of the Executive Summary.

To summarize, I discuss many of the decisions that the writer must make. For example, I state that every paragraph must be written in a way that reflects its relative importance (based on evaluation factors and win themes) and its visual impact on the reader (titles, length, key words, etc.). Since the length of a paragraph is a good measure of the importance of the message therein, the most important messages merit the longer paragraphs. Remember, every paragraph must be focused, no wordiness, no evasion.

The first sentence in each paragraph of the Executive Summary must begin with a strong statement, with the following sentences expanding on the first sentence. Some examples of strong first sentences which became the topics for important paragraphs include:

Personnel Unit First Sentences

We have committed Dr. Kornreich to work as the Project Manager for the NCIC Project in a full-time capacity throughout the contract.

We have assigned a cadre of engineers, scientists, and analysts to begin work immediately after contract award and to remain as key personnel on a long-term basis.

Every member of our project staff has demonstrated their commitment to high quality work in support of many critical Navy programs, work that has been delivered on-time.

Contract Experience First Sentences

Our team has successfully completed over 20 contracts with your organization and has received numerous commendations for our on-time, on-budget performance.

Our team has extensive research experience in all of the technologies that are key to the development of the Strategic Defense Initiative.

We have successfully completed over 3,000 contracts and delivery orders in the past 20 years without an adverse performance rating by the customer.

Management Approach First Sentences

We have selected a suite of management tools, systems, and data bases that have been tailored to the exact requirements of this project.

Our commitment to the delivery of quality products is the result of our initiatives in the planning, organization, and activities of our Quality Control team.

Our Project Manager and Chief Engineer has demonstrated their ability to deliver advanced systems that fully satisfy the customers' performance requirements in every respect.

Problem Understanding First Sentences

The U. S. Air Force has been testing an airborne laser weapons system for use Against theater ballistic missiles for over 20 years.

The development of an improved respirator for use in underground coal mines has been mandated by the U. S. Congress in recent legislation.

Blue noise, which is caused by underwater nuclear detonations, is a serious concern for the Navy because of its long-term effect on sound-based detection and tracking systems.

Facilities and Resources First Sentences

We have established a major state-of-the-art research laboratory in close proximity to Fort Belvoir that will specialize in testing the effects of electromagnetic pulses on personnel.

Our project staff will have direct access to a wide range of computer resources, including corporate computer centers, wide area networks, and special CASE tools.

Our Corporate Information Center has direct access to over 40 computerized technical data bases that can be provided to our project staff in less than an hour.

Technical Approach First Sentences

Our work will be organized into three major phases: planning the data collection effort, collecting the data, and analyzing the data.

Our approach to the development of a computerized data base for deaths and injuries in underground coal mines will begin with an extensive survey of all existing sources of such data.

Our approach to the development of algorithms for forecasting the effects of laser radiation on aerospace materials will begin with the collection of data from USN, USA, and USAF tests.

Preparing the Graphics - During the planning of the graphics for the Executive Summary, the topics and general format for each graphics item was specified; now it is time to sketch the graphics to be prepared by the Graphics Specialist in the Production Center. Along with each sketch, the writer must specify the overall size of the graphics, the minimum type size, the preferred font of the type, and the special matters to be emphasized. I have always written a note to the Graphics Specialist that accompanies my sketch of the graphics. This note provides the exact title (with correct spelling) of the graphics, the orientation (portrait or landscape) of the graphics, the use of color (if any), and the special visual impact needs. This note, which is prepared for each graphics item, no matter how simple the graphics might be, is greatly appreciated by the Graphics Specialist.

Integrating the Text and Graphics Seamlessly - If you have prepared the page layouts and page mockups for the Executive Summary, you will know exactly what text and graphics will be included in the one-page or two-page units. Since each unit must be limited to the pages allocated to a specific topic (such as Contract Experience, Personnel, etc.), there cannot be any overflow of text or graphics onto the pages of the next unit.

Plan your writing and graphics so that you are within one sentence of the page budget, and know which sentence you plan to delete if the work overflows and which sentence you plan to add if a page has extra lines available at the end of the unit. If you have located the graphics in close proximity to the paragraph that it supports, you can delete the graphics callout and the title of the graphics, saving lines and making the page look integrated.

Above all, keep the writing style consistent in all units of the Executive Summary, which is best achieved by good planning, good writing, and good editing.

Good Rules Governing the Text and Graphics - The ability of your Executive Summary to influence the reader can be greatly increased by the observance of a few simple rules, like:

- Control the length of the paragraphs. Paragraph length is particularly critical in dual column page formats. Try to limit paragraphs to five or six sentences. Avoid single sentence paragraphs like the plague.

- Control the topics of the paragraphs. Limit the paragraph to a single major topic. Use either the chain or daisy style of paragraph for your writing style. However, if multiple items must be discussed, use an introduction sentence followed by a bullet listing.

- Control the grade level of the text. Try to limit the sentences to 26 words or less and reduce the number of polysyllabic words in the sentences. Use software programs to measure the grade level of the text. A grade level of eight is good as the upper limit.

- Ensure that the text is immanently readable. Use everyday words as much as possible. Avoid the use of abbreviations and acronyms. Avoid esoteric terms and awkward sentence constructions. Ensure that the text flows smoothly. Vary the length of sentences.

- Keep the graphics simple and easily understandable. Limit the number of items in a graphics to seven. Avoid tedious graphics such as wiring diagrams or lines of code. Keep graphics on the same page or on a facing page immediately after it is mentioned in the text.

- Maintain balance in the paragraphs. Ensure that the number of lines of text reflect the relative importance of the subject. Examples: the Project Manager gets more lines of text than any other person and the prime contractor gets more lines of text than subcontractors.

- Avoid distractive items. Whenever possible, avoid graphics callouts by having the graphics integrated into the text and avoid callouts for graphics on a following or previous page. Avoid referring to other parts of the proposal, and avoid repetition of text.

**TYPICAL TOPICS FOR PARAGRAPHS
AND GRAPHICS
IN THE EXECUTIVE SUMMARY**

Personnel and Staffing
Qualifications of the Project Manager, qualifications of the Chief Engineer or Chief Scientist, corporate commitment of project personnel, experience and education of the project staff, availability of additional personnel, approach to staff buildup and build-down, retention of personnel skills

Contract Experience
Contract experience with the customer, expertise in key technologies, experience in types of works to be performed, performance on the contracts, specific contracts related to the proposed work, major accomplishments in past work

Project Organization
The corporate organizational structure, the team and its qualifications, the project structure, lines of communication, and authority. The roles of subcontractors during contract performance and interfaces with Government representatives and associated contractors

Project Management
The management tools and systems to be used, management of subcontractors, approach to risk management, approach to major procurements, top-level project schedule, reports and deliverables, systems to ensure on-cost and on-budget performance, managing project of comparable scope and complexity. Authorities of personnel in leadership roles

Problem Understanding
Understanding of the customer's requirements, the technologies involved, and the special skills needed. Understanding of the operational requirement for a system or a study and the associated risks, Understanding of the special tools, facilities, and personnel skills needed

Technical Approach
The key technical issues, the technical tools and methodologies to be employed, the major technical risks, the technical back-up plans, the types and sources of data and models to be employed, A flow diagram for the work to be performed, list of technical deliverables to be submitted

System Design/Development Features
A top-level diagram of the system architecture, the system engineering approaches and tools to be used, the engineering facilities and resources committed to the design and development work, and the key technical features of the design, the major technical risks, and CADD and CAM tools to be employed.

Facilities and Resources
A brief description of major offices, laboratories, computer centers, engineering centers, technical libraries, vehicles, storage facilities, CAD-CAM systems, and LANs-WANs. A graphic showing location of offices and other facilities providing technical and administrative support

IRAD Related Projects
Overview of major IRAD projects completed or ongoing, IRAD projects directly related to the project, special tools, data bases, or software developed during IRAD projects that will be used in the project

---

27.3 ASSIGNING YOUR BEST PEOPLE TO THE EXECUTIVE SUMMARY

Assigning Your Best Writer - Even though the Executive Summary is not evaluated by the customer, it is so important that the best writer must be assigned to this writing task. The best writer is defined as someone who:

- knows the customer, the RFP, and the proposal
- displays structure, discipline, and commitment in all writing assignments
- delivers his text and graphics on-time and on-budget
- displays superior, proven writing skills in material that convinces
- respects and understands the customer and the customer's values
- appreciates the importance of a superior design for the Executive Summary
- uses graphics and visual impact techniques for pleasing-looking pages

Assigning Your Best Editor - The Editor, a member of the production staff, is critical to the preparation of a superior Executive Summary, because the Executive Summary is probably the most important means for impressing customer personnel. Gaffes such as misspellings, awkward sentence structures, and unduly high grade levels for the text create a negative feeling among the readers, evaluators, and reviewers. The editor ensures that the editorial policy and good editorial standards are reflected in every possible way in the text and the graphics. Matters such as the selection of a font that is easily readable and the identification of changes in the grade level of the text may be a responsibility of the Editor. Just do not allow the writer of the Executive Summary to be the Editor, and do not use engineers and scientists as Editors either.

Assigning Your Best Graphics Specialist - The Graphics Specialist, a key member of the production staff assigned to the Executive Summary, ensures that the graphics items do not look as if they were prepared by an engineer or writer. The writer for the Executive Summary must listen to the Graphics Specialist in all matters related to the cover design and the graphics that are integrated into the text.

The Graphics Specialist ensures that every graphics item has a good layout, has good visual impact, is imminently readable, and is integrated into the text seamlessly.

Assigning Your Best Printing/Binding Personnel - The printing of the cover and those pages with color graphics is a very important activity during the production of the Executive Summary. The Printer/Binder is responsible for ensuring that the Executive Summary is properly bound, that colors do not bleed, and pages are printed with more margin on the binding side than on the edge side. The method of binding, whether saddle-stitched, three-ring binder, GBC or Velo binding, must appear professional, so the Printer/Binder is important to the team.

27.4 ENSURING THE EXECUTIVE SUMMARY IS CONVINCING

The Importance of Knowing the Proposal and the Design - A convincing Executive Summary can be prepared only by a writer who believes that your technical approach, problem understanding, technical and management staff, resources, and management tools are the best of any offeror. Executive Summary writers who have been closely associated with the design team and the proposal team will develop a full understanding of the proposal requirements, design requirements, and the responses to these requirements. Truly, the most effective writer for the Executive Summary is usually an individual that has worked on the proposal team or design team, has developed an in-depth understanding of the key issues, the win strategy, and the win themes.

Writing in A Confident Style - One of the biggest problems that I have experienced in writing the Executive Summary is that my confident writing style is considered by many reviewers to be the height of arrogance. I believe that they do not understand the difference between confidence and arrogance. I reply to those reviewers that we have prepared a proposal superior to any of the competitors and that my corporation and its team members are the "best buy" for the customer. Sometimes, I have compromised somewhat by having a fellow proposal specialist to review my Executive Summary and to make it more modest. However, it hurts me to submit to the demand for modesty when we are clearly the best.

Note: I have talked to Government Contracting Officers and members of the evaluation boards about my aggressive (arrogant?) writing style. Their comments were surprisingly consistent, in that, initially they felt that I wrote with an air of arrogance, but later, they felt that I was merely displaying an air of confidence. I believe that there is nothing wrong about making claims about being the best offeror when you are clearly the best offeror.

Showing Respect for the Customer - One of the surest means for alienating the SSA, Contracting Officer, COTR, SSEB, and SSAC is to write in a style that can be interpreted as condescending by these customer personnel. After all, most Government employees involved in a major procurement have great depth in their technical skills, management expertise, problem understandings, and related experience. Never write in a manner that the customer could interpret as "talking down"; and never intimate that the customer's technical personnel have outdated skills and understandings.

When you show disrespect for Government personnel, you will almost certainly lose the competition for several reasons. First of all, the Government technical, management, and administrative staff members will dread the thought of working with your corporation or your team. Secondly, the Government personnel are correct in thinking that the customer is due a large measure of respect and that the contractor should appreciate receiving their money. And thirdly, the customer's staff thinks that life is too short to work with disrespectful contractors.

One of the major means for showing respect for the customer in the Executive Summary is to spell out the full name of the customer. Do not, in the Executive Summary, use an abbreviation such as USN instead of the Navy or the U. S. Navy. Of course it is permissible to use abbreviations when they are used as adjectives, such as "the

NSSC facilities" or "the OMB publication".

27.5 SOME IMPORTANT ADVICE ON EXECUTIVE SUMMARIES

Preventing Meddlers From Inserting Their Sentences - A skilled writer of Executive Summaries knows the value of paragraph integrity and the need to get the readers involved with the text. Further, the writer of the Executive Summary establishes a rhythm to the text that keeps the reader engrossed in the text. But there are times when higher level management, in an effort to put their fingerprints on the Executive Summary, will write a sentence and dictate that their sentence be incorporated into a certain paragraph. Even worse, the senior managers may insert more than one sentence.

Keeping The Grade Level Consistent in All Parts - The writer of the Executive Summary determines the grade level for the text and writes the sentences and paragraphs so that the grade level of all parts of the Executive Summary are the same. While this may present some problems, particularly in the technical approach part of the Executive Summary, it is still possible to keep a near-consistent grade level. It only requires that the writer control the length of sentences and the ratio of poly-syllabic words to mono-syllabic words; these two matters are the principal drivers for high-grade levels which may lose many of the readers and evaluators. So, use simpler words and shorter sentences so that the Executive Summary will be understandable to all readers.

When assigned to work under Norman Polmar, a noted Naval historian, I learned some hard lessons related to controlling the grade level of one's text. I was chosen to work with Norm because I had worked over four years in support of the Navy program associated with the development of a high-energy laser weapon system for defense against incoming cruise missiles. Our assignment was to prepare an overview of the High Energy Laser program for presentation to the House Armed Services Committee, which was inclined to terminate the program.

Norm is not a scientist or engineer, but he is a great communicator, and he forced me to write about the technologies associated with high energy lasers at a fairly low grade level. He kept telling me that Walt Disney produced a movie about men in space which was technically correct but was understandable by an audience that ranged in age from six to sixty. And he insisted that I do the same. It was both frustrating and educational to write for Norman Polmar, because he was a relentless taskmaster who specialized in communicating with decision-makers.

Later, we were told by a congressional staffer that for the first time in over 10 years they finally understood the Navy's High Energy Laser program.

Working in One-Page or Two-Page Units - When designing and preparing the Executive Summary, the writer should design the Executive Summary so that each topic is addressed in one or two-page units. The typical 16-page Executive Summary is normally comprised of nine one or two-page units, which will include:

- Introductory Letter Always a one-page unit
- Problem Understanding Normally a two page unit
- Technical Approach Normally a two-page unit
- Management Approach Normally a two-page unit
- Personnel Qualifications Normally a two-page unit
- Contract Experience Normally a two-page unit
- Program Organization Normally a two-page unit
- Facilities and Resources Can be a one-page or two-page unit
- Related IRAD Projects Normally a one-page unit

It is critical that the writer of the Executive Summary limit his/her material to the allocated number of pages. Writers should not ever allow text from one unit to overflow onto the pages of the next unit and should not ever permit any pages to be only partially filled (No major white space). Readers, reviewers, and evaluators will form a very favorable image of your corporation (i. e., very efficient, very structured, and much disciplined) after reading a well-organized Executive Summary.

Issuing Instructions to Reviewers - The Proposal Manager must issue specific instructions to the proposal staff and the design staff who are reviewing the Executive Summary; such instructions should include:

- ensure all facts or data in the Executive Summary are true
- ensure all assertions in the Executive Summary are supported elsewhere in the proposal
- ensure that the win themes and win strategy are addressed in the Executive Summary
- identify material (text and graphics) that might improve the Executive Summary
- do not recommend material be added without denoting what material should be deleted
- do not change the page allocations within the Executive Summary
- do not attempt to rewrite or redesign the Executive Summary during the review

Remember, reviewers can make recommendations and suggest major and minor changes to the draft of the Executive Summary but reviewers cannot require changes to be made in the Executive Summary; only the Proposal Manager has such authority.

27.6 SOME DISASTERS ASSOCIATED WITH EXECUTIVE SUMMARIES

Making Assertions Not Proven in the Proposal - Probably the most fatal flaw associated with Executive Summaries is making statements (assertions) that are not supported in other parts of the proposal. This situation occurs because every Executive Summary is basically an organized compilation of claims or assertions and because page limitations preclude the inclusion of proofs for the claims-assertions. It is the nature of the Executive Summary. Examples of assertions that require proof include major statements such as:

- our contract experience encompasses every technology essential to the SDI architecture
- our project staff is distinguished by their many awards and accomplishments
- our facilities include state-of-the-art research and development laboratories
- we have leased major facilities in close proximity to the agency headquarters

The Volume Leaders must review the Executive Summary and ensure that their volumes provide proof of the assertions (claims). It is recommended that the Volume Leaders compile a list of all assertions (or claims) in the Executive Summary that must support their volumes. Do not overlook this very important activity, because unproved or unsupported assertions create serious concern with the Contracting Officer, the Source Selection Evaluation Board, and the Source Selection Advisory Council. These members quickly develop a cynical attitude toward your proposal when proof is not provided.

Not Supporting the Win Strategy or Win Themes - In many competitions, in the Executive Summary, we made strong statements (assertions) that were not supported by or were contradicted by later sections of the proposal, like:

- In a major procurement, one of our more important win themes was that we would provide a highly qualified technical staff who would bring fresh insights into the problems facing a major Navy system; in another win theme, we stated that our staff was not tied to the errors of the incumbent contractor. However, in our staffing plan, we explained in detail that we intended to hire virtually all of the employees of the incumbent contractor, replacing only about four members of their management staff with our own key personnel.
- In a technical services procurement, we stated that our staff of logistics experts would provide quick-response technical,

management, and administrative services to a Naval Supply Facility in Pennsylvania from a nearby office. Yet in the discussion of facilities and interfaces with our Navy counterparts, we admitted in our management volume that our offices would be over 90 miles and two hours travel time from the Navy facility.

- One of our favorite win themes was that our senior management and administrative staff would be closely involved with the day to day operations of a SETA support team working at a Government facility. Yet the security section of the management volume noted that the Government's special security requirements precluded the managers and administrators from access to the facility at which the work was performed.

Highlighting a Lack of Qualifications - Too often, the Executive Summary becomes the place where our corporation was quickly eliminated from the competitive range because we made some incredibly dumb statements in this part of the proposal. For example:

- In a major proposal to the Department of Energy for the operation of a National Laboratory, the first page of the Executive Summary stated that our corporation had no experience in the operation and maintenance of such a facility (We eliminated our corporation as a competent offeror with this single sentence).
- In a proposal to the Naval Weapons Laboratory at Dahlgren, we highlighted in the personnel section of the Executive Summary the fact that we intended to replace our key personnel with new hires within 180 days after contract award. (We virtually eliminated our corporation as a viable offeror because we scored very low in the ensuing personnel evaluation).
- In the Executive Summary for a major proposal to the Air Force for the development of a high priority system, we promised to establish a major engineering center near the Atlantic Missile

Range after award of contract (We provided proof that, since we did not have the facilities needed to perform the work, we were not a qualified bidder).

- In a major proposal to the Government to operate the Sandia Laboratories, a facility with personnel-related costs of about $3-billion per year, we attached our annual report to the Executive Summary. The annual report showed that we had less than $350,000 in cash and cash equivalents. We lost because we were not a competent bidder. (We documented the fact that we could not finance the operation of the laboratory for more than several hours).

Having Misspellings on the First Page of the Executive Summary - While these matters did not occur on proposals to which I was assigned; the proposals did originate within our corporate proposal center. While one may laugh at these mistakes, it is doubtful that the customer thought that the mistakes were really funny. Consider two instances in which Proposal Managers relied on the spell-check feature of their word processing software instead of paying for the services of an Editor:

- On the first page of the Executive Summary of a proposal to the Air Force for a billion- dollar procurement, our text referred to "...one of the basic tenants of our approach is .....". The text should have read "...one of the basic tenets of our approach is ..." We lost the procurement, and it is possible that the Air Force did not intend to do business with a firm that cannot spell.
- On the first page of the Executive Summary of a proposal to the Defense Nuclear Agency, our proposal referred to "...our Strategic Unclear Policy..." instead of "... our Strategic Nuclear Policy..." We lost the competition, hopefully for other reasons, but it was difficult to convince the DNA staff that we would produce high-quality documentation.

Being Inconsistent in the Use of "We"- It is imperative that the word "we" mean only one thing either your company the prime contractor or your team which includes your company and your subcontractors. When readers of the Executive Summary are not sure which organization (your corporation, your team, your project) is being described, the readers will be uncertain in their assessments and their conclusions can go amiss easily. I have read Executive Summaries in which, because of my first-hand knowledge of the team and my corporation, I knew which organizational entity was being addressed. But I have read Executive Summaries in which it was impossible to determine with any rigidity who "we" meant.

CHAPTER 28

PREPARING THE COVER LETTER AND OTHER ITEMS

28.1 PREPARING A COVER LETTER WITH A STRONG MESSAGE

A Government Contracting Officer once stated that he could not understand why offerors continually sent a form letter as the covering letter for a proposal. He could not understand how the proposal manager, who had produced a good proposal, could spoil the submission with a stereotyped letter. He wanted a letter written to him, the man who would sign the contract some day in the future. I believe that he felt that form-letter submissions were a way of saying that his opinion did not really matter or that the offeror was too lazy to prepare a good forwarding letter.

If you use the general format for the covering letter that most proposal managers seem to prefer, since they do not have to do any creative thinking after weeks of hectic work, most such form letters seem to follow the format, detail, and imagination of the following example:

Naval Sea Systems Command
Department of the Navy
2301 Jefferson Davis Highway
Arlington, VA   22302

28 February 1977

Attention: Mr. ------------------, Contracting Officer

Dear Sir:

Science Applications International Corporation is pleased to submit a proposal to provide technical and engineering services to the Naval Sea Systems Command. Our proposal (No. 001-71-2755-004) is submitted in response to your Request For Proposal, N0054-345987, System Engineering Support for PMS 405, dated 27 December 1976.

Our proposal is fully responsive to the requirements of the solicitation and reflects our commitment to providing superior engineering services to a vital Navy program. We have shown that our staff understands the Navy's requirements and we have described our approach to your complex operational problems. We have been working for PMS-405 for the past five years and look forward to another five years.

If you have any technical or management questions, please do not hesitate to call me at 703-827-4400. You can contact Ms Brenda ------- at 703-827-4430 on financial matters.

Yours truly.

Dr. John I C--------
Vice President

The letter above uses a block-style format for letters, with no indentation, which ensures that the cover letter will be dull to look at and dull to read. So, I suggest something like the following cover letter that I prepared for a proposal in which our corporation made a major effort to present an important message to the Government Contracting Officer.

15 July 19---

U. S. Army Ballistics Research Laboratory
Aberdeen Proving Grounds
Aberdeen, MD

Attention: Mr. George ----------- , Contracting Officer

Reference: RFP 00327-R-177683

Dear Mr. _____ ,

    During my thirty years of active duty as an officer in the Ordnance Corps of the U. S. Army, I worked long and hard to ensure that our combat forces had the best weapons possible. While in stateside assignments, I worked in the testing, development, and modernization of existing weapons. Overseas, I ensured that the weapons used by our troops were supported and maintained by the best personnel and facilities possible. In fact, my entire professional career has been devoted to improving and supporting Army weapon systems.

    I have assembled a project team that has extensive technical and engineering skills, many years of experience on Army weapon systems, and an in-depth understanding of Army operational requirements. This staff is committed to working under my direct supervision at our offices in the Joppatown, MD, area; these offices are located less than ten miles from the Aberdeen Proving Ground. This local office will be supported by a major SAIC corporate technology center in nearby McLean, VA, from which we will have access to computer centers, laboratories, technical libraries, art-graphics centers, and many other resources.

    I am looking forward to continuing my work in support of the Army of the future, and I am committed to working in a full-time, long-term basis on this important Army program. Do not hesitate to contact me at my office (703-555-5555) or at my home (301-555-5555). I am eager to respond to any questions and I look forward to working with you and the BRL staff.

Yours truly,

Dr. Robert T. -------------
Program Manager
Colonel, USA Retired

Attachment: SAIC Proposal

In this personalized letter to the Contracting Officer, we present several major proposal themes: "We know and care about Army ordnance", "We are committed to working closely with you from nearby offices", "We have the right mix of personnel committed to the program", "Our Program Manager will always have the best interests of the Army in his heart". Don't you agree that this second letter is much more likely to attract the attention of the Contracting Officer and to impress the Evaluation Board?

In summary, use your covering letter to present major win themes, to establish rapport with the customer, to express a commitment, to appear like a company that the customer would like to have under contract. Remember, this is the first page that the Contracting Officer and the evaluation team see.

28.2 DESIGNING THE COVER OF THE PROPOSAL

The most telling adverse comment relative to proposal covers is that most covers have too many items, too many colors, and too many distractions. The second most common adverse comment related to proposal covers is that they do not project a message to the customer and are not really relevant to the win themes. The third most adverse comment is that one cannot even guess what the cover is supposed to tell the reader and the evaluator. Finally many, if not most, covers show little appreciation for the values and legacies of the customer.

Most proposal covers in the past ten years are not of the subliminal message type; instead they rank close to the pie-in-the-face message type. It is almost a universal rule that the cover should be conservative, should transmit a quiet message to the customer, and should be related to the win strategy and the win themes. Given a choice, it is far better to under-design a cover than to over-design the cover. The title page must have a rather large number of items in its design, but the cover does not have to include many items found on the title page such as the security downgrading paragraph or the propriety statement.

In a proposal to a Naval Sea Systems Command installation, we prepared the proposal from an office that supported the Naval Air System Command. So, our aviation-oriented staff prepared a proposal cover that depicted a Navy fighter aircraft in flight. I am sure that the staff at the NSSC facility was not impressed with our understanding of the work to be performed and the state of the art in surface ship systems. We lost, and I will always believe that the cover played some role in the loss.

In a proposal to an Army field artillery and missile center, the proposal cover used the corporate blue color for the border. Yet the color of the artillery and missile units in the Army has always been red. Anyone who knows anything about the Army knows this. We may have lost this competition because we demonstrated on our cover that we knew very little about the Army.

In a proposal to the Coast Guard, which is known for an attachment to its early history, we prepared a cover that included a photograph of the USCG training ship, the Ranger. The Ranger is a large, square-rigged sailing ship, and it is dear to the heart of every Coast Guard officer. Although our proposal did not win the competition, our contacts in the USCG complemented us on our cover design.

In a winning proposal to the Government for network services, our cover depicted an existing network control center, workers installing fiber optics cables, and the key features of our fiber optic cable. Our cover design convinced the Government that our system was real, our system was operational, and our hardware was state-of-the-art. We won this procurement.

The Sikorsky Company has a great design for its proposal covers. All of its covers for reports and proposals to military procurement agencies have a colored strip about three inches wide down the left side of the white cover, with the color stripe being tied directly to the customer's colors, such as dark Navy blue for the USN covers, Air Force sky blue for USAF covers, olive drab for Army covers. Within this colored band, Sikorsky places the emblem on the officer's dress hat, such as the two-anchor emblem of Navy officers or the anchor and globe emblem of Marine officers. Every military person and every civil service person instantly recognizes and identifies with the Sikorsky covers; superbly simple, easily recognizable, greatly appreciated.

The Executive Summary writer must know the customer well enough to prepare a cover that matches the image that they foster and cherish. For example, we knew that the Defense Advanced Research Project Agency considered itself to be on the cutting edge of most technologies; so, in a major proposal to DARPA, our cover design depicted space-based lasers engaging ballistic missiles. In another important procurement, we also knew that the Army had to be ready to fight with existing weapon systems, so our cover had a montage of current artillery weapons.

Perhaps the simplest direction in this important proposal matter (cover design) is to ensure that the proposals cover demonstrates an appreciation of the values of the customer.

28.3 PREPARING A COMPLETE COMPLIANCE MATRIX

The compliance matrix is the offeror's roadmap to the proposal. The compliance matrix ensures that the proposal evaluation team will find your responses to the evaluation factors, evaluation sub factors, and evaluation standards. Remember, evaluators seldom, if ever, read the proposal; they search for your responses to the RFP requirements and they evaluate your responses. Remember, evaluating is not the same as reading.

The Proposal Planner or the Volume Leaders must identify all of the RFP requirements for the each volume and prepare a compliance matrix (actually a table). The compliance matrix includes two major items; a listing of the RFP requirements, and a listing of your responses to those requirements. You tell the Government evaluator where to find your responses, within a very structured format. It is highly recommended that you do not rely on the table of contents to serve as a compliance matrix and that you do not force the evaluators to read the proposal in a search for your responses.

While there are several possible formats for a compliance matrix, the following items must be included in every compliance matrix:

- RFP Requirements - this entry includes a citation of the RFP paragraph number and a brief description of the requirement.
- Response - this entry denotes the location of your response to

the requirement, by volume, section, subsection.

Examples of several entries in a compliance matrix are shown below. It is recommended that an applications software system such as EXCEL or Lotus be used for the matrix.

Rqmt. No.	RFP Para. No.	Description of RFP Requirement	Location of Response
17	L.15.a.1	Proposal shall include a Cost Volume	Vol III
26	M.6.a.3	Evaluation factor- Management	Vol II Sect 2
110	C.3.1.7	Contract deliverables shall include a Quality Plan	Vol 1 Sect 6.5
119	H.17	Offeror shall submit a Drugfree Workplace Plan	Vol II App A
121	L.23.a	Offeror shall address Cost Realism	Vol III Sect 5

Compliance matrices can easily include over 100 RFP requirements, which means that a matrix of this size will probably require at least three pages in the proposal. In proposals with severe page limitations, the Proposal Manager will not be able to allocate that many pages to an item that is not required by the RFP. In such instances, I have always put the compliance matrix at the end of the proposal, so that if the Government discards all pages above the limit, the compliance matrix will be the item discarded. However, I have never found an instance in which the evaluation team discarded the compliance matrix because the matrix made their evaluation task much easier.

28.4 PREPARING THE TABLE OF CONTENTS

The Table of Contents is prepared by one of the following persons: the Proposal Planner, the Proposal Manager, or the Volume Leaders. The Table of Contents is particularly important because it serves many purposes, such as:

1. Members of the customer's proposal evaluation team can readily see the structure of the proposal and locate the material needed for their evaluation effort.
2. The Proposal Manager or the Volume Leader can organize the proposal team and make assignments to the Proposal Writers,

based on the subjects in the outline.

3. The Production Coordinator can identify and track the proposal text submitted to the production staff and assess the status of the proposal quickly.

4. The Proposal Writers can easily see where their writing assignments fit into the overall proposal.

5. The Proposal Manager and Volume Leaders can assess their staff's productivity and identify material that is behind schedule.

6. The Table of Contents provides the structure needed to ensure responses are prepared to all proposal requirements.

An initial proposal outline is prepared prior to the Gold Team Review, but that outline is revised, sometimes frequently, sometimes extensively, during the preparation of the proposal. But the outline cannot be changed without the approval of the Volume Leader or the Proposal Planner. The Proposal Planner is not in the chain of command and does not have authority for the approval or disapproval of outline changes after the initial outline has been prepared.

It is important that the Table of Contents use the exact words and exact format as the titles in the proposal text. If a title in the text of the proposal is in upper case and bold, then that title in the Table of Contents should be is the same format and style. It is equally important that the page numbers for the proposal text in the Table of Contents be correct.

28.5 PREPARING THE LIST OF REFERENCES

Citing references is frequently necessary to provide proof of the statements that have been presented in the Technical Approach or the Problem Understanding sections. The act of citing references tends to impress the member of the Source Selection Evaluation Board because the references demonstrate that the offeror has done research during the preparation of the proposal. So, if at all possible within the page limitations, include superscripts in the text that refer to the publications used in the preparation of the proposal and included in the List of References.

The List of References can be organized and presented three ways: a list of references at the end of each section or chapter, a master listing at the end of the proposal volume, or a citation of the references at the bottom of the pages where they are applicable. The master listing is probably better on page-limited proposals because redundancy in citations is eliminated. The reference citations at the foot of a page can distract the evaluator from the material in the text.

The Proposal Manager, in the proposal style guide, will state the method used for citing references. If the matter is not included in the proposal style guide, then the Proposal Manager should specify the use of either the University of Chicago Style Guide or the Government Printing Office Style Guide as the standard for the preparation of reference lists or reference footnotes.

If the proposal has severe page limitations and if the inclusion of one or more pages for a List of References takes pages away from critical material, I recommend that the List of References be put in the very last part of the proposal. If the Government intends to delete pages from the proposal that is over the page limit, they will remove the last pages in the volumes. Let the Government delete this non-evaluated, non-required item; it will only hurt their staff.

28.6 PREPARING THE GLOSSARY AND LIST OF ABBREVIATIONS

It is wise to prepare a glossary and a list of abbreviations/acronyms with each volume of the proposal, provided the page limitations are not too restrictive. I suspect that most people would be surprised to learn how many acronyms are used in the typical proposal, in spite of efforts to control their usage. Acronyms and abbreviations have become so much a part of our language that they are almost uncontrollable.

In the preparation of the Proposal Writers Folder which is issued to each Proposal Writer, the instructions therein state that each author is to submit a list of all abbreviations and acronyms with their text. The Production Coordinator is responsible for assembling the master list from the many lists submitted by the writers. At least that is the way things are supposed to be done. In practice, all too often, an Editor prepares the list while editing the text.

A glossary should be prepared for all words or terms that are not found in a Webster's Collegiate Dictionary. These words and terms include the technical jargon, the military-specific words, and special usage items such as drug free workplace, performance bonds, life-cycle-costs, disclosure statement, Actual Cost of Work Performed, and Estimate at Completion.

If the proposal has severe page limitations and if the Glossary and List of Abbreviations and Acronyms takes pages away from critical material, I recommend that these two items be put in the very last part of the proposal. If the Government intends to delete pages from the proposal that is over the page limit, they will remove the last pages in the volumes.

28.7 PREPARING THE TITLE PAGE

The preparation of a title page that looks professional, yet contains all of the RFP-required items, is a near impossibility because the title page must include many types of information, including:

- title of the proposal and proposal identification number
- identification number of the RFP
- name and address of the offeror (your corporation)
- name and address of the contracting agency
- date of the proposal

When the proposal includes classified material or proprietary material, additional information must be included on the title page, including:

- security classification, top and bottom of the page

- security downgrading instructions
- restriction on the use and dissemination of proprietary material

Other items that may appear on the title page are the names of the team members, the logo or emblem of the contracting agency, and the corporate logo. Also, on the back side of the title page, the copyright notice must be inserted if the proposal has copyrighted material. It can be seen that the preparation of the title page is not a simple task, especially if you are hoping to have a simple page. Reconcile yourself to having a very cluttered title page, particularly when classified and proprietary information are included in the proposal.

28.8 PREPARING FLASH PAGES AND TAB PAGES

Flash pages and tab pages are an effective means for indicating the various sections within the proposal, but there are important concerns about the use of flash pages and tab pages when the proposal has severe page limitations. The USAF, as a rule, counts tab pages and flash pages in the page limitations, which can mean that you must give up 8 to 10 pages in a page limited proposal. Navy organizations are inclined to allow tab pages and flash pages to be used without counting them against the page limitations. When the customer allows tab pages and flash pages, use them because they appear to be sign of organization within the proposal.

Notes: (1) Flash pages and tab pages are heavier stock pages that allow readers to open a volume to specific places. (2) Flash pages are similar to tab pages but do not have tabs extending beyond the 8.5" x 11" pages.

ABBREVIATIONS

A & E Architects and Engineers
ACO Administrative Contracting Officer
AMC Air Mobility Command
AMS American Management Systems
AMSDL Automated Material Distribution List
BAFO Best and Final Offer
B & P Bid and Proposal
BDM Braddock, Dunn and MacDonald
BRL Ballistics Research Laboratory
CASE Computer-Aided Software Engineering
CBD Commerce Business Daily
CBS Cost Breakdown Structure
CDRL Contract Data Requirements List
CFR Code of Federal Regulations
CLIN Contract Line Item Numbers
CLIN Contract Line Number
CO Contracting Officer
COCO Government Owned-Contractor Operated
COCOMO Construction Cost Model
COLA Cost of Living Adjustment
COR Corporate Officer Responsible
COTR Contracting Officer's Technical Representative
CPA Certified Public Accountant
CSCS Cost Schedule Control System

CSCS Cost Schedule Control Systems
CSSR Cost Schedule Status Report
DAR Defense Acquisition Regulations
DARPA Defense Advanced Research Project Agency
DARS Defense Acquisition Regulations
DCAA Defense Contract Audit Agency
DCAS Division of Compensation and Analysis Support
DID Data Item Descriptions
DNA Defense Nuclear Agency
DOD Department of Defense
DOS Department of State
DSMC Defense Systems Management College
EMI-EMC Electromagnetic Interference- Electromagnetic Compatible
EMP Electromagnetic Poles
FAR Federal Acquisition Regulation
FBI Federal Bureau of Investigation
FBO Foreign Building Operations
FCMHSA Federal Coal Mine Health and Safety Act
FCRC Federal Contract Research Center
FCRC Federal Contract Research Center
FIPS Federal Information Processing Systems
G & A General and Administrative
GFE Government Furnished Equipment
GFF Government Furnished Facilities
GFI Government Furnished Information
GFM Government Furnished Information
HCFA Health Care Finance Agency
ID-IQ Indefinite Delivery - Indefinite Quantity
IFB Information for a Bid
IFB Invitation for a Bid
IRAD Independent Research and Development
MM Martin Marietta
MSHA Mine Safety and Health Administration
NAVAIR Naval Air Systems Command

NBS National Bureau of Standards
NRL Naval Research Laboratory
NSSC NASA Shared Services Center
NTE Not to Exceed
O & M Operations and Maintenance
OCD Other Direct Costs
OCI Organizational Conflicts of Interest
OMB Office of Management and Budget
PLO Project Liaison Office
QA Quality Assurance
R & D Research and Development
RFP Request for Proposal
RFQ Request for Quote
RSNF Royal Saudi Naval Forces
SAIC Science Applications International Corporation
SDI Strategic Defense Initiative
SDIO Strategic Defense Initiative Office
SETA System Engineering and Technical
SOW Statement of Work
SPCC Ships Parts Control Center
SSA Source Selection Authority
SSAC Source Selection Advisory Council
SSEB Source Selection Evaluation Board
SWAGS Sophisticated Wild Ass Guess
TARS Transportation Acquisition Regulations
TSA Transportation Security Analysis
USBM United States Bureau of Mines
USN United States Navy
WBS Work Breakdown Structure
WSMR White Sands Missile Range

INDEX

A

Accounting system and RFP's, 77
Acquisition Manager, role of, 239
Administrative Contract Officer (ACO), 94
Advanced Research Projects Agency, 91
Adverse weather conditions as terms and conditions matter of
    importance, 87
A&E design contracts cost realism, 381–382
Affirmative action program as terms and conditions matter of
    importance, 87
Anderson, Bob, iii
ANSER, 14
Art-Graphics Specialists, 384
Austin Company, The, iii

B

BDM Corporation, iii, 12, 168
Best and Final Offers, 70, 407–408
Better management strategy, 164
Bid-No Bid Board, 2
Bid-no bid decision, strategies of, 1–7
    axiom about, 2
    form used in decision process, 4
    highest level corporate considerations and, 5–7

E

K

L

M

S

T

U

V

W

CPSIA information can be obtained
at www.ICGtesting.com
Printed in the USA
LVHW022050270321
682691LV00001B/11